THE
EDUCATION
of a
TENNIS
PLAYER

 Frankston Library Service

Please return items by the date printed on your loans docket.
Please report any damage to staff. Fees are charged for items
returned late. To renew loans by phone, quote your library card
number or go to ww.frankston.vic.gov.au/library/

FRANKSTON LIBRARY
60 Playne Street
Frankston 3199
Victoria Australia
Tel: (03) 9784 1020
Fax: (03) 9784 1750
TTY (03) 9784 1707

CARRUM DOWNS LIBRARY
203 Lyrebird Drive
Carrum Downs 3201
Victoria Australia
Tel: (03) 9782 0418
Fax: (03) 9782 0187
TTY. (03) 9782 6871

THE
EDUCATION
of a
TENNIS
PLAYER

ROD LAVER
with
BUD COLLINS

NEW CHAPTER PRESS

The Education of a Tennis Player is published by New Chapter Press
(www.NewChapterMedia.com) and is distributed by the Independent Publisher's
Group. (www.ipgbook.com)

© Rod Laver, 1971, 2009

ISBN: 978-094-2257-625

Cover photo courtesy of Getty Images. Back cover photo courtesy of Corbis.
Bud Collins/Rod Laver photo (prior to Introduction) courtesy of Getty Images.
Photo of Laver wedding (page 13), BBC photo shoot (page 65), French Open trophy
ceremony (page 108) and Wimbledon photo (page 178) are also courtesy of Getty
Images. Photo of 1969 US Open (page 216) courtesy of Corbis.

New Chapter Press wishes to thank Kirsten Navin, Bill Mountford, Robert Geist,
Andrew Tasiopoulos and Irene Tan for help with this project.

Cover & book design by Kirsten Navin

Printed in Canada

ACKNOWLEDGEMENTS

IT DIDN'T HURT TO BE BORN AN AUSTRALIAN. CERTAINLY I can't thank my Mum and Dad, Melba and Roy Laver, enough for their part in my tennis life—for always having a court wherever we lived, and thus making it possible for me to play a game all my life, for fun and a living. (I have long since forgiven Dad for his early judgment that my older brothers had the tennis talent in the family.)

I'd also like to thank:

Those same brothers, Trevor and Bob, who hit with me even when it was a bother.

Charlie Hollis, who showed me what the game was really about—and how to get where I had to go.

Harry Hopman, who made me and the rest of his dynasty, from Sedgman to Newcombe, realize that talent is nothing without fitness.

Roy Emerson, good friend and remarkable doubles partner—strong enough to have carried me.

Ken Rosewall and Lew Hoad, who finally convinced me to turn pro by offering to back the guarantee with their own money. (I hadn't realized anybody was that anxious to beat me.)

Bud Collins, who yanked the whole story out of me, and who suffered as much as I did when I lost. (After all, he shares in the royalties from this book.)

For Randy Walker, our current publisher, who was excited about republishing this book after forty years.

And to Anita Ruthling Klaussen for her endless and caring editing.

And for Mary, who made it the grandest slam.

R.L.

CONTENTS

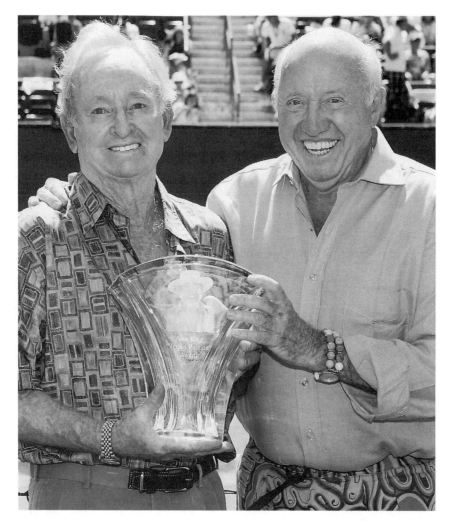

Bud Collins and I go way back – we first met in 1956 at the Longwood Cricket Club just outside of Boston at the U.S. National Doubles Championships. It was a good thing that he didn't tell me that if I didn't win the Grand Slam in 1969 that this book would not have been published. I was inducted into the International Tennis Hall of Fame in 1981 and Bud joined me there in 1994 in recognition for his lifelong contributions to the sport, particularly his excellent writing for the *Boston Globe* and his entertaining television commentary. He has received a lot of attention through the years for his colorful wardrobe – especially his pants. It makes it easy to pick him out of a crowd. We are photographed here during an on-court ceremony in Indian Wells, Calif., in 2008.

INTRODUCTIONS

WHY DID I WRITE A BOOK? ME, WITH NO LITERARY BACK-ground, foreground, inclinations, or even interests.

One of the reasons might have been that I received an advance from a publisher with instructions: write a book. There is something about an advance that inspires almost anybody to thoughts of literary creation. Some take the money and run. Others pull up lame in the typing fingers (or finger). Publishers learn to adjust to those breaks of their game just as I did to bad bounces.

But most of us literary-set types, with an eye to supplementing the advance with further royalties, press on and deliver a manuscript which in time becomes a tome to be peddled in bookstores. In this case, this one.

Sports personalities have been doing this for a long time. First to appear in the English language was Dame Juliana Berners in 1486, whose *Book of St. Albans* was about hunting and fishing. Dame Juliana liked to hunt and fish, and so do I. I hope we prove to have something else in common. Her book is still selling. If mine is four centuries from now my heirs will be extremely pleased.

After Dame Juliana came a deluge of boxers, football, basketball and baseball players, cricketers, horsemen, golfers and tennis players putting their stories in print.

My story, focusing particularly on the year 1969, is part of what I want to tell you. In winning the four majors -- singles championships of Australia, France, Britain (Wimbledon) and the United States to register the first open Grand Slam in tennis history -- I owned 1969 as much as any athlete can own a year. There were other important championships, too, and $124,000 in prize money. And the honor of being selected not only Player of the Year but No. 3 in the all-time rankings behind Bill Tilden and Don Budge.

I don't think any athlete has had such far-flung success as I enjoyed in 1969, winning tournaments on four continents, my second Grand Slam. I wonder if a tennis player will ever have a season like that again? I rather doubt it. Even though I won more money in 1970 (cash pours into the game at ever increasing rates), I couldn't equal the achievements of 1969. That was my special year, and I wanted to set it all down.

But there was more to 1969 than winning, and more that I want to tell you apart from my story. Even though I'd been playing tennis for more than twenty years, I was still learning in 1969, and I'm going to pass along some things I learned then and in other years on to you.

It's funny how the most simple tenets of the game, like keeping your eye on the ball, are overlooked at times by even the top players. You can be the best player in the world and still butcher a lot of routine points and situations, just as I have done. When I blew an easy smash at the net you could see that the hacker within me was still alive and well. I'm sure this must comfort those who are the backbone of the game—the hackers everywhere.

While there is some doubt that an Australian, collaborating with an American, could actually write a book in English, Bud and I felt it was worth giving a try.

Rod Laver
Carlsbad, Calif.
2009

I'VE KNOWN ROD SINCE 1956 WHEN WE MET ON THE BROAD porch of Boston's venerable Longwood Cricket Club, overseeing a sporting meadow, acres of grass courts, soothing to the eye, tricky to master. Neither of us could have imagined that eight years up the line he would master a nor-easter – a furious rainstorm – as well as a furious foe, the great Pancho Gonzalez, to win the first of his five U.S. Professional Championships, laying out his credentials at Longwood as the universe's best tennis player.

He didn't look it as an 18-year-old who had come to Boston to play doubles alongside another young Aussie, muscular Bob Mark. Not much meat on that short Laverian frame, and Mark's presence made him look anemic. This was 12 years before the tennis revolution that made all players – pros and amateurs – equal in open competition, striving for prize money.

The initial U.S. Open in 1968 at Forest Hills in New York threw all five championships into one pot: men's and women's singles and doubles plus mixed doubles. But before that it was a two tournament split: U.S. Doubles at Longwood, preceding the U.S. Singles at Forest Hills in New York. Laver and Mark won a couple of rounds before losing to countrymen Roy Emerson and Mal Anderson, a pair of country boys like Laver himself, raised with cattle in the Queensland bush.

At Forest Hills, Laver was out fast, unluckily drawing the foremost American, Ham Richardson. Still, he was enjoying himself, unnoticed at the U.S. major, and thrilled by the final, embracing two more Aussies, world Nos. 1-2 Lew Hoad and Kenny Rosewall. Heady talk was floating about, a possible Grand Slam for the powerful Hoad, who already had the Australian, French and Wimbledon titles in his satchel.

Sorry Lew, no Slam, because Rosewall, another little guy, was too quick and sharp for his fellow Sydneysider in the four set final. There would not be a Grand Slam – all four majors conquered within a calendar year – until none other than Laver, in 1962, emulated Don Budge (1938) and Maureen Connolly (1953).

I was disappointed. In my second year as a sports reporter for the *Boston Herald*, I had driven to Forest Hills with a friend, hoping to see

Hoad make an historic triumph, and write about it. But once Lew lost, my sports editor also lost interest in an almost-Slam. I didn't get there in time to see Laver lose his first rounder, but I had a feeling he'd be a fine player. He had won the U.S. Junior title prior to Boston, and I knew Australian tennis management wouldn't support a kid on a round-the-world campaign if he weren't an extraordinary prospect.

He was justifiably proud to be traveling with the Aussie squad. Rosewall's victory was the first of seven straight U.S. singles titles for the Down Under-takers. In Rod's future was the seventh, 1962, and battles with Hoad and Rosewall on the pro tours – as well as stinging losses to ageless Kenny in several important tournaments. The original open, the British Hard Court, and the first major open, the French, were two of them in 1968.

Rosewall remained a friend – but a thorny one whose backhand could give you an ulcer. After Rod took the money and ran away with the pro circus in 1963, the rivalry with Rosewall at times seemed a secret. Until the pros were let back into respectable society at the birth of opens, they seemed to disappear for long stretches, receiving minimal or no publicity. Nevertheless, the small band of outlaws were hustling across the globe, willing to go anywhere customers might be available, and put on a good show.

As rivalries go, the most renowned was the in-your-face showdowns of Martina Navratilova and Chris Evert, amounting to 80 clashes over 16 years, Martina ahead 43-37. They had the attention of the fans, press and TV. There have also been Helen Wills and Helen Jacobs, Bill Tilden and Little Bill Johnston, Pete Sampras and Andre Agassi, Roger Federer and Rafael Nadal, among others.

Rod and Kenny played twice as many times as anybody else but were hardly noticed, some results weren't even recorded. It has taken sleuthing on the part of historians Andrew Tasiopoulos in Australia (Laver leading series 80-67, all confirmed) and Robert Geist in Austria (Laver leading series 79-71, including 22-7 in the open era) to come up with the best figures.

As the years passed, and I moved to the *Boston Globe*, I saw more of Rod at various tournaments. Mainly Jimmy Van Alen's uproarious VASSS (Van Alen's Streamined Scoring System) affairs at Newport, Rhode Island, and the U.S. Pro at Longwood. We became friends, and in 1969 I got a call from Rod's agent, wondering if I'd like to be involved in a Laver memoir. Although the agent had other ideas, Rod had put forth my name, and I was flattered.

Fine. But first I had to meet the editor-to-be, Peter Schwed at Simon and Schuster in New York. Peter was first-rate, had edited P.G. Wodehouse among other literary stars, and was an enthusiastic tennis player. However, he was less than encouraging, pointing out that Rod wasn't that well known at that stage (the second year of opens unfolding), and would have to play sensationally, reap a lot of headlines to make a book worthwhile.

"What about a Grand Slam?" the editor said. "That would give us a big send-off. Do you think Laver can do that? No man has since [Don] Budge 31 years ago, and he's the only one. Hoad had a chance, but Rosewall wrecked that. Well...what about it?"

"Oh, sure," I said with a seeming confidence I didn't really feel. Rosewall was still in the way, playing better than ever, and Rod would be 31 in August. Budge had Slammed at 23. Moreover, the climate was not that of the 1962 Slam when the pros such as eventual Hall of Famers Rosewall, Hoad, Gonzalez, Butch Buchholz, Andres Gimeno were barred from the majors.

But it became clear: No Slam, no book.

I never revealed that to Rod until much later, long after his second Slam was securely wrapped up. He had enough pressure trying to hold off the rest of the covetous mob below his No. 1 perch without worrying about a book. He left the worrying to me and his stalwart (and pregnant) wife, Mary, while he peerlessly minded the business of putting together the unparalleled season of 1969.

Nobody was happier than Peter Schwed, who didn't have to say, "Maybe next year, fellows." The book he named *The Education of a Tennis Player*, did very well. But that wasn't the end of it, even though, in time, it went out of print.

As the major championships made plans to salute Laver on the 40th anniversary of the mammoth of all seasons, Rod and I decided to join in the fun by bringing out this new edition, including post-1969 days as his career rolled on. And the horrific blind-siding by a deadly stroke that floored him, took him into the dark region of total incapacitation. Nearly took him away altogether.

The "Rockhampton Rocket" had been rocketed within, his brain bleeding perilously. Not with their sharpest thrusts had such Hall of Famers as Neale Fraser, Ken Rosewall, Lew Hoad, Roy Emerson, John Newcombe, Tony Roche, Stan Smith, Arthur Ashe been able to derail him so effectively.

Rod's biggest win was his remarkable fight against the hemorraghic stroke -- not only to survive as his world suddenly fell apart, but to re-gain cognition and the strength to return to his beloved family, tennis, golf and gardening.

It was admirable. I was proud to be his friend. There is more to this man than peerlessly striking tennis balls and tigerishly competing – but the memories of those feats will always cheer me.

Bud Collins
Boston, Mass.
2009

TURN OFF THE RAIN

THE NIGHT MARY HUNG UP ON ME THE YEAR NEARLY WENT sour.

I was almost through the biggest year of any tennis player—maybe any athlete—ever had when the pressure that suddenly grabbed me was one that almost every man has felt: domestic. I had an unhappy, angry wife who wanted me home when I had to be somewhere else 3,000 miles away, and who ended the argument strongly—she stopped talking to me. Although numerous husbands would consider that a lucky break, I did not. There's no way I can play or feel well if there's something wrong between me and Mary.

For a while I worried that it would stay wrong, just when I was within reach of everything. If it had, I couldn't have joined those exceptional athletes who made 1969 such an extraordinary year in sports.

So many wonderfully improbable things happened in 1969: The New York Jets ruled football. Those magnificent antiques, the Boston Celtics, came to life one more time to conquer basketball. The New York Mets climbed out of the trashcan to glitter atop baseball. Arnold Palmer, who had begun to be regarded as a monument to past glories, began to win golf tournaments again. And in tennis, where I had labored practically underground since becoming a professional in 1963, I won the first open Grand Slam and became something of a household name.

This was my year, 1969, and people were becoming aware of me and my sport. I realized this when Americans began asking me for my autograph—on the street and in other public places away from tournaments. This had been going on for a number of years in England and Australia, where there is a substantial tennis public. In Time magazine, an article referred to British talk-show host David Frost as "the Rod Laver of television . . . [who] would consider success in the U.S. the culmination of his own grand slam." A couple of years before, my name would never have been used for that sort of comparison in Time. Sporting references are common but tennis is never the sport cited. Not in the United States. In his World War II memoirs Field Marshal Montgomery could talk about breaking Nazi General Rommel's serve, but that was for British consumption.

It meant more to me than just seeing my face and name more frequently, in wider pictures and taller type. It meant that the game I've devoted my life to was beginning to catch on big and that more and more people were becoming aware of it and recognizing that it was the best game for them.

Life had been very different seven years before, in 1962, the first time I made the Grand Slam. Then the Slam was an affair for amateurs only. Open tennis—the integration of amateurs and professionals in competition-was a long way off, and seemed unlikely to arrive during my career. I was an amateur making a comfortable living from playing. Twenty-four years old without a worry. Single. Free. Hitting a tennis ball. Seeing every bit of the world I could. Having a few beers. Partying a bit. That was all that was on my mind. Most people felt that was about all my mind could hold: another bland, efficient Australian tennis champion. A countrywoman of mine, Lemeau Watt, once remarked at a tennis party: "Rod does his job extremely competently and thoroughly. No show, no emotion. Like a good plumber. A plumber doesn't put on a show down there alone in the basement, does he? On the court Rod is totally oblivious to his surroundings."

I don't think of myself as just another Australian, though I'll agree we aren't the most flamboyant breed. I do have some distinguishing marks, although hardly any that would make you single me out as a big-time athlete. Red hair, scrawny, 49,000 freckles, a crook in my nose and a bow in my legs. Maybe I have a certain appeal to the spectators because I seem ordinary enough to be one of them. Maybe, but are they looking for the ordinary, even if they can identify with it?

There's one thing: my unimpressive body hangs from King Kong's left arm. Of course, it probably doesn't seem that unusual from the grandstand. I was stunned myself when Dave Anderson of *The New York Times* tape-measured me one afternoon in 1968 and reported that my left forearm is twelve inches around—as big as Rocky Marciano's was. And my left wrist is seven inches around. Floyd Patterson, another former heavyweight champion, has a six-inch wrist.

I guess I hit tennis balls more times than Rocky and Floyd hit people, although not as damagingly. The balls still had some bounce when I got through with them. You couldn't say that for many of Rocky's opponents.

I imagine throwing a good punch is as satisfying as punching a winning volley. A lot of things changed for me in the seven years between Slams, but not the indescribably joyful sensation of hitting a tennis ball well. The hacker has to do this only once to sense what I'm talking about, and then he goes in pursuit of a repeat. It may take him ten minutes to find it again, but it's worth it. I'm lucky because I've been hitting the ball well for years. It's still an obsession. I suppose the same is true for a batter in baseball. I know it is for a golfer. I love golf, and shoot in the eighties whenever I can find time to play. The trouble with baseball and golf is you don't get to hit the ball enough. The better you hit the golf ball, the fewer opportunities per round you have to experience that great feeling.

Boxing and tennis, however, give you as much swinging and hitting as you want. Strangely, although they may seem worlds apart, boxing and tennis have a certain kinship. Two individuals head-to-head, probing for weakness and attacking it. Footwork, timing and stamina are essential. Just you and your opponent in there until one of you is beaten. There's no brain damage in tennis – although sometimes I wonder.

The element of inflicting physical harm is meant to be absent in ten-

nis, but it isn't unheard of. This isn't the garden party game that origi-
nated among Victorian gentlemen in England. It's not hockey by any
means, but players get "toey," as we say at home—edgy, annoyed—and
punches get thrown. Probably the stroke-of-the-year for 1969 was the
left hook with which an Englishman, Roger Taylor, gashed and flattened
an Australian, Bob Hewitt, following their acrimonious match in West
Berlin. Taylor won the match and the fight, but lost money because his
hand broke against Hewitt's head and he couldn't play for a while. Even
though he won, Roger was embarrassed. Antagonisms can develop
during a match, but they don't often blossom so violently. Hewitt was
embarrassed, too. We Aussies regard the English—we call them Pom-
mies (for pomegranate eaters)—as below us in sport. In fist fighting, the
English are the ones who get knocked down. But Roger Taylor made up
for all those hopeless English heavyweights in boxing history, and you
won't catch me badgering Roger the way Bob did.

Nor was I going to badger Mary when she boxed my ear by dropping
the receiver resoundingly to end our conversation.

Nothing could bother me the last time around the Slam. Now I was
bothered. Then I didn't understand the workings of mortgages or wives.
I didn't have either. Now I had one of each.

I don't know that my understanding is much greater, but I have
learned that they take some thought and concern and effort, particularly the wife.

I had put through this call from Boston to our home in Corona-del-
Mar, California, on a July night only eight days after I'd won Wimbledon, the tournament that is synonymous with the British championship—and the world singles title. With Australia and France already in
the sack, I was at the three-quarter pole on the run for the Slam and
only a few weeks away from the finish at Forest Hills.

The conversation with Mary wasn't good. It was the worst of my life,
and though I could see why she was furious, there wasn't much I could
do about it. If you know how to stop the rain in Boston, let me know and
we'll make a lot more money in that line than in tennis.

Rain. That was what had put me and Mary in such a long-distance bind. I've heard about that Spanish plain, but it can't be as wet as Long-wood Cricket Club during a tennis tournament. When O. C. Smith, the country singer, went on about the summertime rain in Indianapolis, he should have checked out Boston to really find out about rain.

Like India, Boston has a predictable monsoon season: it arrives when I arrive.

It was my sixth visit to Boston for the U.S. Pro Championships, and I was trying to win the title for the fifth time. Only once in all those years was the tournament not in danger of floating away.

Pancho Gonzalez and I played the 1964 final, the first year I won, in a driving nor'easter, on sloshed grass. In 1968, there was so much rain that we had to abandon the tournament and return two months later to complete it.

At the end of the summer of 1969, when I completed the Slam at swampy Forest Hills—Boston weather had gone South—the reporters marveled at the way I played in the muck, particularly the British journalists. They'd never seen such good tennis under such bad conditions, they wrote following my victory over Tony Roche. But that's only because they'd never covered tennis in Boston where I had trained well to become a bog-runner.

Nobody has drowned yet playing at Longwood, but I've fallen into enough puddles to worry about the possibility. I'm always pleased whenever the club lifeguard, attends the matches.

I don't know what it is with Longwood, but in 1965 it seemed to be the only place rain fell during a New England drought. The club president then, the late John Bottomley, felt a little guilty in church on our semi-finals Sunday. The priest led a prayer for rain—"for the farmers"—and John said he was praying for dry weather for the tennis players. "Actually," he said, "it was a split prayer, because I was with the farmers, too. But I knew I'd lose. We'd get drenched and the farmers would parch."

That's what happened. Mary was well aware of Boston's record, and she was worried that the tournament would drag on, eating into the last time we'd have together before our baby came at the end of the summer.

Pregnancy didn't help her disposition. She hadn't had a baby for seventeen years—there were three of them in her first marriage—and she was getting cumbersome and uncomfortable.

We'd had a marvelous time at Wimbledon, living in a quiet flat at Dolphin Square, a large block of apartments near the Thames. I'd spent very little time with my American wife during a year jammed with frantic traveling. London was pleasant even though I had to concentrate on the tournament. At least we were together.

After Boston, we were going to have nine more days, and then she'd be alone the rest of the summer, alone when the baby was due to come on finals day at Forest Hills.

That was the obstetrician's prediction: September 7. If everything went well for the Laver family, that would be the day of the Grand Slam for me and the Grand Slim for her.

We parted at London airport. I flew to Boston. She went over the Pole to Los Angeles, which is fifty miles from our home that hung over the Pacific at Corona-del-Mar. Her flight was delayed, and arrived several hours late. By the time she got home the glow of London was gone and she was nervous and tired. How else should she have felt?

In the back of my mind I thought I might be joining her in a couple of days. Everybody has a letdown after Wimbledon, and I wouldn't have been startled if somebody had beaten me in Boston. After I won the tournament, Arthur Ashe commented: "Laver has to be inhuman to play that well after Wimbledon. You just have to have a letdown, but he didn't!"

That summer I was inhuman, I guess. Mary probably thought so for a while even more than my opponents.

While I've been complaining about Boston weather, I have nothing but good feeling about the place and the people. It's where pro tennis finally began to grow up, and maybe where the entire game started to turn around and head toward a boom.

The U.S. Pro Championships had been played since 1927, the year after competitive professional tennis began. In 1926, an American sports promoter, C. C. (Cash-and-Carry) Pyle launched a new spectator sport by signing the French Diva, Suzanne Lenglen, ex-U.S. champ Mary K.

Browne, Vincent Richards, Harvey Snodgrass, Paul Feret, and Howard Kinsey to go on tour. Richards won the first U.S. title over Kinsey at a place called Notlek Tennis Courts, a site in Manhattan long since buried beneath a building.

The tournament had good days and mostly bad days in the years that followed, but it hardly became one of the great events. In 1963, my first year as a pro, Ken Rosewall beat me in the final, and the payoff was zero. Attendance at Forest Hills was poor, the promoters went broke, and all they could present us with was "sorry, fellows." Even on toast it wouldn't taste good.

There were no plans to continue the staggering tradition until Ed Hickey, a public relations man for the New England Merchants National Bank—and a tennis nut—talked his bosses into sponsoring us. The bank put up $10,000 in prize money, and Longwood, the second oldest club in America (1877), took us in. Just when it appeared that the pros wouldn't even appear in America in 1964, Boston rescued us, and due to the good name of the bank we were able to line up sponsors in a few other cities and get a small circuit going. Despite the weather, Boston was a success. We were in business unexpectedly in the United States.

That summer on the eight-city American circuit Kenny Rosewall was our leading money winner with $8,800, while I was third with $6,900. At Longwood alone in 1969 I won $8,600, and in 1970 first prize went up to $12,000. The financial advances in pro tennis have been pretty substantial, today dealing in the millions. But we felt like millionaires with the Boston payoffs.

Because of this, we pros have felt an obligation to Boston, the bank and the club and their tournament. They meant new life. That's one reason, that I always wanted play well there. No letdowns in Boston, although, as I said, it wouldn't have surprised me to do badly.

There was more than the $8,600 first prize on my mind. There was Mary and my first child.

Still, with luck, I told her in London, we'd be seeing each other in a week's time and have those nine days together, to fix up the nursery, to relax in the lovely home I seldom lived in.

"See you next Monday," she smiled, "and tell them to turn off the rain this time."

For five days it was perfect. Then on Saturday the inevitable downpour began. "We'll play the final Monday. See you Tuesday," I told Mary over the phone confidently. I was playing well and believed I'd be in the final.

"Look, it isn't fair," she said, "for them to keep you there if the rain goes on and on. Last year you came back later to finish it. They could do the same thing this year if it rains again Sunday."

And it did rain. And I had to call Mary. This call I dreaded. Now my arrival was pushed back to Wednesday—if the rain stopped, that is. Maybe later.

"They can't keep you there indefinitely," she reasoned. "Tell them you're leaving Tuesday regardless of what happens. I want you to leave Tuesday . . ."

"But I can't just walk out, Mary," I replied.

"It wouldn't be walking out if you tell them now. Tell them that you've made plans, and you're already staying over. Just explain that you have to leave Tuesday and they'll juggle the schedule or reschedule entirely."

We talked that over for a while, and her mood wasn't good. Then, abruptly she said, "Well, Rod, if you aren't home Tuesday, don't bother to come . . ."

Bang! went the receiver in California. The click went through me like a sonic boom. Mary is a strong girl. She slams a receiver as hard as I slam an overhead.

What did she mean? I wasn't about to redial and ask.

Was one more day away that big a deal? Before Mary begins to seem the villainness of this piece, I'd like to make it clear that she's the heroine. Without her and the sense of purpose she's brought to my wandering life, there'd have been no Grand Slam of 1969. I'd be a very good player if she weren't sharing my life, I'll concede that. But I'd be a very lonely one, and not so good as I became.

Our marriage is one thing we're sure of, but it hasn't been easy for either of us. It isn't easy for any athlete's wife, with all the traveling her man does and all the time he's away from home. But I believe it's the worst for a tennis player's wife. The other sports stick to fixed schedules; tennis' schedule is often erratic, and the weather plays a greater part in altering it. A baseball player is gone, on the road, for at most two weeks. Football players are away a few weekends, and the trips for basketball and hockey players are brief. For the most part the golf circuit is within the United States, and the players can often drive between tournaments. A golfer can even take his family along in a trailer when the kids are young.

With me, it's Sydney one day and Philadelphia two days later. My season is the entire year, my places every time zone, every continent. I may be gone six weeks or more at a time. This was my 1969 itinerary, between January 10 and December 4: To Australia—Sydney for the New South Wales Open . . . up to Brisbane for the Australian Open . . . over to Auckland for the New Zealand Open . . . off to Philadelphia for an indoor open at the Spectrum . . . down to Florida for pro tournaments in Orlando and Miami . . . home for five days . . . up the coast to Oakland, Portland, and Seattle for small pro tournaments . . . home, commuting to the pro tourney in Los Angeles . . . and then our "vacation," nine days in Hawaii . . . from there to New York for the Madison Square Garden Open . . . a long flight to Johannesburg for the South African Open . . . back home for a few days, while commuting to a pro tournament in Anaheim . . . then to Tokyo for a pro tournament . . . home for two days en route to New York for the Madison Square Garden Pro tourney . . . on to London for the BBC-TV match . . . over the Channel for a pro tournament in Amsterdam . . . up to Paris for the French Open . . . rebounding over the Channel to Bristol for the West of England Open . . . then settling three weeks in London for the open at Queen's Club followed by the Wimbledon fortnight . . . a jump to Boston for the U.S. Pro Championships . . . home a few days prior to pro tournaments in St. Louis, Binghamton, N.Y., Ft. Worth, and Baltimore . . . now New York for two weeks and the Grand Slam climax at Forest Hills . . . back home to welcome the baby and play the Pacific Southwest Open at Los Angeles . . . a hop to Las Vegas for the Howard Hughes Open . . . a few days at home before revisiting Europe for pro tourneys at Cologne and Hamburg . . . home to change shirts, then once more to Europe (via business stops in Boston and New York) to play tournaments in Barcelona, London, Stockholm, Basel, and Madrid.

One season—on the road 259 days; nearly 200,000 miles.

Countless take-offs and landings, hotel rooms, packings, and un-packings. The beer labels, from Sapporo in Tokyo to Foster's in Sydney to Narragansett in Boston to Coors in Vegas, ran together in a blurred montage. Within a year's time, beginning with the Argentine Open in November of 1968, I played every continent except for Antarctica. The only reason I missed that is Admiral Byrd spoiled the commercial pos-sibilities by not charging the penguins to watch a visiting attraction.

I spent more time over the Atlantic than under my own roof, and that isn't a good basis for a marriage. Sometimes Mary must think she's mar-ried to a left-handed yo-yo, and naturally we've had our fights.

But Mary wouldn't ask me to give up the game, even though we'd be all right financially if I did. She's a trained accountant, and I too could get some sort of job. But she realizes that I'd be miserable in a nine-to-five job, that I've got to be hitting that tennis ball for a while yet.

At first I thought she was being unreasonable when she gave me the ultimatum and hung up on me. But one of her statements kept coming back: "The year just gets whittled down to nothing."

She was right about that. My contract called for an annual guarantee of $90,000 from my boss. In 1969, that was National Tennis League, an organization of pros run by George MacCall and Fred Podesta. That's $10,000 a month for nine months with three months off. I went to play wherever they told me, and I got that money if I didn't win a match. The prize money I earned applied against the guarantee, and in 1969 I won $124,000. That meant I went $34,000 above the guarantee, which de-lighted the bosses. They had to pay me nothing, but they had to make up the differences between earnings and guarantees for a couple of other players.

In addition, they paid my air fares or other travel, while I was respon-sible for all my living expenses. How does a promoter make any money?

They haven't been too successful. The theory is that they'll be able to profit by charging management fees to various tournaments for supplying our bodies. Or by running their own tournaments. It has worked out well only for the players.

Now, three months off sounds nice until you begin breaking it down. If the average worker gets a three-week vacation, two days off a week plus seven legal holidays, he has 126 days free compared to my 93. Of course, I like the $90,000 guarantee, and I'm not moaning. But I am pointing out what it can do to your family life. My three months off are spaced in dribs and drabs of five days here and eight somewhere else.

Once in 1969, because of rain and flying difficulties and a medical problem with my elbow, an eight-day holiday was whittled to eight hours. Mary met an incoming plane, drove me to a doctor's office for treatment, and then back to the airport to catch another plane.

It's been like this from the start, when we even had trouble getting married. We were supposed to have a week's honeymoon after a tournament in St. Louis in June of 1966, and it turned out to be one day when another tournament was added to the schedule.

"Spare me from long honeymoons," was Mary's reaction. She took it pretty well, although only a day earlier she thought even that much was going to disappear.

Where was the groom, everybody wondered at the bridal dinner. I wasn't sure myself. I was in the singles and doubles finals at St. Louis and lost them both, being a little shakier than usual with the wedding set for the next day. Lew Hoad and I grabbed our rental car and headed for the airport to catch a plane for San Francisco. On the way to the airport the car gagged and quit. "I think we're out of gas," said Lew, reading the gauge astutely.

"I think we're out of one bridal dinner and wedding rehearsal in San Rafael, California," I said. "And maybe one wedding."

"With your footwork they'll never let you go through a wedding without a rehearsal," Lew said cheerfully. "Let's have a beer somewhere."

I thought we should try for gas first, and eventually both needs were filled, and later on there was a plane on which we flew all night, arriving about 3:00 a.m. Nobody to meet us at the airport then. We rented another car and were about to try and find where we were staying when, "For God's sake, Lew, I left my travel folder, air tickets . . . all my vital stuff on that plane." I was in tip-top shape for the biggest day of my life.

By that time the plane was in a hangar somewhere, but we tracked it down, found the folder and spent the next four hours driving around the San Rafael area, trying to discover where we were. At daybreak, we got un-lost and found the house. We did get some breakfast and a shave en route to the church.

Graciously, after all that, Mary showed up, too, and we did get married. She got an idea of what it was going to be like, and she became reconciled to it.

But the whittling down of the time we're supposed to have together gets to her, and this was magnified—with everything else—by her pregnancy.

Her mood was not magnanimous, and all through that Monday I wondered, what kind of man am I? Wasn't my commitment to my wife and child as important as a tennis tournament? Shouldn't I explain my position to the tournament officials, excuse myself and leave?

Several times I thought of doing just that. I even made a plane reservation for Tuesday morning. If I defaulted early, the tournament wouldn't really be left in the lurch, I tried to tell myself. I was to play Rosewall in the semis Monday night. I could forfeit the match to him beforehand and be on my way. The crowd would get to see the other semi—John Newcombe against Fred Stolle—plus some doubles. They would feel cheated by my withdrawal, I suppose, but there would still be an excellent final on the Tuesday between Rosewall and the Newcombe-Stolle winner. I'd won the tournament four times in five years. It might be nice for somebody else to win. I didn't believe it, but you know how you can rationalize almost anything in those inner arguments—especially with those angry words of hers bouncing back and forth inside my brain like a long baseline rally.

I didn't think long about a default. I couldn't do that. I had to play

Making Mary my wife was indeed my grandest triumph. I'm glad that many of the boys were on hand for the ceremony - and very happy that I made it there myself after quite an adventure with Lew Hoad the day and night before.

Rosewall, but I was beginning to get fatalistic, which was something new for me. I started to tell myself that it was no disgrace losing to Kenny. He's often beaten me when I was playing splendidly. I would try, but my concentration would be broken and he'd probably beat me. Well . . . so what?

I was really building myself up for a loss, convincing myself that it was all for the best. Mary wanted me to walk out on the final. It wouldn't be necessary. In my state of mind I wasn't going to be in the final. The sound of that phone clicking was in my ear, and I was worried about Mary and the baby.

Kenny and I walked onto the court, and my head was buzzing like mission control. Our argument was being replayed along with a soliloquy of my own. I was saying why doesn't Mary understand, and replying that maybe it was me that didn't understand. What difference can one match make? None, but this might be our only baby, and weren't Mary and the little fellow everything?

As we began warming up, I welcomed this inner conflict because I knew it would jam my concentration. There's no way you can play well with ruptured concentration. So Rosewall would beat me but I wouldn't be taking a dive. If you can't concentrate, you'll lose. It was comforting.

And it didn't work out. It was a lovely evening. The stands were full, more than 5,000 people, which outside of London, Paris, or New York is a big tennis crowd. Well, we're all bloody ham actors. Put a crowd in the place and we haven't got time to worry about our wives running off with the milkman, or having a miscarriage, or spending the prize money before we've won it. We stop having soap operas in our brains—or at least I do.

Kenny and I were ready to go. There he was, Kenneth Robert (Muscles) Rosewall across the net. A friend, yet for seven years a deadly enemy. My most difficult opponent. And you know, everything bugging me just vanished. It's funny—and I don't understand why—but I just don't know how to play a match without trying. There was no way to keep myself from doing everything I could to beat Rosewall.

I was a winner before I was a husband. I'm a victim of a wanting-to-win that has been inside me since the first time I hit a tennis ball, and this wanting has more control over me than family, money, anything.

I won.

Then it started again, the cerebral soap opera . . . "Can Rodney the Rocket win the tennis tournament and the game of marriage, too? Or is it one or the other?"

As I walked to the clubhouse, the debate came along with and within me. The plane reservation is set for tomorrow morning, Tuesday, the day of the ultimatum. But so is the final. Walk out now? Would I be the first man to win the Grand Slam, welcome his firstborn and get a divorce all in the same day—while being sued by the New England Merchants Bank for betraying their tournament?

I had to talk it over with somebody. A friend, who knew me mostly as an athlete—a competitor—had a couple of beers with me, and I told him the whole thing. It felt better to talk it out. Finally he said, "You're not going to be on that plane tomorrow. You're going to be playing tennis tomorrow night."

"I guess you're right," I agreed. We had another beer, and I said good night. I slept well.

The next day, I knocked off Newcombe, and in the doubles old Pancho Gonzalez and I, playing our first tournament together, beat the Wimbledon champions, Newcombe and Roche. It was an $8,600 evening for me. Vinnie Richards, the first U.S. Pro champ, won the tournament four times. Now I was one up on him, but still three singles titles behind Gonzalez.

I was on the first plane to the West Coast the next morning, and Mary was waiting for me at the L.A. airport with a big kiss. I was apprehensive, a day late. She didn't mention it. Neither did I. She didn't mention the phone call, and never has.

LESSON • 1

Mental Preparation

PANCHO GONZALEZ once told me about the night before his Davis Cup debut against Australia, the final in 1949. He and Ted Schroeder, who were to be the singles players for the U.S., were terribly nervous. After dinner they settled into a bridge game with Alrick Man, their captain. "Alrick kept looking at his watch," Pancho said, "and around midnight he finally said, 'Aren't you fellows going to bed? You've got a big match tomorrow.' We told him to relax and enjoy his bridge. There was no sense going to bed when we were so keyed up that we knew we'd just lie there and think about the next day's matches. It would be anything but restful. Finally, at about three a.m., we got tired and quit playing cards. We were tired enough to sleep, and the few hours sleep we got were good ones." Both won their singles and the U.S. retained the Cup.

I know the feeling. At Forest Hills in 1969, my semifinal with Arthur Ashe was halted by darkness with me leading. It's a tough situation when you have to come back the next day to finish. You could drive yourself bonkers thinking about it. So I stayed up a little later than usual, had an extra beer to make sure that when I got into bed I'd go right to sleep.

Otherwise you can get up more tired and psyched than when you turned out the lights.

A match played in your mind can be harder than one on the court. I know of club players so determined to be rested for a match that they'll go to bed at nine, planning to get about twelve hours sleep. Instead they think about the match and play it about five times and sleep fitfully, if at all. I'm not recommending that you stay out all night. It's an individual thing. But I do think it's silly to get in bed before you're tired and risk counting shots that don't bound over the net.

I try not to think about a match at all until a few minutes before I go onto the court. Then I welcome the rush of nervousness. It tells me the adrenaline is pouring. If I'm not nervous I worry because my mind and body aren't getting me up for a match.

The mental and the physical are very close. If I'm not in tune physically I'm going to be lazy-minded. With the amount of tennis I play over nearly the entire year I never feel really unfit. Thus my daily practice sessions are pretty strenuous. I like to practice an hour and a half the day of a match—in the morning if I'm playing in the afternoon, or in the afternoon if I'm playing at night.

Obviously that's too much for the ordinary player, but I think the principle is important. By playing a fair bit the system wakes up, mentally and physically. For you it might be a ten- or fifteen-minute knock, but I think practice on a match day is vital.

It's easy to say don't think about a match until just before you play it, but how do I manage to avoid those thoughts? Well, I try to keep myself busy in other ways, doing errands and other things. If I can keep moving about, doing something—not strenuous—my mind will shut out the coming match. I also try not to arrive at the court much before my match is scheduled. If I did absolutely nothing during those hours preceding a match, I really would get fidgety and edgy.

2

SOMETHING CALLED
THE GRAND SLAM

THERE WAS PLENTY TO DO IN THE FEW DAYS I WAS HOME.
A nursery to set up and decorate. Some golf for relaxation. Some tennis, too—with Mary—which was also relaxing. She played until she was
seven-and-a-half-months pregnant, and tennis kept her feeling fit, and
from going crazy when she was alone.

She hadn't been playing very long, but she's enthusiastic. Although
she doesn't expect me to hit with her, I like to. Picasso shared his work
with his roommates by using them for models, didn't he? Why shouldn't
I share my talent at home, too? I don't know if Muhammad Ali practiced swings with his wife, but it all depends on your line of work. Tennis is fun and laughs we can have together. That's why it's such a good
family game. More people are discovering that tennis is an agreeable
way to keep trim.

After a week, I was ready to go again. Corona-del-Mar restores me
nicely. I like looking out at the ocean, watching the surf. From our house,
you had a good look at a great surfing area called the Wedge. You may
have seen it in that movie, The Endless Summer. I love to body surf, but
not in California. Too cold. I reckon the water back home in Queensland
is just right for it, and it amazes me to see all those Californians in the
water.

If I was that cold-blooded I'd never lose a match.

But I was pretty cold-blooded the rest of the summer after leaving home and heading East. This was the stretch run, the last quarter on the way to the winner's circle and the Slam at Forest Hills, and I didn't lose a match.

Grand Slam varies in meaning in the games of bridge, baseball, golf, and tennis. A sweep of the tricks, or a home run with the bases loaded, is unusual but not rare. The bridge table and the ball diamond offer the possibility daily.

In golf and tennis, a series of triumphs within a calendar year make up a Slam. Golf's has been singular, celebrated only in 1930 when Bobby Jones, the phenomenal Georgian, won the amateur and open championships in both Britain and the United States. I can't imagine there'll ever be another just like that one, since only an amateur is eligible to enter all four tournaments, and the amateur who can compete evenly with pros in golf and tennis no longer exists. Today golf's Grand Slam is considered the winning of both the U.S. and British Opens plus the Masters and the PGA. No one has ever done it.

The Slam in tennis is also an obstacle course of four national championships to be won in one year, though farther flung in time and location: the Australian in January, the French in June, the British in July, and the U.S. in September.

I like to think the tennis Slam is the hardest of all because you have to get your game up to top level four times over an eight-month stretch, and of course you're playing other tournaments in between, too. Much travel and changing conditions are involved. In 1969, I started in the tropical summer heat of Brisbane and wound up in the autumn rain of New York.

I'm not sure when I first heard the term Grand Slam, but it was Don Budge—the original Slammer—who cleared up the meaning for me. Don explained that the only countries to win the Davis Cup—Australia, the U.S., France, and Britain—became known as the Big Four, the world's tennis powers, and when Budge was the first to sweep the Big Four titles in 1938—the year I was born—his feat was called the Grand Slam.

Five years earlier, an Australian, Jack Crawford, came very close.

Jack won the Australian, French, and Wimbledon (British). The official name is The Lawn Tennis Championships, period, (but everybody calls this event Wimbledon.) At Forest Hills for the U.S. Championship, Crawford led Fred Perry two sets to one, and it appeared that he would have a Slam.

Crawford hadn't set out specifically to win all four, as did Budge in 1938, and numerous others including myself later. He just won the first three, and that had never happened before. But there was little, if any, ballyhoo about a Grand Slam preceding his bid to complete it.

In his column in *The New York Times*, John Kieran did write: "If Crawford wins, that would be something like scoring a grand slam on the courts, doubled and vulnerable."

And when Crawford fell short, Allison Danzig reported in paragraph three of his account in the *Times* that "Crawford's quest of the Grand Slam was frustrated."

With his 2-1 lead in sets Crawford may have looked the winner, but he was through, exhausted. He was having trouble with his asthma, and even occasional slugs of brandy taken during the fourth and fifth sets couldn't turn him back on. Jack won one more game, and Perry won the match, 6-3, 11-13, 4-6, 6-0, 6-1.

The next year Perry, the dashing Englishman, took three of the major titles, but he was cut off early, losing in the fourth round of the French. But he won the French in 1935 and became the first to win all four major titles, though not within a calendar year.

Budge not only made the first Slam, he says he invented it. "I take certain whimsical pride in . . . creating it [the Slam]," he wrote in his autobiography. "Crawford almost won something that didn't exist. There was only passing notice at the time that I had won all four titles, but with time and publicity the stature of the Grand Slam grew. The expression became popular and it was what I came to be best known for.

"In 1938 I had set my goal to win these four titles, but only my good friend and doubles partner, Gene Mako, was aware of it.

"The fact that there was no such acknowledged entity as the Grand Slam made it somewhat easier for me because I wasn't bothered by the cumulative pressure of the press and fans that Laver and Lew Hoad [in 1956] had forced on them. But the pressure from within was no less intense for me than for them."

The *Times*' "passing notice," as Budge calls it, was just that after he beat Mako in the Forest Hills final. "Feat Sets a Precedent" was the fourth deck in the headline, and well down in his story Danzig noted: ". . . a grand slam that invites comparison with the accomplishment of Bobby Jones in golf."

Budge relates that his biggest goal had been attained in 1937 when he led the United States to its first Davis Cup success in ten years. He was clearly the master of the amateur world, and he wanted another goal to keep his interest high in 1938 before he helped in the defense of the Cup and then turned pro.

He set out to make a Slam, an original contribution to sporting lore, and a target for those who followed.

Thanks to his pioneering, the Slam received plenty of ballyhoo thereafter, and was uppermost when I made the rounds.

In Budge's time, obviously, few non-Australians made the twenty-one-day haul Down Under to play in our championship. The boat trip was forbidding and expensive. In 1938, only Budge, Mako, and three or four Australians even played all four Major tournaments. By my day the jets opened up the world to everyone and squeezed it together, making it relatively easy for a squad of tourists to hit all the major stops. The same tough crowd was everywhere—there was no avoiding them.

In Budge's Grand Slam, six of his 24 victories were over men ranked along with him in the world's top ten. In mine of 1969, I won 26 matches, 12 of them against others in the top ten. I also won the South African championship, the British Indoor, the U.S. Pro, and 11 other tournaments, a total of 18 titles in 33 tournaments. The pace had accelerated. We were playing every month of the year, probably too much for our own good. But the money was there, and we went after it.

Tennis wasn't a year-round occupation in the Budge era. It is now. I think it's more demanding, flitting between time zones, and there's more pressure with so much money being pumped into the game. But I like it this way, the money and the constant movement.

When I make comparisons between today and the more leisurely Budge period, I'm certainly not trying to make my triumphs sound any grander than his, just pointing up differences. At the end of 1969, a panel of the most respected tennis writers drew up an all-time ranking. It was headed by Bill Tilden. Second was Budge, followed by me. I don't think anybody can really say who was the greatest, but I am happy to accept that ranking. Moreover, I considered Don a friend, and I'll always be grateful to him for the way he treated me in 1962 when I was on the verge of my first Grand Slam.

Another man might have been resentful of my claiming a piece of the property that had been his alone for twenty-four years. Not Don. He had been through the tension, and knew what it could be like. He helped me relax by spiriting me away for a day in the country before Forest Hills began that year. We drove to the Grossinger's resort in the Catskills where I could take it easy. Nobody asking questions, no phones ringing. We even played a couple of nonchalant sets. He was great.

In Don's year, he was unquestionably the best player in the world, though an amateur. I couldn't very well consider myself the best when I won the amateur Grand Slam in 1962 so long as such splendid pros as Pancho Gonzalez, Ken Rosewall, and Lew Hoad were at large. Plus Butch Buchholz, Alex Olmedo, Andres Gimeno, Barry MacKay, and Mal Anderson. I was excited and tremendously pleased at making the Grand Slam in 1962. The collection of titles raised my asking price when I turned pro a few months later—but I knew I wasn't the best.

Probably Rosewall was then. Knowing that took something out of my satisfaction at dominating amateur tennis. I had my Grand Slam; now I wanted a shot at Rosewall, Gonzalez, and the others. To get it I had to drop into limbo with them on the pro circuit and give up any thought of ever repeating the Grand Slam.

It was either glory or money in those days prior to open tennis. You took your choice: glory (and, of course, enough money to get by on) with the amateurs; or very good money and anonymity with the pros. It was time for me to make the good money, and to satisfy my competitive urge against the blokes I knew were the strongest. But no more Slams . . . I thought then.

I'd heard about Budge's Grand Slam, and Californian Maureen Connolly's, too. Until Aussie Margaret Smith Court did it in 1970, and German Steffi Graf in 1988, Maureen had won the only women's Slam in 1953. My first year away from Australia, 1956, I was a witness to a near-thing. Lew Hoad was the world's No. 1 amateur then, one of my early heroes, and I was able to watch almost all of his matches as he took the Australian, French, Wimbledon, and came into the final at Forest Hills. One match away, but across the net was Kenny Rosewall.

I sat there marveling at Rosewall, along with the rest of the crowd, as he destroyed Lew's bid, 4-6, 6-2, 6-3, 6-3. I never stopped marveling at him. Thirteen years later, he was still around trying to break up my second Grand Slam. He had his shot at me in the final of the French, but I played the clay court match of my life and avoided the treatment he gave Lew.

But in 1956, it was exciting enough just to be at Forest Hills and follow Lew's progress. I was eighteen, awed, and unknown. A few aficionados recognized my name because I'd won the U.S. junior title a month before, but I could wander around getting the feel of the place completely unnoticed.

I was out of that tournament fast. Ham Richardson, then the No. 1 American, was my first-round opponent, and by virtue of the company I was keeping I played for the first time in the Forest Hills Stadium. Ham got me out of there before you could say one-two-three: 6-1, 6-2, 6-3. My Queensland mate, Roy Emerson, got to the quarters, and I was glad for him. It was fun for a young Australian to watch as his countrymen dominated the championship of their great rival, America, with Hoad, Rosewall, and Neale Fraser surrounding a solitary Yank, Vic Seixas, in the semis.

I didn't mind the passive role of spectator at the final. I figured I'd be there in one of the starring roles one day, but the thought of a Grand Slam for Laver didn't occur to me until four years later.

In 1960, I won the Australian title for the first time, and since that's the only way you can begin a Grand Slam, I wondered: Why not me? After beating Neale Fraser—coming from two sets down—I had that feeling that it was going to be a big Laver year. Hadn't I been Wimbledon finalist to Alex Olmedo in 1959? So why couldn't I make a Grand Slam?

Manolo Santana, the gifted Spaniard, showed me why. He and that slow clay in Paris abruptly brought me back to the real world. Parisian clay may look harmless, but it's quicksand for us outsiders from Australia and America, a trap that clogs our power and swallows us.

Europeans are like kids snapping up peanut butter sandwiches when they operate on the home ground against big hitters. My visions of a Grand Slam were almost blacked out in the first round of the French by a Pole named Andrzej Licis, who pushed me all over for five sets. Weird luck was the only way I beat him—with a no-hope shot made up on the run, a backhand topspin lob at match point that floated over his head, plunked on the baseline and left the ball stained with a big white chalkspot. I had never heard of Licis before, and seldom after, but that afternoon I thought he was one of the greatest players in the world. I doubt he felt the same respect for me.

I wasn't thinking Grand Slam anymore, just wondering how much longer I could last. Not another round. Santana, who really was one of the best, and plays a clay court as artistically as Isaac Stern plays the violin, put me out with little trouble.

I had to learn to play on clay, to firm up my patience and prepare my way to the net better. The Grand Slam was three-quarters grass [today hard courts replace lawns in Australia and the U.S.], and I wasn't worried about myself there. The other quarter, the French, is something else, more challenging than the others, more difficult to win, more satisfying from the standpoint of having survived a terrific test.

There isn't as much pressure, perhaps, because it's early in the season and the prestige isn't as great as Wimbledon or Forest Hills. But in Paris you know you've been in a fight. You come off the court exhausted, looking battle-stained, your clothes and body smudged with red clay.

I promised myself that in 1961 it would be different for me in Paris. It was to the extent that I got to the semifinals before running into Santana, who was the top seed. And I gave him a better match. After four sets we were even—in the score anyway, two sets each, and I'd had a fine chance to win in four, leading 4-1. But I was through, and Manolo wrapped me in a lovely web of shotmaking, 6-0 in the fifth. I believe that's the only time it's happened to me since I've been a world-class player. It happened so fast it was almost painless.

In the second set Manolo sprained his left ankle. He took off his shoe and hobbled around, testing, to see if he could go on. I followed him to commiserate, but not to step on his bare foot as I should have. I missed my chance. Still, it didn't seem to matter when I had that 4-1 lead in the fourth set.

Then Manolo exploded. He was sure of his ankle again, and he rang up eleven straight games and the match. I never got close until we shook hands.

Five weeks later, I won Wimbledon and was considered No. 1 in the world. Was that a nice thing to do to your leader, Manolo—blitz me in Paris with all those people watching? The next time I'll jump on your foot with both of mine.

LESSON • 2

The Killer Instinct

WHEN I WAS A KID, and beginning to play well, a little better than the ordinary, I first experienced the enjoyment of playing to a crowd. It was a good feeling to have my strokes admired, and I was in no hurry to get off the court. As a result I let too many opponents off the hook. I found out that you have to play with the intention of making it a short day, of doing the job quickly and thoroughly.

I don't mean rush it. Anything but that. But when you have the opportunity you strike then, and you realize that no lead is as big as it looks. If your opponent is serving at 1-4, you feel pretty good: three games ahead. But that's only one service break, and you want to keep the pressure on, or you're going to be in trouble. It's no time to experiment with new shots or to show off for the "sheilas" in the crowd.

I've heard it said that you're either born with the killer instinct or you're not. I don't agree with that. I feel I had to develop that killer outlook which, to me, means making the shot called for to win the point and resisting certain temptations. You don't try to blast a ball 200 mph crosscourt into a corner when you have an easy sitter and your opponent is way out of position. If a soft, unimpressive-looking dink is called for, you hit it and make the point.

The good chances don't come that frequently, and the killer knocks them off surely when presented with them. The killer doesn't let up or ease off when he gets a good lead. This can be learned. Make sure of the easy shots—concentrate extra hard on those. Everybody has problems with difficult shots, but the killer gets his edge because he is meticulous with the setups.

Don't compose eulogies to yourself when you get ahead. Concentrate on staying there. When Charlie Hollis, my coach, decided that I wasn't homicidal enough, he sent me out with the intent of winning every match 6-0, 6-0. That seems grim for the usual player, but Charlie's theme was good and clear: run scared and don't let anybody up.

CHARLIE HOLLIS

THERE WERE DECIDED SIMILARITIES BETWEEN THE GRAND Slammers Budge and Laver. Both redheads, freckled, a bit shy and reticent. Conscientious about learning to hit a tennis ball harder and better. Conscientious about winning.

Although Don came along first, conditions where I grew up were a good deal more primitive out in the never-never land of the Queensland cow country. I'll bet Don never sat in the rain to watch a movie. The movie houses in Oakland undoubtedly had roofs, but not the one in Rockhampton where I saw my first cowboy film—and became permanently hooked on John Wayne and others of that celluloid style. It was just an outdoor screen with folding chairs set up in rows. If it rained the movie kept going, and I stayed. You don't walk out on John Wayne, do you? And risk getting shot in the back?

I think we got started on roughly similar courts though. Don describes the public park court where he took his first swings as gravel. I would take that to mean a gritty surface, unlike the concrete more common to California on which he really developed and refined his game. My first court was ant bed, homemade by my Dad and the boys in the family. It's common stuff in the Australian Outback. You knock over an anthill, which has become quite hard, crush it and spread the grit on a level piece of ground where the grass has been skinned off. It plays a lot like clay.

About a month before Don, who was then twenty-two, concluded his Grand Slam, I was born at the Tamachy Hospital in Rockhampton, August 9, 1938. As far as I know, there is no plaque on the wall of the hospital to mark the occasion. A lot of people are surprised to learn that there were even walls, but Queensland isn't quite that rugged. And we weren't that far out in the Outback. It was far enough that we boys could hunt kangaroos, though; and when we built a tennis court, we had to clear quite a determined scrub growth.

It was a thoroughly outdoor life, but I didn't shoot up majestically as Budge did. I was a midget, five feet four, the first time I played at Wimbledon. I'm glad I grew a little more as I left my teens, to my present height of five feet, eight-and-a-half inches.

We Lavers aren't big people, but we're sturdy and athletic, as were the Roffeys, my mother's people. My grandmother, Mrs. Alice Roffey, was still riding horseback in 1967, the year she died. She was ninety. Uncle Frank Laver made a name as captain of an Australian national cricket side, but then a fellow should be pretty good if he is brought up on a team. There were eleven boys—my Dad, Roy Laver, the youngest—and that was just right for cricket. They were known as the Laver family side around Gipsland, the cattle country in Victoria where dad came from.

Dad was raised in the cattle business. He went north, to Queensland, to go on his own, and he did well with various properties—what Americans call ranches. He met Melba Roffey, my mother (like many Australian girls named for Dame Nellie Melba, the great opera singer of the time), married her, and they settled in the Rockhampton area. We moved around a bit in those parts. Rocky is on the coast, above Brisbane, tropical country, a town of about 30,000 then.

Until I was nine, we were on a property called Langdale. Then we were in a tiny town called Marlborough, where Dad ran the butcher shop. He was fifty now, and easing out of the cattle business where he'd done well. After his brief stint as a butcher, we moved into Rocky. Dad wanted us closer to school and closer to organized tennis.

We'd had a court on the Langdale property, and on the weekends the "neighbors" from properties in the area—sometimes from miles away—

would gather at our place to play. When there was a tournament in Rockhampton, Mum and Dad would gather us up and we'd all go in. They'd play all the events, mixed doubles together.

They were keen on the game, and Dad was very ambitious for us three boys. Trevor is six years older than I, and Bob four years. Lois, the only girl, is a good deal younger. She was born when I was nine, and didn't figure much in the family tennis. Dad wanted us to be good at tennis, and he felt Trevor could be a fine tournament player.

He didn't think much of my chances because I was so small, but soon after Charlie Hollis took over coaching us in Rocky, Charlie told Dad that I'd be the best. "They're like you, Roy," was the appraisal of Trevor and Bob that Charlie Hollis gave my Dad. "Quick-tempered. They blow up too fast. Rodney has the more easygoing manner of his mother. If we can build the killer instinct in him, then it'll be the perfect blend."

Charlie was always after me to beat my opponent as badly as I could. "Your job is to go out there and win as quickly as possible, Rodney. If you can beat him 6-0, 6-0, do it. Give them no chance to come back at you."

In Rocky, where Dad was semiretired, working a little in contracting business, we cleared trees and scrub and built ourselves another court. Lighted, too, although the five 1500-watt bulbs we strung overhead were about as strong as candles in a London fog. We were eager, though, and our sharp young eyes could have sighted a ball in a coal mine.

It was one of those nights I sneaked out of bed for my introduction to Charlie Hollis. I was a little over ten. He was having a knock with Dad, Trev, and Bob, and when he spied me in my pajamas, my nose sticking through the chicken wire, he said, "Let the little bugger have a hit." Pajamas and bare feet may be the costume for some pretty good games, but not tennis. I went out there anyway and kept the ball going with Charlie.

Later he advised Dad, "Rodney's got the eye of a hawk. I believe we can make a champion out of him."

They were determined to do it. Dad drove me everywhere to play tournaments, even as far as Brisbane, which was 450 shaky, dusty miles over dirt roads. He had started me off, and he made sure I paid attention to

Charlie, whose ability as a teacher he respected.

When we boys began a daily program under Hollis, we'd get up at five in the morning, ride our bicycles five miles to the town courts and play by ourselves until Charlie woke up and supervised us before we had to go to school. After school it was more tennis, and then some more at night with Dad when we finished our homework.

The fences on the town courts didn't last long after Hollis got himself established as the coach in Rocky. He had his class practice serving by knocking the ball at the fence from six feet away. We didn't waste time chasing balls, and a lot of kids could use one court. It was a good way to get grooved in our motion before we actually began playing.

Charlie was a great one for a complete approach. Tennis was more than just hitting a ball if you were going to go someplace in the game. He was a bachelor and he often ate with us. He'd scold me if he thought my table manners were off. "You have to know which fork to use when you go abroad to play Wimbledon," he'd say.

He was always talking about the great players, holding them up as examples. He'd been a good amateur himself, and had seen Budge when Don toured Australia in 1938. He would describe Budge's wonderful backhand, and he'd quiz us frequently.

"Who was Gentleman Jack?"

"Jack Crawford," I'd answer.

"Why was he called Gentleman Jack?"

"Because he was a fine sportsman, and he always was well groomed, on and off the court."

My brothers still like tennis, but they prefer fishing and skin diving from their boat that they take out to the Barrier Reef. That's my favorite vacation, going out to the Reef to fish, away from everything in marvelous hot weather.

Charlie would come fishing with us—Trevor and I both won local fishing championships—but his mind never left tennis. We'd be reeling in a big one, excited at the catch, and Charlie might remark, "You know, that Fred Perry certainly had a marvelous forehand. . . ."

No amount of work on your game was enough to satisfy Charlie, and he was a good man to coach me because I thrived on work. For the same reason, I enjoyed the tough training and drills Harry Hopman put us through - first when I attended his clinics in Brisbane and later when he was my Davis Cup captain and I was playing for Australia. This wanting within me to be the best drove me to do any amount of work. If Charlie had directed me to walk to the top of the Toowoomba Range on my hands, I would have done it.

During his teaching career, he continued to take a critical interest in me. After I'd made the second Grand Slam, I received a terse cable from him: "Congratulations. Do it again."

Twice around the Grand Slam was not enough for Charlie. Nothing ever was.

LESSON • 3

Conditioning and Equipment

AS AUSTRALIANS, we pride ourselves on being very fit. Harry Hopman, our Davis Cup captain, pushed us hard, and I think conditioning is sometimes more important than ability. You can have the greatest strokes in the world, but you won't be able to hit them very well if you're tired.

I went to a gym as a youngster to build myself up, punched a bag and followed the rest of the strenuous routines of boxers. It depends on how serious you are about the game. Running is a must. After you practice, you go for a run. Once you're tired I reckon the next five or ten minutes—when you really push yourself—is the real benefit you get out of that day, as far as making yourself stronger. You've got to go beyond the limit. If you run four laps, and feel like you've had it—then you'd better run a couple more. Quicker. This is to get in top shape. By staying this way I find I have not only second wind in a match but third and fourth wind. It's a great feeling to know that you have more in reserve when you're playing a tough match. The running and the exercises, the feeling of fitness, are an important part of my enjoyment of tennis.

For the older player, who isn't particularly keen on being able to go five sets with Ken Rosewall on a clay court, tennis itself is a nice conditioner. You go along at your own speed, and you're not going to kill yourself, maybe. But there is this to remember in a match: if you're tired, maybe your opponent is exhausted. By sticking with it just a little longer instead of saying, oh, the hell with it, you'll often come through in a match you thought was lost.

You've got to play at your own pace, however, and maybe that means doubles as you get a little older. You're not covering as much court, but often doubles is more satisfying because the ball stays in play longer—and you pick a spry partner to run down the lobs. Selection of partner—one who can carry you—is the chief consideration in doubles. Why do you think I play with that pillar of fitness, Roy Emerson?

Don't give up the game just because you've slowed down at singles. Jean Borotra, the old French Davis Cup ace who played into his 90s, said, "Never give up singles. If you play one hour per day without fail you can go on forever." And that's just what he did.

One of my most thrilling experiences was being on the same court with Pieter Smith during an exhibition in Johannesburg. Smith was the beneficiary of a heart transplant, and was back playing tennis. Doubles. Sensibly—which means not taking an unnecessary step. This rule doesn't apply to heart patients alone. As you edge into the over-45 senior league (a senior is a person who believes that every day in every way he is getting better—even though his legs aren't), you should learn that it's silly to chase down every ball. I do because it's my living. But unless you have a real play at a ball—forget it.

You should give some thought to preparation for a match. Loosen up the muscles. A few sit-ups, bending and stretching exercises. Run in place for a minute or so. Unless you're warm, you risk pulling a muscle or straining something. I've noticed that few people take enough practice serves. It's very easy to injure your arm or shoulder if you aren't properly warmed up. Don't be one of those "first one in" guys. Take your time and hit a dozen practice serves, easily at first. Pamper that arm and shoulder.

If it's cold, wear a sweater, maybe even a sweat suit at first until you're functioning smoothly. Wear a hat. One of our floppy Aussie fishing hats is best. On the depressingly torrid Australian days I would wear wet cabbage leaves inside my hat. Honestly. It helped. I sometimes wore a dampened handkerchief around my neck in extreme heat. It's refreshing, and kept sun off the neck.

Keep hydrated. During a match it's all right to sip water. I might have a total of five glasses during a long match in the day, which included some used for just rinsing my mouth out. After a match, I would take Gatorade or one of the other drinks that replenish mineral losses. I don't think they help much during a match. For instant energy, I took glucose tablets during a match. Carbonated drinks are not good.

Naturally you don't stuff yourself before a match. I eat three or four hours prior to a match, although that's an individual thing. I don't believe you should eat less than two hours before playing. Your diet is up to you. About the only thing I avoid is potatoes the day of a match.

Now, let's say you're an ordinary player. You aren't going to do backbreaking calisthenics or run as though you were getting ready for the Boston Marathon. Your fitness will come mainly from playing two or three times a week, and the thought of punching a bag is fatiguing. Well, I'd say you could help your condition, without making a project out of it, by walking as much as possible, using the stairs instead of an elevator—unless you work near the top of the Empire State Building—and carrying a tennis ball around with you. Squeeze it on that odd moment you have nothing else to do. You'll be amazed at how this will build up the strength in your racket wrist and arm. A tennis ball can take the place of worry beads. I imagine if Captain Queeg had fiddled with a tennis ball instead of those ball bearings he might have fattened up his forehand instead of his neuroses.

BRING A COAT AND TIE

BRISBANE WAS THE FIRST BIG CITY IN MY LIFE, A HUGE PLACE to me as a boy. Not anymore. In Sydney and Melbourne, they think of Brisbane as a country town, and I suppose it is the least sophisticated of the five major Australian cities. Hot. And I hope you don't land there on a Sunday when it used to be closed up tighter than a drum. Centuries—the days when the temperature goes over 100—are common during the summer as the humidity encloses you like a wet shroud. The best thing to do in Brisbane in the summer is leave—head for the beach. There are so many beaches on the Queensland coast that you should be able to find one all for yourself, if you like solitude. Most people prefer Surfers Paradise on the Gold Coast below Brisbane. Surfers' style is early Ft. Lauderdale. It's a seaside town where the three B's harmonize sweetly—birds, bikinis, and beer. I don't think Australian birds will ever go for nudity, but considering the bikinis at Surfers, who'd know the difference?

Despite this, and other evidence of the generally relaxed nature of Australians, for years it was difficult to dine out in Queensland without coat and tie, regardless of the temperature. Like a lot of things in Australia, such propriety was a hangover from the days when we looked to Britain for our customs. Without a coat and tie, you were a thug in the eyes of a headwaiter, who was usually encased in boiled shirt and tails. You approached him and it was a confrontation. You'd have an easier time getting past the Chicago police. An American friend of mine, stopping at Lennon's Hotel between planes, had left his luggage at the airport and strolled into the dining room in a neat sports shirt. It was Sunday. Lennon's had the only dining room open. Only after much pleading, arguing, and finally threatening to roll on the floor and die of hunger tremens did my friend persuade the maitre d' to relent. Although the room was practically empty, he was seated in a distant corner, hidden by a screen, where the waiters regarded him as though he were a Red Sox fan at Yankee Stadium.

Lew Hoad giggled about getting that same treatment at a sleazy hotel in the bush, a town called Cloncurry where the heat— 110 degrees, and no air conditioning—was only slightly less oppressive than the flies. The pros were on a tour. Cloncurry wasn't a glamour spot for them even in the vagabond days of 1958, but they'd been booked there.

"Get coats and ties or get out, you mugs," snarled the unshaven innkeeper. They couldn't believe it. But the man presided over the only beer tap in town. They complied.

So I had a coat and a tie in my bag when I returned to Brisbane in 1969 to play the Australian Championship for the first time in seven years. It was finally an open tournament, the last of the Big Four to abandon its amateurs-only policy and welcome the pros in the new era of integrated tennis that began in 1968.

The Grand Slam was totally open, and here I was to try to launch another one—this time a universal Grand Slam.

It was good to be back. This was home. Though I came from Rockhampton, I moved to Brisbane and went to work for the Dunlop Sporting Goods Company when I became really serious about a career in tennis and quit school. I was fifteen.

It was no country town to me. Brisbane had streetcars! Long gray things that looked like destroyers. And the lights were pretty bright for a kid off a cattle property. You didn't take a chance on getting rained on when you went to the movies. The theater had a roof.

Charlie Hollis decided I was ready to try on metropolitan life in 1951, and Dad drove me to Brisbane for the state championship for boys fourteen and under.

"Don't come back if you don't win," were Charlie's instructions. I think Dad would have brought me back, but I got the idea. Charlie didn't temporize. I won, and was pretty happy. Being a state champion was a very big thing to a thirteen-year-old.

The next year, Dad took me down again to attend the clinics that Harry Hopman was giving as a promotion for the newspaper, the *Brisbane Courier-Mail*. That made me very nervous at first. Everybody in Australia—and, I thought, the world—knew and admired Harry Hopman. He'd been a fine player, then captained the Australian Davis Cup team of Frank Sedgman and Ken McGregor that broke America's postwar grip on the Cup in 1950. He was working with Hoad and Rosewall, who were about to burst forth as young world-beaters, and here I was, getting instruction from this important man who was respected everywhere—Wimbledon, Forest Hills, Paris, Rome.

He had a nice way with kids, though. Firm, but good-humored. He seemed to treat us as though we all had the potential of Hoad and Rosewall. He could explain everything clearly and make you work.

Charlie Hollis told Hop I was going to be a champion. I was embarrassed, but I appreciated Charlie's testimonial, knowing well that I looked like I'd been on a hunger strike most of my life. I was short, skinny, and not too quick either.

After a couple of days, Hop remarked, "You're the Rockhampton Rocket, aren't you?" "Rocket" stuck.

"He was the Rocket—because he wasn't. You know how those nicknames are," Hop said. "Rocket was one of the slowest lads in the class. But his speed picked up as he grew stronger."

I became determined to build up my strength; if I couldn't grow much bigger—I weighed 143 when I finished the 1969 Grand Slam—I would at least get stronger. One of the simple things I did to build up arm strength for my wristy game was to carry an old tennis ball around and squeeze it every time I had a chance. This would help any player.

One of our group at Hopman's clinic was a good little player, Brian Littleproud, from a cattle crossing called Chinchilla out west. Sometimes

I wonder what became of him. Too bad he didn't become a champion. Wouldn't that have been a marvelous name for the sportswriters to play with: Brian Littleproud, the cowboy from Chinchilla?

There was tremendous interest in playing tennis in Brisbane, and in watching good tennis. Americans found it a dead town, amused by the numerous houses built on stilts, to allow air to circulate underneath. But never in the populous U.S. had there been a tennis crowd to equal the mob at Milton Grounds in 1958. Not anywhere else either, except Sydney and Melbourne.

Until 1958, Brisbane had been considered too small to support a Davis Cup Challenge Round, the grand final in the worldwide tournament. A Queenslander was on the team then, Mal Anderson, who'd also been coached by Charlie Hollis, and the local officials convinced the Australian Lawn Tennis Association that the support would be forthcoming.

Milton had seats for about 6,500, then larger than any U.S. tennis stadium but Forest Hills. Huge Bill Edwards, who wrapped his 300 pounds in suit, vest, starched collar, and tie every day no matter what the weather, ran tennis in Brisbane and was determined the town would make a marvelous showing when the U.S. team arrived to play for the Cup. Up went the temporary bleachers, up, up so high they could have used Sherpa guides for ushers. I'm glad I didn't have to sit on the top row because the stands seemed to quiver all the time. Each day for three days 17,886 people crowded themselves onto those precarious perches. With the exception of Wimbledon, no tennis event in the world came close to those figures, and that was 1958 in a small city.

It was an exciting match with the Peruvian Alex Olmedo carrying the U.S. to a 3-2 win, one of the infrequent times that the Americans have been able to carry off the Cup from Australia.

Those were the days of tremendous U.S.-Australia rivalry in the Davis Cup, when attendances of 25,578 at Sydney and 22,000 at Melbourne were the largest in the game's history. Sadly, that day is over. The last time Brisbane was host to a Cup final, 1967, total attendance for three days was 14,500. Nobody seemed much interested. Spain was the opponent and the sporting public knew it would be no contest. Australians won't buy tickets for a lower grade product, and the Davis Cup, once the high spot of the season, had lost its glamour until all pros became eligible to play in 1973 – a shocking delay five years after the acceptance of open tennis.

Dominating the barroom of the Milton Club, covering practically one wall, was a gigantic photograph of that 1958 mob scene. It was almost a shrine, and many a glass was lifted wistfully to that portrait of another era, with the prayer that it might return. I hope it does, and a very positive sign was the 2009 opening of a new tennis center, named for Hall of Famer Patrick Rafter, replacing deteriorated-and-abandoned Milton. It has a date on the world-wide tour. We found that out when we arrived in Brisbane for Australia's first open championship, 1969, France, England, Germany, Ireland, the U.S., Argentina, and even Switzerland had staged national opens in 1968, all these after the Australian season had closed in January. Australian tennis officials had nearly a year to prepare for their first open and the experience of other countries to learn from. Nobody bothered to learn or prepare in Brisbane and the first Australian Open was a terrible flop.

It shouldn't have been held in Brisbane anyway. Sydney or Melbourne were the only places for the first big one. But it was Brisbane's turn since the nationals was shared in rotation with the other three eastern cities, Sydney, Melbourne, and Adelaide. It was understandable that the stands weren't filled in 1967 for the Davis Cup against Spain, but I for one thought Brisbane would reawaken for an open because the standard would be the highest again, and the Australians who hadn't played in the championships for one or more years—Rosewall, Stolle, Roche, Emerson, Newcombe, and I—would be back. We weren't looking for the crowds of 1958. Those temporary bleachers had been taken down long ago, but we thought we could fill the permanent stadium of 6,500. We didn't. The biggest crowd was 4,500 when I beat Emerson in a match between the hometown boys. Other days it was lonely there. Thousands and thousands of people were watching all right, but they were at the beach, accompanied by TV sets. The tournament organizers had given away the TV rights, and they didn't have enough foresight to black out the Brisbane area. Why would a bloke pay for a seat in that bloody heat at Milton when he could sit in his bathing suit with a beer at Surfers Paradise and catch a wave or squeeze a bird during the lulls on the screen?

Brisbane was the last place I thought I'd encounter tennis apathy. It would have surprised me less to learn that Las Vegas had lost interest in blackjack.

The sporting climate in the No. 1 tennis nation had changed, no doubt about it. For one thing, the press had soured on inept officials who persisted in maintaining the phony "amateur" game and ostracizing pros. These officials, backward in just about everything they did, felt they didn't have to promote tennis and compete for spectator dollars. They continued to live in the past, when tennis could command a huge following without any effort. In the postwar years, there was great national pride in tennis and the fact that our small country—in terms of population—could defy the world and smash the mighty U.S., our idol. U.S.-Australia Davis Cup conflict guaranteed sellouts. Times changed. Listen to Fred Stolle:

"When I was a kid, tennis was a great future, a way to travel and represent your country. We worked our butts off for the chance and the competition was phenomenal. There were tennis courts everywhere. Now, because of building demands a lot of courts have disappeared, and kids have more to occupy their minds as Australia grows up and becomes more like the United States. They have cars, there's surfing, golf, they have more money. They think of college, which we never did. They're just not as bloody hungry. The press has knocked tennis so much in recent years that the public has grown to regard it as inferior. In the old days, the sports pages were packed with tennis. That's changed and it isn't going to come back overnight. The market has been hurt, and the officials are going to have to realize that nothing is automatic anymore. You have to hustle your product, as they say in America. Just announcing the open championship wasn't enough, but that's all they did."

Fred and I and others feel that tennis can make a comeback in Australia, but it will take much hard organizational work by younger officials who realize that the game is now merely one of many diversions for the public. In my day as an amateur, you could sell a youngster on the benefits of being a career "amateur" athlete. That was the system. You can't anymore. If he's going to devote himself to a game, he has to know there's a sound professional future so that he can support himself openly and well. You won't get the best athletes to play tennis otherwise. The United States is an example of that. Their best athletes play baseball, basketball, football, even golf.

Tennis always got its share of our top athletes, but not so many in recent years. I hope that intelligent organizers will reverse the trend and restore Australia's old interest, get the assembly line running again. The way the game is improving all over the world, I'm not sure Australia could ever be in such a dominant position again, and I'm not sure it would be a good thing. Too much success did have something to do with spoiling the game. Winning the Davis Cup year after year became boring to an extent, but only, I think, because other countries—specifically the U.S.—couldn't make a good match of the final. Many people, of course, are glad to see Australia decline. "Break up the Aussies!" would be the cry in baseball, but I can't agree with that.

I'm not apologizing now. There may not have been great depth to that 1969 tournament, but I had to beat Emerson, Stolle, Roche, and Gimeno – all Hall of Famers – in succession to win, and that's just about as tough a lineup as you can find.

There was some doubt that our pro group would play Australia at all. Prize money was low ($25,000), and the most I could win in singles was $5,000. That's not much when you consider the expenses of that trip, and the boss, George MacCall, was having trouble negotiating with the tournament officials for the price he thought he should get for transporting his troupe, National Tennis League, to Brisbane.

Nevertheless, the Grand Slam was uppermost in my mind, and George sympathized. He agreed that I could enter on my own even if he held the rest of his group out of the tournament. In this case, the title meant a lot more to me than the money.

I was relieved when George, along with Bob Briner of World Championship Tennis (the other pro group), was able to make a deal for all the pros. Without the rest of them there, trying to make life miserable for me, I would have been truly miserable. It would have been an easy, empty victory, no fun. I've never looked for tournaments I could steal.

LESSON • 4

Tennis Anyone? Any Age?

IS THERE AN IDEAL AGE to begin tennis? Depends on what you expect to accomplish. I'm convinced of this: you can start late in life and still learn to play respectably, so that you can have a lot of fun. And that's the most important aspect, isn't it? In California, where I live, it's remarkable the number of people giving up golf in their forties and taking up tennis. They want the exercise which makes them feel better, and they don't have to devote the best part of the day to a game. My wife, Mary, was a late starter and now she bats the ball around fine. Not great. But she enjoys it as much as anybody. Mostly these people will play doubles. You don't have to be so accurate or cover so much court.

In regard to becoming quite good, the younger you start the better. But a kid shouldn't be pushed. I've seen five and six-year-olds with wonderful coordination and ball sense who go right at it. But they were also strong enough to handle the racket comfortably. Usually a youngster isn't ready for it until eight or nine, and not then unless he has a genuine interest. The "tennis parent" who drags his youngster onto the court isn't doing the child a favor. There was a case of an American man who started his kids off with full-size rackets almost as soon as they could walk. His theory was that they would build a tennis sense immediately and increase their strength even if all they did was drag the rackets around the court. His kids did become very good at early ages, won national junior titles—and then became sick of the game before they were out of their teens.

There have been striking exceptions to the general rule of starting young. Orlando Sirola, the Italian, first played at twenty-two. He had strength, size, and aptitude, and four years later was a Davis Cupper. Stan Smith, one of America's best, hadn't been playing very long competitively before he won the U.S. junior title at age eighteen.

If a very young child shows an interest, but doesn't have the strength, you could saw off a racket for him, lower the net, and cut down the dimensions of the court. Some teachers have experimented successfully with smaller courts laid out especially for kids, the dimensions of the court and net reduced proportionately as in Little League baseball. The size of the racket and court and the height of the net can be very discouraging for young beginners. In fact, the height of the net is often very discouraging to me.

41

THE FIRST LEG ON THE GRAND SLAM: THE AUSTRALIAN

THREE YEARS HAD PASSED SINCE I'D BEEN HOME, AND I WAS very anxious to see my parents. They were getting older, and there wouldn't be too many more times together. Tennis means a big sacrifice in family life. More so if you're an Australian because almost everything is happening somewhere else. I left when I was fifteen to make tennis my career and have spent precious little time at home since.

You wonder, quite a lot in the beginning, if the loneliness and the being away from the family is worth it. I've really been a gypsy more than half my life. I've made good friends and enjoyed seeing the world and I believed I was doing the right thing to secure my future. But, remember, I've done extremely well. That fact helps combat the loneliness. I've known young Australians who seemed to have as much promise as I, who were my friends, but couldn't fight the homesickness. This kept them from being outstanding, and they had to find something else to go into.

During the Australian Open, I learned that Mary was going to have the baby. Only that, and seeing my folks, made Brisbane bearable. The tournament was the most discouraging I've ever played in. There have been worse conditions while barnstorming as a pro, and fewer spectators. But when you come into Milton Courts, where your memories are so good, and then this long-awaited open turns out as a terribly bush league production—well, it hurt.

Bill Edwards and several of his fellow officials snubbed the tournament one day to go to the races. We knew Bill didn't care for the pros and the idea of open tennis, but did he have to insult us by acting that way—to the detriment of an event that could have made money for Milton, his club? Australia's tennis old guard needed to be excused from the scene.

I arrived at Milton and walked out onto the stadium grass to look around and I thought back nine years. My first major title was the Australian in 1960, when I got that premature notion I could keep going through a Grand Slam. It was a marvelous win for everybody, not just me, because by beating Neale Fraser of Melbourne in the five-set final I became only the second Queenslander to win the national championship since 1905.

Eight thousand were in the stands, among them a good-sized gathering of friends from Rockhampton, crowing for me every chance they got. Of course it was my crowd, considering the circumstances. Fraser was the No. 1 amateur in the world then and he had a match point on me in the fourth set. I slipped away and had seven of them on him at 7-6 in the fifth on my serve. He busted loose every time, but finally I held serve for the title.

A lot of people thought it was the most exciting match they'd ever seen. That was how I remembered Milton, for that struggling, unexpected triumph which had Australia talking, and started my collection of major championships. Others may have remembered it, too, but few bought tickets to witness the hero's return. Neale Fraser showed up, only as a spectator. And he was in on a free ticket.

A young Italian named Massimo di Domenico gets a mention as the first of twenty-six victims in the Grand Slam. The grass wasn't as fast as usual at Milton, and I could experiment and get the feel in beating him, 6-2, 6-3, 6-3. Brisbane is always hot, but the heat seemed more blistering to me, though I'd grown up in the area. I wasn't used to it after years away from Queensland.

I knew it in my next match against Roy Emerson, and I'm happy we played at night. Dew makes night tennis on grass a bad, slippery idea.

But we didn't miss the sun at all, and the crowds improved a little.

If there was one match that did revive some of the old tennis feeling in the town it was Emerson and Laver.

We were the local boys who had made it better than any Queenslanders. We'd played so many times that sometimes our matches seemed as familiar as summertime reruns on TV. No matter what happened, though, we became better and better friends, doubles partners, very close, but Emmo would cut out his heart to beat me. He's a tremendous competitor, unbelievable when it comes to fitness. I think he's the hardest-working athlete I've ever seen.

Emmo and I come from the same kind of background, out in the bush. He was brought up on a dairy farm at a little place called Blackbutt, and he got those really strong wrists by milking cows. I don't know whether he used the continental grip on the cows, but they knew he was going to hang on until they produced their daily quota. He must have milked thousands of them. When Emmo began to show a high aptitude for tennis, his family sold the place and moved to Brisbane. They had a court on their property, but his father wanted Emmo to be able to get the best competition and instruction.

At first, in Brisbane, Emmo couldn't get used to taking a bath whenever he felt like it. "Out on our place, water was scarce and precious. It was almost rationed," he told his new friends. "I thought we were going to run out in Brisbane, and I never used much until I was certain we could have as much as we wanted."

Emmo has a very rigid code for himself, and we like to think this is the way of a dinkum (honest-to-God) Aussie. Although he has had numerous injuries during his career, one of them costing him his fourth Wimbledon title and the other possibly costing him a fifth—and making it easier on my Grand Slam in 1962—he never, never talks about them or implies that an injury was the cause for defeat.

"Once you walk onto that court," said Emmo, "you're signifying that you're in perfect shape. Otherwise don't go on. Only two things happen. You win, or your opponent beats you. Injuries have nothing to do with it." Any talk of injury, as an excuse, grates on Emmo. He once snorted about the chronic moaner, Niki Pilic: "I never beat Niki when he was well." You'll never hear Emmo complain, but you will hear his footsteps all through a match as he charges the net incessantly, and sometimes you'll hear that piercing laugh of his, and be glad. That's Emmo's way of releasing the tension when he's bungled a shot he should have had.

Emmo gleamed on a court, the sun or the lights glistening off his patent-leather hair and the gold fillings so prominent in his front teeth.

The sight of him is as much with me as anything else in the game because we've played each other so often in important matches. He has been my downfall, and I his. Titles of our own nation - and numerous others - have been at stake often when we've met, and we've meant a lot of disappointment for each other. During the two Slams, in eight tournaments, I've had to get past Emmo five times.

By 1960, Emmo and I were the rising players in Australia while Neale Fraser was briefly at the top. In the semis of the nationals at Brisbane, I somehow pulled up from 2-5 in the fifth to win five straight games and beat Emmo. Then I knocked off Fraser in that wild final. That delayed Emmo's winning his first Australian title, which he got a year later by going through me in the final. Later, in 1961, after winning Wimbledon, I was favored to win my first U.S. Championship. But there was Emmo in the final, winning his first instead, and me shaking his hand and saying, "Well played, Emmo."

Although Emerson never attained a Grand Slam, he won more of the major titles than anybody else, a total of twelve singles — six Australian, two U.S., English, and French - and 16 doubles. At the close of 1969, I was one behind him in singles with eleven, ready to pass - but didn't. Even though Pete Sampras did surpass him in 2002 with a 14th major singles title, probably no one will overtake his total stash of majors: 28. Laughed Emmo, "I didn't even know I held the singles record until it came out in the press that Pete was chasing me. We didn't pay any attention to records."

The grass was slick when we went on. Because of the slipshod scheduling it was after 9:00p.m. Emmo's a slow starter. So am I, but he was slower and I got the first set pretty quickly. And the second. But he took the third, and he had a break and was serving at 7-6 in the fourth, looking like he'd catch up. It was just about midnight now, the crowd excited. The year would be marked by patches like the one I struck then. I began hitting my returns harder, and they were buzzing with topspin. Emmo was charging in, but he missed a couple of volleys. I broke back, and kept going for a run of three straight games and the match, 6-2, 6-3, 3-6, 9-7.

There wasn't much time to have a beer and relax because after I'd showered and talked to the reporters it was one in the morning and I was due back to play Fred Stolle in the quarterfinals in ten hours. Hardly time for breakfast.

Stolle, a tall, slim blond, probably would have been a basketball player if he'd grown up in the United States instead of Sydney. He was quite a good cricketer, a wicket keeper, which corresponds to catcher in baseball, but he was always getting his hands banged up and his mother didn't like that. She encouraged him to play more tennis, and he had a talent for it. We're the same age, but Fred was a late developer and first made a name as a doubles player. I didn't consider him a rival when we were both amateurs but with his rifling serve, good volleys and backhand, he came along strongly in 1964 and won Forest Hills in 1966.

We had a terribly long second set, and I had to serve well to stave off a set point, but Fred couldn't get into the match after that and I won 6-4, 18-16, 6-2.

Like Emmo and I, Tony Roche is a country boy. He grew up in Tarcutta, a tiny New South Wales settlement surrounded by nothing and sheep, about 200 miles from Sydney. His father, Andy Roche, was the town butcher, as my Dad had been briefly in Marlborough, and Tony has the strokes to do a splendid job with a cleaver. He prefers a racket, and is as threatening with that.

After pounding a ball against the side of his house so much that he nearly knocked it off the foundation, Tony decided he'd have to get out of Tarcutta if he was going to be a serious tennis player. He was missed. His departure cut the population noticeably, by almost one per cent. Moving on to Sydney, he was quick to be noticed as an exceptional prospect.

All through 1969, Tony was trouble for me - the main trouble. He beat me five out of nine times, giving me my own medicine—a lot of left-handed spin—and making it clear that he thought my time was over and his had come. It seems strange with all the millions of tennis players in the world that two left-handers from the Australian bush, from places called Rockhampton and Tarcutta, would be one-two for 1969.

One reason Tony got a jump on me, I think, is that he had more opportunity to play against left-handers. For years I was the only lefty among the touring pros. This was a decided edge for me because the only time my opponents encountered left-handed spin was against me, while I was well accustomed to the right-handed spin.

When Roche went pro with Dave Dixon's Handsome Eight, two other lefties went with him, Taylor and Pilic, so that he became well grooved in opposing his own kind. The abundance of lefthanders in their troupe probably was a reason that Newcombe, Drysdale, and Ralston were able to give me exceptional trouble.

I wish I had more time during a match to watch Tony, but I'm pretty busy following the ball. When he signed with the World Championship Tennis pro troupe, with seven others, they were called the Handsome Eight. Roger Taylor, John Newcombe, Niki Pilic, Pierre Barthes, Butch Buchholz, Cliff Drysdale, all have movie star looks, or what we used to think of that way, in the pre-anti-hero days. Denny Ralston has an All-American appearance, but Tony? Ask him where he ranked in beauty among the Handsome Eight, and he replies "fourteenth." The movie star he resembles is Victor McLaglen. He has a plastic face that he's always trying to rearrange with his right hand when he makes a bad shot. Tony's facial expressions are fantastic. He may not be pretty, but he does have a rugged Aussie look about him with his shocks of blond hair, his heavy jaw and sturdy chest. He could have been a fine boxer or football player, I think. Tennis was lucky to get him.

Just before we got to Brisbane, Tony beat me in the New South Wales final in Sydney, which was our country's first actual open. He took a lead on me that he never gave up over the year, but he couldn't beat me in the matches that mattered most—and paid best.

I brought three sunhats to the court that Saturday to play Tony in the semifinals, and each one was thoroughly soaked when we finished over four hours later. We started at noon. My brother Trevor was coming down from Rocky for the weekend, and since he keeps his sports goods shop open a half-day, he phoned me: "I won't be there till two. Try to keep it going so I can see something of it." We laughed about that later. Trevor got to see more than enough of me and Tony struggling away with the temperature at 105 and no shade anywhere. We kept towels in an icebox beside the court and draped ourselves with them every change game. It was only momentary relief. I kept taking glucose and salt pills, but I got groggy. It turned out to be the longest match I ever played—90 games—and by far the hardest. Ten years back, at Wimbledon, I got by big Barry MacKay in 87 games, also a semifinal. But the London climate was a lot easier to take than Brisbane.

There wasn't much to choose between us after Tony got into the match. It looked like I had him when I won the first two sets, 7-5, 22-20 [no tie-breakers until 1970], but I was getting tired. At that point of the season Tony was fitter than I, and when he grabbed the third set 11-9, you could see him begin to puff up with confidence. That brought merciful intermission with a shower in the dressing room, one of those showers you never want to leave. Too quickly we returned to the oven, and Tony came back eagerly to resume with the same heavy serves and stiff volleys. I was in a daze as he ran off five games. The set was gone. I conceded that much as I served the sixth game, but I wanted badly to hold serve so that I could lead off in the fifth set. It was hard to do because Tony was playing full-tilt now and felt he had me. He'd already beaten me in Sydney and he was going to do it again.

Confidence is the thing in tennis, as I'm sure it is in any sport. I hear other athletes talk that way. Confidence separates athletes of similar ability.

Tony had it . . . and in an instant during the decisive set he lost it, through no fault of his own, on what may have been a very bad break. I'll never be certain, but Tony Roche will go through life thinking he was bad-lucked out of that victory by a linesman's decision. Maybe he was.

We went to deuce in the sixth game of the fourth set but I worked to make sure I got the game. It was important to me, even though Tony and I both saw that the set would be his. Maybe he didn't sense the importance. He served out in the next game for 6-1. We were even, and the momentum was his.

But serving first in the fifth set picked me up a bit. It's a psychological help to go into the lead every time you win your serve in a close match, and that's why I tried so hard for a seemingly meaningless game when I was down 0–5 in the fourth. I wanted to serve that leadoff game.

Naturally, now I had to hold my serve, and I hadn't been serving too well. Tony had broken me three of the last four times. He was returning serve better than I was, and returning was tricky business on that court. It was freshly re-sodded and playing badly. Any time a ball landed on the court, hitting it was guesswork. That's unusual for Australian grass, but this was Brisbane '69, with everything schemozzled. Bad courts were just one more factor in a general screw-up.

Now I knew I had to get my first serves in because Tony would be jumping all over the second ball. I tried to pull myself together and make sure the first serve was a good one and that I was up to the net in position to make a good volley. I figured one break of serve would decide the match, the condition we were in. Tony was stronger, but he'd never been in a fifth set with me, and he'd have just a little more pressure on him, serving second.

Every time I held, the situation would be just a little dicier for him. My serve began to work all right. His continued too. One love for me, but he tied it. Two-one, and then 2-2. Three–two. I was feeling a little better. He wasn't blasting me off the court the way he had in the fourth set, and my confidence was beginning to come back. I've lost five-set matches, but not many, and I'd have to think hard to remember one. Three-all as Tony held, but his volleys didn't have quite the zip. I served to 4-3 and we changed courts. Slowly. The wet towels from the icebox felt good on my head. I wrung out my sun hat and it was like squeezing a sponge. One of the things I used to do on hot days was put a piece of wet cabbage inside my hat. That was a pretty good trick for keeping cool.

Nothing like a green salad on your head, although I don't know if oil and vinegar does much for your scalp. But I had no greens this day, and Tony and I felt like the cabbage that lies alongside boiled corned beef.

It was his turn to serve and I screwed my mind into working for every point as though it were the last. If you do that when you come down the stretch in a tight match you'll be surprised how often a superhuman effort will come out of you. "It's 3-4 in the last set, and I'm going to hack and grub," I told myself. "Just do anything to get the ball over the net. It doesn't matter how you look. Form won't win this one."

You learn to hack, as we call it, when you join the pros. Get balls back, and the hell with trying to slap a winning shot that doesn't have too much chance. It looks great if you make it, but at this stage you can't give away points.

A big shot may look lovely, but anything that goes over the net now will look lovely. You still win matches by getting the ball over the net one more time than your opponent.

You face up to that when you leave the amateurs. You settle down. You can slam away when your opponent isn't too sound, or you clearly dominate him, but I was in with Tony Roche in the decisive set, and it was no time for pride and flamboyance. I was going to scratch and dig and bloop the ball over any way I could.

I was chipping my returns now, trying to squib them onto his feet. With the ball skipping erratically on those courts, the opportunities to hit full out were limited, and the best thing was just to meet the ball.

So Tony was serving at 3-4, and this was the place for me to do my utmost. He knew it; everybody who hadn't passed out from the heat in the stands knew it. Win this one and I'd be serving for the match at 5-3. This had to make it even a little more tense for Tony. We split the first two points: 15-all. Then he missed a volley. The 15-30 point is an awfully big one in this spot. He came in with a good serve, down the middle, spinning into my body. I sliced under it with my backhand to chip the ball crosscourt with underspin. Tony looked relieved because he thought the ball was going out. He was sure it was out, but there was no sound. Tony turned around and looked at the sidelines-man sitting behind the court. The official held out his hands, parallel to the ground, like a baseball umpire signaling "safe." It meant my shot was good, and the umpire called: "Fifteen-forty!"

Tony was furious, and I can hold his hand and sympathize . . . now. It was such a big point, and the ball may have been out. I didn't have a good view, but I had the feeling when I hit the ball that it might be going wide. I wouldn't have been surprised if it had been called out because it was terribly close.

It was a judgment call. Nobody—and I know Tony agrees—can blame a linesman if he misses one on a day like that. He'd been sitting there broiling for more than four hours, trying to stay sharp and alert. And maybe the ball was good and the man was correct. No matter. It stands as good forever because the linesman said so.

"Fifteen-forty" was the best thing I'd heard all day. Two break points, and Tony was riled. Tony swung hard on his serve, and I knocked the ball back to him. He was at the net to make a backhand volley and sent the ball crosscourt to my backhand. Now this was a shot I love—the backhand down the line. Tony realized it and began moving to his left to cover it. But in this situation—two points to break—I was going for it with everything. I got the racket back and drove at the ball, snapping my wrist to load the ball with topspin. Tony and I had been through all this before. But even though he anticipated me, he was going to have a hard time volleying that top-spinning ball down his sideline whenever I hit it that well. Out went his arm in the reach that failed. His racket probed for the ball and found it, but he couldn't control it. One of the most beautiful sights of 1969 was that ball clunking into the net.

Tony's game was knocked apart by that line call, and he couldn't get himself to function in the last game. He was mad and frustrated. He hadn't quit, but it all seemed so unfair to him. In that moment of his anguish, I served through the game promptly, getting only token opposition.

Ninety games, the eighth longest singles match ever played: 7-5, 22-20, 9-11, 1-6, 6-3. It's a good thing that players customarily shake hands at the end of a match. It was an effective way of holding each other up.

Even though Roche has been around, and at the highest level, he let himself get flapped out of that match like a novice, forgetting that you have to play the calls, as we say. Let's assume the decision that upset Tony was outrageously wrong, and everybody thought so.

You can ask the linesman if he's sure of his call. Sometimes he'll change it or ask the umpire's advice. But if he won't there's nothing you can do. You have to forget it, and make yourself work harder for the next point.

Serving on grass at 15-40, Tony still had something like an even chance of winning that game. When he didn't, he still had a shot at my serve. But by the time he pulled himself together the match was over. You mustn't let the worst call in the world fluster you. I'm glad to offer this advice to Tony today.

Physically, that was the toughest match of the year, certainly of the Grand Slam. But the element of pressure wasn't there. Not for me. The Grand Slam hadn't even begun. I'd won nothing, and there was nothing to be concerned about. It was only the second tournament of the year, and though I wanted the Grand Slam, I really had no idea the year would turn out so incredibly well.

It could all have ended there as easily as not, on the center court at Milton. How many thousands of shots did I need to make the Grand Slam? I don't know. Nobody counted. This isn't baseball. But that one shot, the questionable call, could have changed the whole thing. Roche, of course, is convinced that it did, and I can't argue with him. It's funny, the hours and hours you practice, the miles and time you put in, and maybe the whole thing hinged on a bloke sitting in a chair, looking down the sideline, whose job it was to decide whether a ball was out or in. I like to think he was right, that he was wide awake and decisive and that my shot was a deftly hit winner. It reads better that way. But it doesn't matter. Over the years the calls even up, Tony, but that one will hurt even a century from now when you're playing mixed doubles against Bonnie and Clyde at the River Styx Sauna and Racket Club, won't it?

But it may have been more than just a point—15-40 instead of 30-all— for both of us. If Tony had won the game, he might have won the match. That would have given him three straight victories over me, and a substantial heightening of his confidence. It wouldn't have helped mine. I can still see that backhand return of mine streaking for the sideline. Was a season for two men riding on that shot? That's one way to look at it, but maybe I'm getting too dramatic.

Nevertheless it's weird how a simple mistake can change not only a match but perhaps a career. To my mind the most fantastic example occurred in Brisbane during the Queensland Championships of 1955. Nineteen-year-old Ashley Cooper, just out of the junior ranks, was playing and losing a first-round match to a local entry, tall Les Flanders. At match point, Flanders stood at the net about to crush a sitter. It was all over, Cooper was reconciled to that, and he didn't much care where Les put the ball. He was astonished when Les butchered the smash, knocking the ball way out of court.

The reprieve turned Coop into a tiger, and he went on to win the match. His confidence soared and he was the sensation of the tournament, beating Mal Anderson and Merv Rose (then No. 10 in the world) on the way to the final where he played well in losing to Rosewall.

Cooper never should have gotten to the second round, Flanders' carelessness let him live one more point, and somehow the spark he needed was kindled. Less than three years later, Coop was Wimbledon champion, No. 1 man in the amateur world. Those wins over Anderson and Rose gave him faith in himself, put him in a position to battle Rosewall impressively. But I wonder if Coop would have gone to the top if Les Flanders had finished off that easy shot properly.

The championship match in which I met Andres Gimeno was an anticlimax. Andres wasn't spirited, not strutting the way he usually does. He dislikes grass and extreme heat. Few Spaniards brought up on clay, care for grass, and for Andres, bad grass is more agonizing than eating dinner before 10:00 p.m. Nevertheless he'd had a good tournament, beating Kenny Rosewall, Butch Buchholz, and the amateur Ray Ruffels, without losing a set.

I think he felt he'd done enough, and he seemed pretty much resigned to defeat when he played me. I hadn't lost to Andres in a long time, and though he had several chances to break my serve in the third set, I took him pretty much as I knew I should, 6-3, 6-4, 7-5. I got my $5,000 although the tournament went broke, and now the Grand Slam was a definite possibility. I hoped my troublesome elbow would hold up, and I was pretty sure that there'd be no more 100-degree days along the way. Emerson and I won the doubles over Rosewall and Stolle, so we had a chance for a Grand Slam there, too. Only three teams have completed doubles Grand Slams: Aussies Frank Sedgman and Ken McGregor in 1951; Americans Martina Navratilova and Pam Shriver in 1984; Aussies Margaret Court and Ken Fletcher in 1963 (mixed).

I was so disgusted with the mismanagement of the tournament that I wanted to get out of Brisbane before I said some things I'd regret. The best part of it was seeing my family. We stayed together in a motel. Though it was pleasant, a reunion like that is spent mostly in talking about old times. You're not really a part of the family anymore, and you aren't planning any future as a group. You talk about things you've done together, a lot of good times, but you know there won't be a lot of time together in the future. My life just isn't built that way.

LESSON • 5

Confidence and Shrugging off Bad Luck

AMNESIA, that's what a tennis player needs. Well, maybe not quite a total loss of memory, but I can't stress too much the importance of shoving the last point right out of your mind. Forget it. A point won't come back no matter how much you think about it. If you played it badly there's no way you can reverse it; if you played it well, it won't help you on the next point.

The next point—that's all you must think about. "Gotta get the next point!" is what you tell yourself. "Gotta get the next point."

Sure, it hurts when you get a bad call or you blow an easy shot. Worse still is brooding about it. I've seen this sulking about what-might-have-been tear players apart and cost them matches.

You beat yourself by thinking about your bad luck. It's unfortunate for a fine player like Dennis Ralston that he can throw himself off for two or three games by getting upset at something that you have to regard as ancient history and beyond your control. This is something, I guess, you have to start early. But maybe it's a mark of maturing.

You can't change the last point—forget it.

Get the next one.

LIVING WITH PAIN

TONY ROCHE WASN'T BY ANY MEANS DESTROYED BY THAT semifinal in Brisbane. The next week in Auckland, he handled me in four sets to take the New Zealand Open. My left elbow was aching again. A cortisone shot prior to the Australian had quelled the pain and I was able to play as I wanted. But in Auckland I was hurting.

The long hauls were beginning. Two days out of Auckland we were back in snow country, in Philadelphia for the indoor open at the Spectrum. En route I stopped in Los Angeles for a quick visit to Dr. Robert Kerlan, an orthopedic specialist well-known to athletes, who had helped another left-hander with his aches, Sandy Koufax of the Los Angeles Dodgers.

I suppose anybody who's played tennis for any length of time has had a sore arm or elbow. Dr. Kerlan told me that the way I flick the ball he's surprised the elbow was functioning at all.

He gave me another injection, and I was okay in Philadelphia, beating Tony in the final. But by March, the arm was seizing up so that I could hardly straighten it. If I played more than an hour the pain was terrific.

The injury went back to June of 1968 when I fell on my wrist going for a ball in Boston. With the wrist weakened, I think I put too much strain on the elbow. I won Wimbledon all right, but then everything gave way and I was beaten at Forest Hills by Cliff Drysdale (now the ESPN commentator). Six months later, it still wasn't right, but I had to keep playing. You do that in tennis when you're a pro. It's not a team game. There's nobody to take your place. Pancho Gonzalez found that out fast in his rookie year in 1949. He'd twisted his ankle badly and didn't think he'd be able to play against Jack Kramer on the tour. Kramer was also the promoter, thus Pancho's boss. "I don't think I can make it tonight, Jack," said Pancho, sincerely regretful. "Don't be silly," said Kramer. "We always play." They taped the ankle, shot it with novocaine and Pancho went on. He and all the rest have played with injuries often. The way we travel and play you can't expect to be 100 percent all the time, but if you can get onto the court, you play.

When my cortisone wore off, there were decagesic pills. Those worked for a while, but when I got to New York for the Madison Square Garden Open, my arm hurt so much I couldn't bear to practice. I figured the adrenaline flow during a match and the usual competitive flame would keep me heated up.

Dr. Kerlan had given me something to think about: "There may come a time, and nobody can predict when, that you hit one tennis ball too many. When a bathtub is filled to the top, it only takes an eyedropper to make it overflow. Your elbow could be near the point when just one little swing will finish it."

Cheery observation. Koufax reached that point with his elbow and decided against going any farther.

Was I there? I began to wonder in New York on the most ironic day of my life as I went from hero to zero within hours. At a luncheon in my honor, I was presented with the 1968 Player of the Year trophy, the top award in the game, sponsored by the Martini & Rossi distillers and selected by the foremost tennis writers. It was very nice. Free lunch. Roast beef. And then a scrappy Young Texan, Cliff Richey, roasted me. To a turn.

I won the first set, had good leads in the second and third sets of the best-of-three match, and came completely apart. When I seemed to have the match won at 3-1 in the third set, I started double faulting all over the place. I was a public spectacle, a perfect example of how a good player can lose his cool in an instant and play the game he usually owns like an outsider. Sure, the pain was fierce, but it shouldn't have made me stop thinking so completely that I lost five straight games, all but giving them away. You can't do that against anybody, least of all a tiger like Richey.

I began to rush my serve. That's fatal. You lose your rhythm. As a result I wasn't throwing the ball high enough. That's common when you get anxious and speed up. You have to slow yourself down and make yourself go through the phases of your serve carefully. The first phase is throwing the ball up properly.

Even when I didn't double fault, I usually missed the first serve. But I came storming into the net behind the second, as though I were serving beautifully. I should have noticed that Cliff was knocking the ball by me. Didn't I have the best view in the house? Racing to the net is a wonderful tactic—if you prepare your way. I was like one of those Polish cavalrymen in World War II, gallantly charging a Nazi tank on horseback.

Unless you're playing an unseasoned opponent that you can disconcert merely by showing yourself at the net, you've got no business up there on less than forcing strokes. Richey wasn't disconcerted by a close-up of my freckled face. He kept passing me. I didn't seem to notice. Panic— your magic spell was everywhere.

The Player of the Year had panicked, forgetting all the fundamentals. Cliff Richey, playing his first prize money event, came off with a first-round victory, an unexpected check ($900), and a scalp (Laver's).

Not since my first visit in 1956 when I ran into top-seeded Ham Richardson at Forest Hills, had I lost an opening-round match in New York. It was embarrassing, particularly the timing. In the papers the next day: photo of Player of the Year receiving his Tiffany trophy . . . and below, the story about him receiving his Richey thrashing.

My humility was high that morning. And my confidence was lower than the Grand Central subway station. I wondered if I'd ever be able to play well again. Confidence is that flighty. Even when you're not playing particularly badly. Arthur Ashe once said, "Before a Davis Cup match I'm so gripped with self-doubt that I actually wonder if I'll be able to hit the ball over the net. Suppose I never get one ball back? That's what I wonder." I know what he means.

I had a long time to wonder and worry, a flight from New York to Johannesburg. Would the elbow be any good for anything but bartending? I've known Australian bartenders who got tennis elbow from working too hard during the maelstrom of the Six O'clock Swill—those last desperate minutes before closing time. It didn't affect their careers, but my line of work was different. I thought about it, and Dr. Kerlan's advice that I would have to learn to live with some pain. A lot of people do.

He'd also given me another decagesic prescription, and suggested a stronger dose. The pain had started on the outside of the elbow and moved inside. Needing more than pills, I became the pots-and-pans man of tennis as Kerlan recommended equipment as vital to me as my rackets: a hydroculator and a pot to heat it in. A hydroculator is a canvas pad which retains steam heat after being boiled.

He instructed me to wrap the elbow in the hydroculator for twenty minutes before I played and to pack it in ice afterward. I felt like a frozen daiquiri every night. The pots were too cumbersome to pack, so I bought one every place I went.

"I'd like to see your pots," was my line to the dime store salesgirls.

"What do you want to cook?" she'd inquire.

"Elbow," I'd answer.

"Oh . . ." she'd say, as though I were some kind of nut, or a cannibal.

Mine got well cooked, and I have to say I couldn't have won the Grand Slam without my dear hydroculator. And the pots. Plus thousands of ice cubes. Ice cubes meant more to me than they did to W. C. Fields—and he kept a refrigerator in every bedroom for emergency use.

Those treatments, combined with the pills, allowed me to regain my customary rhythm. I was determined not to become a pill-gobbler, and took them only a couple of other times during the year, prior to the biggest tournaments.

LESSON • 6

Handling Injuries, and Other Props

IT SEEMS TO ME that people can put up with more pain than they tend to. I don't think you can hurt yourself that drastically by playing with slight muscle pulls. Doctors may disagree with me, but I think you can work these things out by playing. It's like stiffness. They'll stay with you twice as long if you don't run them out.

I guess I feel that the average player tends to pamper himself, but it may seem that way to me because we can't do it as pros. We frequently play with injuries. It's the way our business is.

Stretching exercises before you begin playing will reduce the possibilities of muscle pulls and will get a pulled muscle ready for play.

Blisters on the feet and racket hand can be bothersome. The best way to prevent them on the feet is to wear two pairs of socks, to cut down on friction. It's common to wear a light pair under a heavy wool pair. I generally wore two reasonably heavy wool pairs because I changed directions so quickly and for me two pairs of wool are more comfortable. Pancho Gonzalez had trouble with blisters on his fingers. He taped his fingers very carefully before he played. There are gloves on the market, similar to golf gloves, that protect the racket hand and also help keep a firm grip if your hands are sweaty.

Wristlets, or sweatbands, are available to prevent sweat from running down the arms onto the racket handle. On scorching days, it can still be difficult to keep your hand from slipping. Back in the day, I think an old-fashioned answer to this was simple sawdust. You can keep a supply in your shorts pocket and beside the court, and sawdust will take care of the moisture and keep the handle dry. Grip tapes that are placed over the original handle of the racket have become increasingly popular in recent years.

Shoes should be lightweight, durable and comfortable, and there are plenty of brands that fit the description, although I feel that the Adidas is the best. Don't forget to put on two pairs of socks when fitting shoes.

Dead is the rigid idea that white is the only suitable shade for tennis clothing. We pros have led the way in breaking the textile color bar, and many clubs are relaxing their white-only rules of apparel. Once I became used to wearing colors, white seemed bland. Color peps up our appearance as it does in other forms of athletics.

In the days of Tilden, players used to feel unequipped without polo coats in which they swathed themselves after matches. The idea was good. You need a cover-up costume to ward off chills. Track suits replaced the polo coats and players don't look as dapper as they did in the 1920s, but a track suit is more useful, easier to warm up in, and easier to launder.

Most tennis clothes are drip-dry and quickly cared for. A quick way we itinerants sometimes do our washing is to wear our tennis clothes right into the shower and soap them down.

I traveled with several changes, but Tony Roche, for one, limited himself to one pair of tennis shorts. "It saves space in packing," said Tony back in the day, "and I haven't met a tennis player yet who wears more than one pair at a time."

SOUTH AFRICA

SLOW HARD COURTS ARE THE SURFACE FOR THE SOUTH African championships. You have to be able to keep the ball going, hit ground strokes and play patiently. It's the kind of game people like to watch, and the stands at Ellis Park were always crowded. Good tennis was one reason; the other shrewd promotion by Owen Williams, the man in charge. Owen's management raised the South African Open to a high position in Johannesburg, but the problems of apartheid led to its decline.

After failed attempts to obtain a visa from the racist government, Arthur Ashe was finally admitted to play the South African Open in 1973. He made it to the final, losing to Jimmy Connors. It was a breakthrough of sorts, well publicized, but there was no softening until apartheid collapsed in 1994. Then Nelson Mandela, permitted to play tennis during his long prison confinement, revealed himself as an Ashe fan, and welcomed Arthur as an honored guest, no longer shadowed by the secret police as he had been in 1973.

South Africa was reassuring because my arm didn't fall off. It didn't even come loose through six rounds of singles. The tournament was a good test—Frew McMillan in the fourth round, Bob Hewitt in the quarters, Cliff Drysdale in the semis, and Tom Okker in the final. Drysdale, who has been troublesome for me with his deceptive, two-handed backhand, was the only one of them to take a set in a match of strangely one-sided sets: 6-1, 1-6, 6-1, 6-2.

Only for one set did Okker press me in the final, 6-3, 10-8, 6-3. It was a long way to go to win $2,800, my smallest first prize of the year, but right then I would have gone to the South Pole for nothing to get the same result—to know that the elbow would hold up. The way I packed it in ice after every match, the South Pole wouldn't have been a bad place for me to play.

Although I was the winner, a guy named Gonzalez stole the show from me as he had so many times. When I first came with the pros, I was annoyed that the only man in the troupe who got much attention from the public was Pancho Gonzalez. I guess Kenny Rosewall and I resented it because we knew we were now consistently better players than Pancho, and yet in the public's mind—especially the American public—Pancho was the champion. Always was and always would be. I've heard about Americans who still regard Jack Dempsey as the heavyweight champion, and are oblivious to anyone who has followed. That's the way many American sports fans seem to be about Pancho. To them he's the only tennis player worth discussing, and I will say that at least until my second Grand Slam I had to acknowledge the fact that, in the U.S., Gonzalez was the only tennis name immediately recognizable to any group of sports nuts. Rosewall and I have as much pride as anybody else. We were bothered by the general feeling that Pancho was the only name who could sell tickets in the U.S.

"Without Pancho you guys would be out of business." We heard that over and over, and it cheesed us off. We reckoned that people wanted to see us, too, especially since we were the big winners. It was disheartening even to consider that Pancho was holding the pro game together through the force of his fiery personality. Could our game be so shaky that its success depended on a player who was past his prime?

This bothered us, and so did Pancho's attitude in the mid-1960s. He was ungracious to say the least, a loner, and an absolute jerk on the court. He tried to take every advantage.

Various Gonzalez incidents widened the affection gap between him and his competitive colleagues. But here we were in Johannesburg, shortly before Pancho's forty-first birthday, and I found my old distaste for him gone. He was still a bastard in a match. Off-duty, he'd mellowed. We all used to secretly, and openly, cheer against him, but now I was finding myself enthralled to watch him, just like any other spectator.

He captivated Johannesburg completely by outlasting Fred Stolle, 11-9, in the fifth set after losing the fourth, 12-14, in the longest match of the tournament, 73 games. Next, in the quarters, he showed no signs of wear until the end of another five-setter. He grabbed the first two sets from Drysdale, barely lost the third, 10-8, and the fifth, 7-5.

In 1968, the first year of open tennis, Pancho had a few bright moments, but he really wasn't ready for the transition from the shorter matches and tournaments of the pro tour to the week and two-week major events involving best-of-five-set matches. He faltered badly in England, the first pro to lose to an amateur (Mark Cox) at the British Hard Court Open, and wilted at Wimbledon against the Soviet Alex Metreveli.

But 1969 found Richard Alonzo Gonzalez, one of the world's more resilient grandfathers, ready. South Africa was important to both of us. Pancho showed us he was going to be a factor, not just a relic worth watching out of curiosity. He was really playing better tennis at forty-one than he did when I first encountered him at thirty-five. Much better. There were times when I wished he'd just give it up and disappear, but he proved that if a man takes care of himself and is determined, he can play this game productively for longer than I'd thought. Pancho was ten years older than I, and I was pleased he was around as an inspiration.

When he was out of the singles at Johannesburg, Pancho kept going with the young hipster of the courts, South African Ray Moore, to win the doubles. This was one of the beautiful combinations—Moore, the Wolfman, and Pancho, the Old Wolf. Moore's now-generation coiffure—the frizzy blond hair that made his head seem a sunburst—and his mustache and headband identified him as a freaky son of staid South Africa. Ray is such a pleasant, kind guy that he's a favorite everywhere. At home, they didn't know quite what to make of him except that he ought to get a haircut. He did cover himself with psychedelic T-shirts on occa-

This fun photo shoot for BBC television in England featured (from left to right) me, fellow Aussies Kenny Rosewall and Tony Roche and Tom Okker of The Netherlands. After I beat Okker in the final of the South African Open, I knew my elbow would hold up.

sion, although these were a bit much for the tournament officials in Johannesburg who insisted on all-nice-and-white. Deviation from white is just that—deviation—in South Africa. Ray didn't make much fuss. He just played good tennis with the man eighteen years his senior, permitting no generation gap to form down the middle which they covered with sharp volleying. Ray and Pancho had never played together before, but they got it together, as Ray would say, for a few days, and soon had the crowd backing their improbable run to the title. "Pancho's really all right for a man his age," Ray enjoyed saying. "He listens to my Led Zeppelin records and I can communicate with him. He's a nice man." I guess I'd agree although I wouldn't have some years ago.

Moore seemed to be an odd character in his hippie style, but there was depth to him. While it was easy to condemn South Africa from a distance, Ray had done it where the heat was—at home—and one of the results was that he was barred from playing in the Eastern Province. He was outspoken on the racial question, and even campaigned on behalf of the Progressive Party, which opposed apartheid. This brought public criticism down on him in South Africa, but bravely he wasn't afraid to speak up.

Ray considered boycotting the 1970 Open as his protest of the pre-1973 refusal to give Ashe a visa. But he decided that he could do more good by appearing in his country and working however he could for a change. He was the only South African athlete to oppose his government so vigorously, and today Moore is partnered with Charlie Pasarell in operating one of the planet's most important tournaments in Indian Wells, California.

I took a title out of Johannesburg, and so did Pancho. We were going to do all right this year, even though we probably didn't imagine how well. I was glad my elbow responded, but I still had my doubts about its going the distance through Forest Hills, which was five months off.

LESSON • 7

Changing Your Game as You Grow Older

IN 1963 AT ADELAIDE, when the American team of Chuck McKinley and Denny Ralston took the Davis Cup away from Australia, the pivotal victory was the doubles match. The Yanks beat Neale Fraser and Roy Emerson largely because Fraser couldn't hit his overheads. McKinley and Ralston obliged by feeding him lobs whenever they could, and Fraser's failure caused an astute observer, Jack Kramer, to say: "The first thing that goes in an aging tennis player is not his legs—but his overhead."

Now Fraser was by no means an antique. He was thirty, but he hadn't been playing quite as much as the others. It was a good lesson to remember. The overhead is the most tiring stroke to hit, and if you can make older opponents hit a lot of them, you're going to cause a breakdown. (Unless the older opponent you have in mind is Pancho Gonzalez—although Pancho could be wearied a bit by good lobs, too.)

Pancho, by the way, was a good example of a prudent change by a man over forty. He used a much lighter racket than he did years ago, barely 13 ounces. Red Hoehn, former teaching pro at the Badminton & Tennis Club in Boston who has done stringing for Pancho, was jolted back in the day when he weighed Pancho's rackets. "This is the same weight my twelve-year-old daughter uses," said Hoehn.

The lighter racket is easier to whip around, causing less strain. Pancho became a devotee of the metal racket. Again, it can be swished easily, offering less resistance with the split shaft. Serving with the metal rackets is not as tiring.

On the serve, it's doubly important for the older player to get the first ball in, for this is a fatiguing stroke, too, and you want to hit as few serves as possible.

Elderly players -- there are people in their nineties who continue to play -- might consider using VASSS (Van Alen Streamlined Scoring System) rules, in either single-point or no-ad form. Single-point is similar to table tennis scoring, with the serve changing every five points. No-ad eliminates deuce; thus the first to reach four points wins the game. Both reduce the strain of serving long deuce games or sets. Jimmy Van Alen, the audacious enemy of conventional scoring, also conceived the sudden death tie-breaker, a revolutionary newcomer at Forest Hills in 1970. This outlaws deuce sets, going into force at 6-6 in games. Sudden death is a best-of-nine sequence of points ending the set. The professional tours have adopted no-ad for doubles, and a tie-breaker in place of a decisive third set. Jimmy would be delighted. Complete rules of VASSS are available on request from the International Tennis Hall of Fame, Newport, Rhode Island.

Older players may be surprised at finding themselves better in many ways than as youths, having learned not to blast away all the time with the gusto of bygone days, and to must play more thoughtfully, mixing up strokes. Hitting the ball on the rise takes advantage of the pace the opponent puts on the ball and uses less energy. Don't run for a ball obviously out of reach, or on a point that probably doesn't mean much, say at 40-0 or 0-40.

Gonzalez was a good example, mustering his energy, saving the big serve for when he really needed it. He kept his returns low and soft, and used the lob often and well. When he came to the net he made sure it was behind a worthwhile shot. He felt that his eyes and reflexes had gone just a little and had trouble with balls hit directly at him at net. This is always a good tactic to use with a volleyer—bang it right at him—and it pays off more against an older opponent.

Older players are more likely to pull muscles, so they should be sure to be warmed up properly, and should take it easy if they haven't been playing regularly.

It's a great game at any age. So take it easy and enjoy it.

THE DAVIS CUP JITTERS

EVEN IN THE JET AGE, AUSTRALIA IS A LONG WAY FROM ANY place. Getting out to any place takes time and money, and there aren't very many opportunities. Tennis is one of them, a good one, a privilege as well as an opportunity. And an honor because anybody sent away by Tennis Australia represents Australia. Playing ability is important, but so is behavior. A few Australians have made fools of themselves with temper displays and have been caught with their sportsmanship down. Very few. That doesn't mean that Australia doesn't breed racket-throwers and whiners. It's just that those types don't get sent abroad.

When we went away on a team headed by Harry Hopman—or any other captain during a non-Davis Cup tour—the man in charge had our parents' blessing to lay on the discipline. We'd get no sympathy at home if we complained, because this was a great opportunity for us. Travel came much harder for us than for Americans.

We're an easygoing people, but we're very competitive, too, somehow different from the Americans whom we consider our best friends and hottest rivals. Australians have handled the pressure of tight situations in tennis better than Americans. We don't blow up. That's not 100 percent true but it does seem that way, and when our players collapse or choke they don't rave and fume like Americans. I think it's because of the difference in the societies. We're competitive in sports all right, as much as anybody in the world, but the Americans are competitive in everything, every waking minute.

The pressures are much greater on American tennis players, and it's no wonder they explode. A young Californian isn't much different from a young Aussie. They grow up in tennis climates and tennis atmospheres. At fifteen years old, the American may even be ahead of the Australian, but life is much more complex for the American. There is the pressure of school: he has to be thinking about his marks so that he'll qualify for a good college. At the same age, the Australian with a future in tennis quits school and goes headlong into tennis.

There's no stigma attached to leaving school at that age in Australia. By fifteen, you complete a segment of education that is nearly the equivalent of high school in America, and it is as much education as most Australians get, although more emphasis is now being placed on completion of high school and entering university than in my day. We're still a very young country and higher education is for only a few. I didn't even have the usual amount of schooling. When I was fourteen, I lost a year when I came down with hepatitis. My father took me away to a farm where I could recover my strength, and when I was ready for school, they said I'd have to repeat the entire year.

I was never that crazy about school anyway. I was sure tennis was going to be my life, so I wanted to get into it. Charlie Hollis, my coach, helped me get a job with a sporting goods company, the usual thing for a boy who wanted a career playing, but he had trouble doing that. Finally Dunlop took me on to do odd jobs around their plant in Brisbane, but Charlie had several turndowns before that. I was too scrawny and didn't look like much for the long haul as an athlete.

With that kind of job it was understood that I'd have time to practice and to go away to tournaments. I'd be giving clinics and exhibitions on behalf of the firm wherever they wanted to send me, and I'd be kept in equipment. The pay was nothing to speak of, but my parents found me a place to lodge, and I didn't need much money. What I needed was pretty clear to me: to hit thousands of tennis balls, get stronger and more accurate, and to accumulate tournament experience.

This is the way it was and is. Many times I regret my lack of education.

At a party or with non-tennis friends, occasionally I felt uncomfortable as the conversation swirled about me. I've always been shy, but well-educated people can make me feel shyer, at first, if I don't know them. It's a matter of gaining confidence, and since I've been married and met a wider circle of people, through Mary and living in California, I began to enjoy getting to know people outside of tennis. I read more, and I guess I become more aware.

I can't say I'd stay in school if I had it to do again, or that I'd think about college. I had to get on in tennis, and the way I did it was the best way. This is where the Americans go "wrong," and I've purposely put the word in quotes because it depends on the surroundings you grow up in and what you want out of life.

In American tennis, Cliff Richey, a semifinalist in the French and U.S. in 1970, and a Davis Cupper, was the closest thing to an Australian in outlook. For Cliff, tennis was everything, and to his parents it was, too. They encouraged him in his desire to hit a tennis ball to the exclusion of just about everything else. Cliff did get a high school diploma somehow, although his original class graduated a couple of years before he did. He still shudders when he thinks about biology, which he had to hit a few times before getting the credit. Cliff was dedicated to tennis, and although he didn't have the talent to be a great champion, his determination made him a good living as a pro.

But Cliff was an odd-man-out in America. All his contemporaries in tennis had gone to college—gone "wrong" as I said—and that slowed their tennis development. While I was hitting tennis balls in Italy, learning the slow court game against a tenacious opponent and feeling the tensions of an alien environment and a hostile crowd, Ronnie Holmberg—who beat me in the Junior Wimbledon final of 1956—was juggling tennis with classes at Tulane.

There is plenty of tennis for American college players, but they're essentially part-timers fitting the sport into education. That's the right way for Americans, a fortunate way. But how could Holmberg keep up with me? From the age of fifteen I was a tennis professional. I didn't sign a contract until much later, but obviously I was a pro. Tennis was my life; it supported me. Holmberg and I were equals at eighteen, but thereafter I shot far ahead. We Aussies were on subsidies from sporting goods firms, an advantage not permitted then by U.S. amateur rules.

Frank Froehling, who gave me a good match at Forest Hills when I completed my first Grand Slam in 1962, was one of the Americans who tried to have it both ways by attending college and filling in the spare hours with big-time tennis. "It's pretty funny that we Americans would always be criticized for our Davis Cup failures," said Frank, "when to be a Davis Cup player on the Australian level you have to play tennis full time. So then when you'd play full time, somebody would call you a tennis bum, or say, how come you're not in college. They never asked Laver or Emerson why they weren't in college. Everybody accepted them as career amateurs. That wasn't nice for American boys, yet we were expected to rise up on the big occasions and beat them. People would say what's wrong with American tennis?

"After four or five years of tennis and college, a guy would graduate and decide he'd give the game a couple of all-out years. For all but the exceptional players this was too late, but many would try. They'd have to put up with this comment from their friends: 'Are you still playing tennis? When are you going to get a job?'

"How could you win?

"Things are better now, though, with more realistic rules, and the opportunities to make prize money from tournaments. It's honorable for a college graduate to go into pro football, basketball and baseball, and now at last there are the same legitimate career opportunities on the tennis circuit as there are in golf."

That's the pressure in the United States that has never been felt by an Australian. The background of the game in the U.S., as a rich man's sport, made a career of playing tennis seem improper. A player had to seem to be doing something else as his principal occupation. It was ridiculous. We had the amateur hang-up in Australia too, but a career as an amateur tennis player was perfectly acceptable. In fact it was choice, with all the travel, glory and privileges involved. Nobody asked when are you going to get a job, because we all had connections with sporting goods firms and because playing tennis was considered a very nice job. In the United States, with wider economic opportunities, a tennis player was expected to get educated and really go to work.

Occasionally a player would come along who, for a brief time, could blend college with tennis and play at the top. Chuck McKinley did that in 1963 when he won Wimbledon and spurred America to one of its then rare Davis Cup wins. Arthur Ashe had his big five-month drive in 1968 when he won the U.S. Amateur, the U.S. Open, and led the victorious Davis Cup charge, but Arthur's five years at UCLA and two years in the U.S. Army could have been time that he'd never make up in the game. However, he did, winning Wimbledon in 1975. Arthur was a very diversified guy, his life broader than a game. His uniqueness as the only black man in big-time tennis opened many business and social opportunities to him, each reducing the time available to hit balls and concentrate on the game. But he was up to it. Extraordinary.

Undoubtedly the time will come in Australia when higher education is as sought after as in the United States. Then tennis players will be like other professional athletes. They'll mix college with their game and wait until after graduation to specialize. But for years the Aussies have had the jump, and they've made the most of it.

I settled into my career young, and I think that helped my temperament. I knew what I was doing; I was beginning my adult role at fifteen. The American kid is bewildered about what he wants to do then, and he's got so many options.

When I was twenty-one, I was a seasoned pro and ready for my role in the cooker at Wimbledon and in the Davis Cup. American kids usually aren't.

In Davis Cup matches, Americans feel strongly about playing for their country, just like everybody else. Ashe said, "Maybe it can get too nationalistic. The Olympics do, but you can't escape the fact and feeling that your country is depending on you and your game. Too much can be made of it, and that's where the pressure comes from. It's built up by the press. It makes Davis Cup an altogether different competitive experience."

Although I played on four Cup-winning teams in four years, I regret that the competition wasn't too keen after the first year, 1959. Then it was as tense as anything I've been through. We had to battle in the early rounds as well as the final when we took the Cup away from the U.S. I lost to Mario Llamas of Mexico and Ramanathan Krishnan of India on the first day of those meetings to keep us in trouble in the best-of-five-match series.

In the Challenge Round, the grand final at Forest Hills, we took the Cup only because Neale Fraser was so sensational, winning both his singles over Alex Olmedo and Barry MacKay, and the doubles with Roy Emerson.

My contribution was mainly applause for Neale and Emmo. It stands as the biggest disappointment of my career that I lost to Olmedo on the third day with Australia ahead, 2-1. I could have clinched the Cup right there. I had set points in every set, but won only one as Alex beat me, 9-7, 4-6, 10-8, 12-10. Fortunately for us, Fraser came through against Mac-Kay in the last match. Neale made me feel doubly glad—to be part of a victorious Australian team, and to be taken off the hook for my failure. All through his struggle with MacKay, which ran over two days because of bad weather, I hated myself for blowing the match with Olmedo.

After that, the Davis Cup wasn't much of a thrill. We were the defenders and had to play only the final against the survivor of the preliminary rounds. It was a letdown that the Americans never made it, and we weren't pushed by the teams that beat them, Italy in 1960-61 and Mexico in 1962. In the six singles and one doubles matches, I played I lost a total of two sets. That was dull. Harry Hopman trained us in his usual thorough manner, as though we were going to run across the Simpson Desert. It was overkill, but Harry believed in running scared— or running any way as long as you kept running.

With the kind of backing he got at home, Hopman could be a "martinet," as the newspapers called him. I felt he was petty at times with his fines for minor training infractions, and failing to pay us the daily allowance if we lost a day crossing the dateline. His harshness probably prevented a few fellows, like Merv Rose and Bob Mark, from realizing their potential. They soured on him early. And his role as a strategist was overvalued. His usual advice during a Cup match: "Relax and hit for the lines."

But I have nothing but gratitude for Hop because his program of working our guts out made me a winner. Conditioning is often the deciding factor in a match between players of similar ability, and at the top there isn't much to choose between individuals in the matter of talent.

Hop showed us how to be the fittest. Running and strenuous exercises and drills were stressed. Fitness means more to you than strategy in a tight Davis Cup match. Hop got us readier than our opponents. That was his strength, getting us up physically and mentally, bringing us to the peak at the right moment. After that he could sit beside the court, mutter "hit for the lines" and appear a genius.

It's easier to bear down and get really fit when you're a member of a team. When you're out on your own as a pro, and have to discipline yourself, that's when it's a test of how much desire you have to get on. Will you make yourself get up early and run? Will you do those double knee jumps faithfully, and work as hard in practice as you would in a Wimbledon final, stretching for every ball in the two-on-one drill? Those of us who have been through the Hopman mill have been molded into these habits, and I reckon the conditioning of four of us in our thirties—Emmo, Stolle, Rosewall, and I—stacks up pretty well against any athlete.

Tennis is an individual game, and it is a game of individualists. The team aspect of Davis Cup competition gives tennis another dimension, a very satisfying one. It was Donald Dell's ability as captain in uniting a group of extreme individualists—Arthur Ashe, Clark Graebner, Bob Lutz, Charlie Pasarell, and Stan Smith—that enabled America to gain control of the Davis Cup in 1968 and establish a long reign. Of that group, Stan Smith was the only one who could be described as a self-sacrificing team man before Dell took over.

The desire to win for your country is common enough, but I had more than that going for me in 1956 when I went on tour for the first time. I wanted to win for the people at home, in Rockhampton. I felt I was playing for them and I didn't want to let down these friends and neighbors. Maybe you feel more that way when you come from a small town. Everybody knows you, and if you do well you'll actually be able to put the town on the map. I guess I did that, in a way, for Rockhampton. It sounds corny, but I played with the feeling that I'd let Rocky down if I lost. Nobody else from the town had ever gone abroad to play. This feeling was strong at first, then, of course, it subsided. But it was a part of me, it was always there. Frequently in Australia townspeople will take up a collection to help send a promising young player away. They did that for Jan Lehane in a little town called Kingsbury, and she felt that her friends were riding with her. "It made me try twice as hard as I thought I could," she said.

It's likely an Australian will feel a special allegiance to his or her hometown because tennis is so prominent a sport in Australia, and all your results are followed closely in the local papers. Dennis Ralston had something of this feeling for Bakersfield, California, an isolated community where tennis was important and he was a leading personality. After he and Chuck McKinley won the Davis Cup for the U.S. in 1963, in Adelaide, Ralston instructed the American correspondents to "tell 'em in Bakersfield that I won it for them." This is the way a small-town boy feels, and I was that boy.

My first world tour was paid for by an industrialist named Arthur Drysdale. It was common in those days for young Aussies to make trips subsidized by wealthy countrymen. Drysdale didn't choose me in particular. He gave the money to Harry Hopman for the purpose of helping develop two promising juniors. Hop chose Bob Mark and me, a pleasant jolt when I learned about it.

When Charlie Hollis was coaching me, he was concerned about the whole picture of life as a tennis player—not just the strokes that supported that life. He drilled me on etiquette and dress, on whatever customs he knew of the countries where I'd be playing, and in the histories and personalities of the great players of the present and the past.

"We want to be proud of you when you're becoming a champion," he'd say over and over. "You have to know how to act the part. You're representing the people of Rockhampton and Queensland and Australia." My parents were with him wholeheartedly.

That might not make much of an impression with kids of today. They seem more sophisticated, but it sank into me.

I feel that I represented Australia pretty well, but there was a summer night in 1958 when I was scared I'd be going home in disgrace. I pictured the headlines in the Rockhampton paper: "Laver Jailed, Deported After Wild Boston Party. Tennis Stars Arrested for Peace Disturbance."

The entire Australian traveling team had been invited to a party at a penthouse in Boston's Back Bay section. Normally, on a night before the finals of the U.S. Doubles, we'd have stayed home because some of us would be playing. That was an unusual tournament. All the Aussies had been knocked out in the quarters or semis, and our manager, Esca Stephens, said we might as well enjoy ourselves.

That we did until a group of policemen suddenly appeared on the roof. "You can hear this party all over Boston," growled the sergeant in charge. "We've had complaints from six blocks away. I'm backing the wagon up to the door, and taking everybody in."

I was terrified, even through my one-beer glow. This was my first trip away with the team, and I was going to jail. It had seemed like such a good party. A bit boisterous, perhaps, when Ashley Cooper defeated the rest of the crowd in a standing broad jump event on the living room floor.

"All right, you're all going in to Station 16," bellowed that cop. That is one precinct number that stays with me: Boston 16. I thought of jumping off the roof, but it was five floors up. Could I escape like a cat burglar? No, we were a team and we'd go to jail as a team.

"Please, officer," one of our hosts, Charlie Cronin, pleaded. "These athletic fellows here are the Australian Davis Cup team. You wouldn't want to cause an international incident, would you?"

The cop, a burly Irishman, paused, looked us over, and replied: "Now what in hell is the Australian Davis Cup team?"

I never felt farther away from home.

But Cronin had enough Irish in him to somehow talk the cops off the roof, promising that the music would be turned off and that everybody would go straight home.

Something else I didn't want to let down was the Australian tradition. This is the way the Green Bay Packers and the old New York Yankees and Cleveland Browns and Boston Celtics felt, I think. As an Australian I was in a very illustrious line that began in 1950 with Frank Sedgman and Ken McGregor. There had been excellent Aussies before that – Jack Crawford, John Bromwich, Adrian Quist, and even earlier, Sir Norman Brookes, Gerald Patterson, and J. O. Anderson. But beginning with Sedge and McGregor, Australia took over the tennis world and began a quarter-century stranglehold ended. Between 1950 and 1968, Australia won the Davis Cup 15 times, and in 1952, Sedgman won Wimbledon (19 years after the last Australian victory by Crawford). Beginning then, Aussies won 14 of 21 Wimbledon men's singles titles, 10 of 20 French and 13 of 21 U.S.

I didn't want to be the one to let the dynasty down. Sedgman, McGregor, Hoad, Rosewall, Rose, Hartwig, Cooper, Anderson, Fraser, Emerson, Laver, Stolle, Newcombe, Roche. That's quite a tradition, and I think you have to play better being a part of it. More was expected of Australians on a tennis court. Even an itinerant like Bob Carmichael. They called him "Nails" because he used to be a coffin maker, and he's a bloke who's seen the world through tennis. He lived in Paris. Not really a great player (though once a Wimbledon quarterfinalist), but when somebody beat him they felt good because they'd beaten an Aussie. They'd even feel good beating Jack Crawford, and Gentleman Jack in his 70s because a win over an Aussie was something to be treasured.

I think lesser Aussies like Carmichael and Terry Addison (two-faced Terry, who wears a beard when he's abroad and shaves when he comes home to Brisbane because his mother wouldn't let a beard into the house) also played better merely trying to hold up their end of the tradition. We've got great pride in this tennis mastery. We liked being the islanders from the bottom of the world who sat on top in the most international game. We probably are a bit boorish about it, too, but—and this is a bit odd—we also like to get beaten once in a while. We cheered for the Spanish and the Italians, the Mexicans, and the Americans each time when they came down to try to take away the Davis Cup, because we thrive on competition, and we want the feeling of a stiff challenge. But when the competition gets too tough, we'll cheer double faults and other mistakes by the enemy and we'll shout three times as loud for our own good shots.

We're sensitive to the fact that wherever we went people groaned, "No, not another all-Australian final." Wimbledon had ten of those in the twenty-one postwar years, and where once the British loved us madly because we broke an American monopoly and won a few titles for the Commonwealth, they now regarded us as automatons. We didn't show enough emotion. We didn't hug everybody in sight when we win like Manolo Santana, the Spaniard. Nor do we throw our rackets and curse so that we can be lectured, like expatriate Bob Hewitt, all-time Aussie rascal, whose bad manners kept him off our Davis Cup team. (You can afford to discipline the bad actors when you have so many good players available). We are dull victors, they complain. I guess we are, but we are victors. And we do show emotion and glee—when we're doing our banking.

LESSON • 8

Pressure

HARRY HOPMAN, our Davis Cup captain, used to say to us during a tense match: "Relax and hit for the lines."

Easy enough to say, isn't it? But how do you do it when you're serving at 15-40 and the match is at stake? At our level this was where all those hours of training and drills came into play. We could pull our concentration together, tell ourselves to hit through the ball, and remind ourselves that the best way to turn the pressure on the other guy is to get the ball over the net. Then it's in his court—and points are usually lost on errors and not won on outright placements.

It's this way at every level. You won't have practiced so much as I have so that you can hit out on all occasions—well, almost all occasions—without clutching a little. But if the situation is tense, chances are the tension is on both sides of the net, and if you can keep hustling and putting balls back, you'll be piling the pressure up on your rival.

Scrambling and running have won more matches than great shot-making.

Determination has a lot to do with dispelling pressure. You've got to go onto the court thinking you're going to win. Be positive. Screw in your concentration. This is the hardest part of tennis. Concentration separates players of equal ability. Ron Holmberg could hit the ball as well as anyone in the game, but he allowed himself to get distracted or bothered by little things.

In concentrating, you have to wipe everything out of your mind but the match, particularly the ball. Nothing but the ball. Glue your eyes on it. Marry it. Don't let it out of your sight. Never mind your opponent, the weather, people watching, or anything. Nothing but the ball. Make that ball an obsession. If you can get yourself into that trance, pressure won't intrude. It's just you and the ball.

I'm not saying it's easy.

If your opponent is playing too fast, slow the match down. Or speed it up. Change courts quicker or slower. Try to throw his tempo off if things are going badly for you. This is all part of changing a losing game.

There are times when you can get so choked up on serve that your elbow feels like it's in a cast. The net seems a million miles away, and the balls are unresponsive lumps.

Stop.

Take a few deep breaths. Take the racket in your other hand and let your racket hand hang out and release its death grip. Try to smile and consider how silly this is. It's only a game. If your motion has deserted you, just hold the ball up and pat it toward the service court. Forget style. Just remember that to get the first ball in—any way—gives you a heck of a chance to win the point. The ball is on the other side now. A double fault gives you no chance.

Above all, don't give up. Hang in. Nobody is immune to the choke. It can leave you and grip your opponent just as strangely. Keep trying.

Maybe it won't be much consolation, but you ought to know this: I've choked. And I haven't met anybody who hasn't.

9

PARIS IN THE SPRING, 1962

THREE OF THE GRAND SLAM TOURNAMENTS ARE HELD IN English-speaking countries, and an Australian gets along all right. The fourth is on alien ground—Parisian clay. The first time I saw Paris, in 1956, I had a few phrases ready in my atrocious French, so that I could eat and get to my hotel room. Bob Mark, who was my doubles partner, and I got taken for a few elaborate rides by the cab drivers, and we had trouble with the money, our pockets stuffed with francs that didn't mean much. This was when the exchange rate was 350 to the dollar. The French seem less sympathetic to foreigners than other people, and the masterpieces of French cooking don't do much for me, since I'm a typical Aussie, a steak-and-eggs man. You don't need Maxim's to fix that for you.

So Paris, as such, isn't one of my favorite places, but I look forward to it because the French Championships is the tournament I enjoy the most from the standpoint of emotional involvement. I love to watch matches in Paris, grim struggles on that slow clay, beauties for the spectators.

When an Australian is playing, the rest of the Aussies show up for moral support because you know, if the opponent is European, and especially if he's French, the gallery will be very anti-Australian. That's Europe. The crowds make more noise, they take it to heart, they cheer and boo. My introduction to Roland Garros, the tennis complex in the Bois de Boulogne, was a shaky experience in 1956. Bob Mark and I were playing a Davis Cup style junior match against a French team of Christian Viron and Mustapha Belkodja. In the doubles, the crowd went all out for their countrymen, hissing us and even throwing small stones. They weren't angry at us, but they didn't leave any doubt about their sentiments. They really psyched us out, but you get used to that in Paris and Rome and Barcelona and Mexico City where the national pride seems to ride with every shot.

When you realize this, the French tournament becomes great fun. I've seen some fantastic matches at Roland Garros. Probably the most fantastic was in 1958 when a Frenchman named Robert Haillet was so far gone in a match with the stylish American, Budge Patty, that he needed extreme unction. Patty was serving and he led 5-0, 40-0 in the fifth set. Triple match point, and two service breaks up. There was no way Haillet could win, so he figured he'd drop dead with a flourish and he swung spectacularly on a return. The ball landed on a line for his point. Nice, but so what? Still match point and that tremendous lead for a Wimbledon champion and one of the world's finest clay court players. Haillet, as loose as Marie Antoinette at the guillotine, thought what the hell and kept swinging at Patty's serves with all he had . . . and the winners poured from his racket. By the time he got to deuce and then won the game, the crowd began to come back to the center court. But Haillet was a long way behind. The chances of the Tour d'Argent serving Rice Krispies were much better than Robert Haillet's winning the match. But that mob was screaming for him as though he were de Gaulle liberating Paris, and Robert flew to victory on the wings of bedlam.

I've never seen anything like it, but on clay a comeback is much more possible than on a fast surface like grass. Grass is more risky. A couple of mistakes, you lose your serve and maybe you're out of it. The serve isn't such a destructive weapon on clay. You can return easier, and anybody willing to work and scramble can hang in there.

Of course, when somebody was working and scrambling and hanging in there against me, I wasn't so fond of the clay. I realized that this was the hardest championship for me to win, and because of that it probably meant more than the other three. It was certainly the toughest in 1962 when either Marty Mulligan, an Australian who revels on clay, or Roy Emerson should have beaten me, and Neale Fraser could have. Those were three straight five-set matches beginning in the quarters with Mulligan. Fraser in the semis went to 7-5 in the fifth, and Emmo in the final won the first two sets before I began to wear him down. Mulligan—or Martino Mulligano, as his pals sometimes call him now—had the best chance, leading me two sets to one and holding a match point in the fourth set.

How do you make an instant Italian out of an Australian? Add two o's and stir some remote Italian blood in the genealogical pot. We kidded Marty about his conversion to the Italian Davis Cup team in 1968, but he was only doing the best he could with his tennis talents and nobody blamed him. Marty came out of Sydney and was a mate of mine on the Australian Cup team of 1959.

He's a little fellow, very steady, and he took to the European clay better than he did to his native grass. His strokes were accurate and consistent, but he lacked the booming game that intrigued Harry Hopman, our captain. He also came along at the wrong time, in the midst of some of the best tennis players any country has developed. So Marty wisely moved to Italy to live. There he went on the payroll of a large club in Milan, becoming available for the interclub matches, very popular in Italy. The Italian clubs buy players from all over to compete in these "amateur" affairs.

Marty fitted well in Italy, learned a few words, fell in love with an Italian girl, and accepted a bid to play on the Italian Davis Cup team. Since he'd never competed for Australia, he was eligible, after declaring himself a resident. This caused a furor in Italy. One faction, backing Marty, wanted only to win, like the Americans in 1958 who broadened the Good Neighbor Policy to include Alex Olmedo of Peru on the U.S. team. But an opposing faction was horrified to think that an Australian would take the place of an Italian boy in representing the homeland.

All Marty wanted to do was play tennis and make as much money as he could. Europe was the place to do that in the amateur game, and he could make even more by playing for Italy, probably as much as

$30,000 a year all told, with very favorable living conditions too. Luckily, he discovered an Italian grandmother in his family tree. She had immigrated to Australia. That made it reasonably okay, and Martino Mulligano wore the insignia of Italy in 1968, for one year. Italy wasn't able to win the European Zone, so Marty was dumped. They figured they could lose just as easily with full-blooded Italians.

But this was in 1962 when we played. He was just plain Marty Mulligan, promising young Australian—and he was one point away from cancelling out that Grand Slam. I was down two sets to one and serving at 4-5, 30-40, the only match point against me in either Grand Slam.

It's hard to get a bunch of Frenchmen excited about two Australians playing tennis, but I was the favorite, the top seed, and here was this nice-looking nobody named Mulligan about to pull the big upset. Momentarily the customers adopted him as though he were St. Martin, the Patron Saint of France.

If Charlie Hollis had been there, he'd have screamed: "Get your first serve in!" It was the only thing to do in a tight spot, and I got mine in all right—into the net. So now I was down to the second serve. I spun the ball to his backhand and came sprinting in to the net behind it. Maybe I should have stayed back, but all through the match he'd been sending his backhand return down the line, and I wanted to move right to the spot and cut off the return. Sure enough, he stuck to the pattern, and I was there to bang a winning volley. It was deuce. The match point was gone, and I held serve for 5-5. I was still in there, but Marty was fighting hard to close it out in four sets, and the crowd let him know they felt that way too.

The set stretched to 8-all, and then a linesman's eyesight was questioned by Marty, and this quiet, polite Australian erupted uncharacteristically. He was serving and I hit an approach shot that sailed over the baseline. At least Marty thought so, and I'll take his word for it. His word didn't count, only the linesman's who said the ball was good. My point.

This was too much for Marty. He began screaming at the man on the line and the umpire. I was shocked. I'd never heard him raise his voice before. Then I was stunned as Marty picked up a ball and smacked a high-speed drive at the linesman. The fellow's eyes were definitely all right; he ducked, avoiding a headache at the least. The ball hit the grandstand loudly and rebounded across the court.

Marty wasn't the only one shouting now. The umpire was shouting back. Neither understood what the other was saying, but they didn't need an interpreter for most of the remarks. The referee marched out to try and stop the argument. You'd think I'd written the script, the way things worked out, but I stood by uncomfortably until Marty got it all out of his system.

When we resumed he'd stopped complaining, but he'd lost his concentration—and he'd lost his followers. Suddenly he was no longer St. Martin to the crowd, and they began jeering him. They had been carrying Marty but now they got on his back, and he couldn't resist that load. I won eight of the last ten games.

In 99 cases out of 100 it's beneficial for you when your opponent blows up over an annoyance like a line call. The 100th case is Pancho Gonzalez. Anger and rage make him play better, but I didn't have to worry about him in those days.

Last in line at the French that year were two more countrymen, Neale Fraser and the ubiquitous Emmo. They were both victims of caution. I learned something extremely valuable from those victories: don't change a winning game.

Fraser had me deader than Custer. But I got away because after surrounding me, he didn't finish the job properly. He was serving at 5-4 in the fifth set, and with the best serve in the game he was 100-to-1 to liquidate me. Strangely, he decided to be very careful. He stopped following his serve to the net, and his moment of indecisiveness was all I needed. I had more time to make my returns, and more room without him crowding the net. I could take the offensive now that he'd relinquished it, and I shot through three straight games to grab a match he should have won.

A player who goes cautious after building up a lead takes a risk. Emerson, of all people, did just that when he led me 2-1 in sets and 3-0 in the fourth. He'd been sweeping me off my feet, but he got too careful and that gave me time to breathe. When you've got your hands around somebody's neck, keep squeezing, don't let up. Your victim might live to victimize you. That's what I did to Fraser and Emmo in winning France in 1962.

Bill Tilden used to say, "Never change a winning game." I used the words "Don't change," which I think is slightly different. "Never" is a bit too rigid. A tennis match is a very fickle proposition that can do a flip-flop with one swing. An opponent can catch on to your winning game, and if you persist in the same tactics he's going to be all over you.

As long as things are going your way, you don't change, but you have to be ready to adjust. There was no reason for Fraser and Emmo to make such abrupt changes, becoming hesitant when they were beating my head in.

LESSON • 9

Don't Change a Winning Game (and Always Change a Losing Game)

I SUPPOSE Bill Tilden was the first to harp on the dual commandments: Never change a winning game. Always change a losing game. He was right, but it's amazing how many players disregard this sound advice. They get ahead and neglect the methods that got them there. They fall behind and keep failing with the tactics that put them down.

Am I serving badly and getting passed? I'd better go to the net only when I can prepare the way with a good approach instead of rushing up there behind an unreliable serve. Am I butchering my overheads? Perhaps I should let them bounce until my timing returns.

Often you can size up your opponent in the warm-up. Give him a variety of shots and see how he handles them. You may be able to discover weaknesses right away. Pound away at those weaknesses and inadequacies. Not necessarily to the exclusion of everything else. You must maintain a fair variety so that your opponent doesn't know that the ball is headed right for that suspect backhand every time. That's one way to build up a guy's backhand, unless it's absolutely hopeless.

There are a couple of tactics you never want to change. Always go hard for the first point of a game and the first two games of a set. I don't mean that you can coast if you win them, but getting in those first licks can frequently strike a big psychological blow.

Roy Emerson said, "I try like anything for those first two points. Get those and you're going to win almost every game." If you can get that first break of serve, either in the opening game or in the second game, you can crack some players right there.

Tilden gloried in a radical method of breaking up the enemy-playing his opponent's strength until he got through it. "This," Tilden said, "is an exception to the rule of not giving an opponent a shot he likes to play. But, believe me, once a player finds his favorite shot won't work for him, his whole game collapses."

Bill found that exciting. I think of it as risky business. But he was a genius. And he didn't have to play Pancho Gonzalez or Ken Rosewall.

THE YEAR OF THE REVOLUTION

I WASN'T TO RETURN TO THE FRENCH CHAMPIONSHIPS until 1968 when it was the first big open. Open tennis came in officially, however, a month before on a rainy morning in Bournemouth, England, April 21, 1968, the first day of the British Hard Court Championships. This is always confusing to Americans, the term "hard court," by which they mean concrete or asphalt. In Australia, Britain, and Europe a hard court is what the Americans call clay.

Some confusion was fitting after all the trouble and chaos progressive tennis officials had gone through to bring about the sensible blending of amateurs and pros in competition that has proved to be tremendously appealing.

It wasn't very appealing that first morning at the West Hants Club in Bournemouth, but it was history when John Clifton, amateur, served to Owen Davidson, professional, to begin this mixed contest. The traditionalists considered it mongrelization, a mixing of champagne and milk of magnesia. Clifton won the first point, on a smash, but Davidson won the match. Hurrah for the milk of magnesiacs.

The crowd numbered 100–99 people and one dog—but the weather was wet and dreary. Later it got better, and so did the crowds, and there was no room for the dog. Too bad for him, because he missed those epics created by Mark Cox, a British left-hander with tight blond curls who looked like an athletic Harpo Marx.

Cox went into the second round against a man as legendary and congenial as the Loch Ness Monster, Pancho Gonzalez (referred to as Ricardo Gonzalez by the British sportswriters, who, in the matter of Christian names, either perplex you by using only an initial, or overwhelm you with the utterly correct baptismal name of someone who has been known as Pancho for thirty-five years). The first set went as Cox had expected: six straight games for Pancho. A blitz. "I could picture myself losing 6-0, 6-0, 6-0," Mark said, "and I was terribly worried."

His worries began to diminish as he hit out, convinced that within an hour he would be stacked in the monumental pile of Pancho's victims. But an hour later Cox was moving the ball—and Gonzalez—around nicely; and Pancho, who hadn't played a five-set match in years, was feeling it in his forty-year-old legs. Cox eventually survived a last charge by the Old Wolf and a couple of Pancho's nerve-shaking rages to win in five sets, 0-6, 6-2, 4-6, 6-3, 6-3.

It was lovely. A tennis player was on the front page of every newspaper in Britain and a good number elsewhere. Mark Cox hasn't been knighted, yet, but he has his niche in sporting history: he was the first amateur to beat a pro. And what a pro! Gonzalez startled everyone by leaving the clubhouse as he had found it—standing on its foundation. The expected post-match tantrum did not develop.

"Somebody had to be the first to lose, so it might as well be me," shrugged a weary Pancho. "This open tennis is a whole new world, and I'm glad I could still be a part of it."

It was indeed a new world, a better one, but a stranger one for us pros, whose existence had been narrow and ingrown. We'd become used to playing one another, and only occasionally did we have a tournament with as many as twelve players. We almost never played best-of-five-set matches, and we knew one another's moves better than a guy at Sing Sing knows his cellmate's. Rosewall and I were the bosses. Gonzalez had his moments, and the rest were aware of their limitations, although the tennis was first rate— "superplayers," Allison Danzig of *The New York Times* called us. We played hard, no doubt about it, but there was an air of exhibition about it in the public mind, and there was nothing we could do to change that feeling. But opens did.

Immediately the pressure was on us pros. We were the ones who had to prove ourselves after all these years of living in the underworld, away from the customary events. We had derided the amateurs and had talked about ourselves so much as a superclass that everybody thought we'd walk right through the poor amateurs.

It didn't happen that way. On the first day at Bournemouth, a shaky Fred Stolle was almost beaten by a young Englishman named Peter Curtis. The next day, he had an even harder time with a lesser Briton, Keith Wooldridge. "We're the ones with the bloody reputations to lose," wailed Fred. "The amateurs can be loose. They're playing for expenses, and they're sure of those. If they lose it means nothing. But if I lose it disgraces my profession."

That was the kind of talk you heard in the early days of the unknown. Cox beat Gonzalez, then kept going to beat Emerson, who was in his first year as a pro. He gave Emmo one of the worst lickings of his life, 6-0, 6-1, 7-5. This was the same Emmo who had no trouble with Cox a few months before when both were amateurs. But wearing the pro label, Emmo choked badly.

We pros were shaken psychologically at Bournemouth, although I beat Cox and got to the final. There Kenny Rosewall, loving the slow, salmon-colored clay courts, knocked me apart, 3-6, 6-2, 6-0, 6-3. I didn't play badly. Once in a while I missed a shot; he never did.

That was the beginning of the most revolutionary year in tennis. More shocks—for us, the acknowledged pros—were to come. In the opening rounds of the first open Wimbledon, we toppled all over the place, and the amateurs were gleeful. "I always said they were overrated," chortled Marty Riessen, "and that amateur competition was a lot tougher."

He was right in some respects. Many of the amateurs were in better physical condition than some of the pros, and their competition was more varied. They weren't playing against the same guys all the time. They were also more accustomed to conditions outdoors. So a lot of strange things happened. Outwardly strange. We took our bumps at Bournemouth and the best amateurs weren't even there. Except for us pros, the field was second-rate. The top-money amateurs like Manolo Santana and Tom Okker were ducking us for the moment. They did have reputations to guard.

Things were a little better in Paris, following Bournemouth. A lot of good amateurs were there, and we were really finding out about new faces and different styles. It was almost like beginning all over again. I ran into a hulking Romanian named Ion Tiriac in the quarterfinals, completely new to me, but a real clay court operator. Europeans feel as hopeless as polar bears in Miami Beach when they go to Australia, England, or the U.S. and have to play on grass. But in Europe, on their clay, their outlook changes. Their competitive spirit goes up and they feel they can beat anybody. That's the way it was with this Tiriac. His strokes weren't much, but he lobbed well and he battled. He won the first two sets, and I had to make up my mind that I'd just stay out there three or four hours and keep running and hitting. Finally, I wore him down, but that kind of match makes you know you've been in a fight. You're covered with that red dirt and look like you've fallen in a mud-hole. You've been running and reaching—up and back, across court—and every point has seemed like a war. It has to be better for the crowd, and more satisfying for an athlete.

The crowds in Paris in 1968 were incredible. We were amazed that the tournament was even held because that was the spring of the student riots, the general strike. It was an exciting time to be in Paris, exasperating, too, and we thought sure the tournament would be called off. Paris seemed absorbed in more pressing matters than tennis. The students were throwing paving stones around on the Left Bank, and the only reason they weren't really dangerous, according to Buddy Weiss, editor of the *International Herald Tribune*, was "they didn't have a childhood background in baseball. Can you imagine the damage American college kids would have done throwing those rocks?" Later those skills were to be demonstrated to greater—sometimes tragic—effect on American campuses.

Public transportation was shut down and there was little gasoline for private cars. So people walked out to Roland Garros, the place named for a gallant French pilot of World War I, and the crowds were immense. Lance Tingay, who wrote for the *Telegraph* of London, remarked, "Well, demonstrations can get to be a bit of a bore after a while, you know. People would just as soon watch Laver crack a tennis ball for a change after weeks of the gendarmes cracking student heads."

They certainly knew how to do that. Those Paris cops were efficient and rough, and we stayed out of their way when we got caught in a mob.

Nobody went to work during the strike, and I guess that was a break for us, because for several days Roland Garros wasn't big enough. For years the French Championships had been going downhill, losing money. In 1968, the tournament rebounded with a huge profit. Our presence and the fact that it was France's first open had a lot to do with it. But the general strike didn't hurt.

Fifteen years before, as a teen-ager, Rosewall had won the French title to mark himself as the best clay court player in the world. Kenny is the doomsday stroking machine. His ground-strokes never end, and his volleying is bitingly sure. On the clay, he has plenty of time to set himself for that magnificent backhand, and you'd better not come to the net on him behind anything that isn't shot out of a 16-inch gun. It was a long time between French Championships for Rosewall, who had signed his first pro contract in 1956, but he made the most of the wait, cutting me up, 6-3, 6-1, 2-6, 6-2.

Despite the early sabotage by amateurs in the first year of opens, Rosewall and I were in our second straight open final at Paris, and Tony Roche and I played the all-pro Wimbledon final.

Amateurs beating pros provided good copy, created debates, and drew welcome attention to the game. Form took a battering in 1968 and that is always newsworthy, but any realist knew that opens were something of an illusion. In effect you were putting one group of pros in with another, a group of wolves in amateurs' clothing clawing at the professed wolves. The difference was labels. Nevertheless, it was stimulating. All the players were together, as they should be, scratching for the top dollars in prize money. Some, like the Iron Curtain delegates, still called themselves amateurs because their countries chose to maintain the fiction, and some were going under the ridiculous guise of "players." The official definition of "player" was a tournament competitor over age eighteen who supports himself from the game and accepts prize money but is not a professional. Tennis officials have ever been capable of splitting hairs on Yul Brynner's head, and the nonsense continued. The end of it was in sight, and soon all competitors were just true-blue amateurs or true-gold pros.

LESSON • 10

Playing on Clay

PATIENCE AND LEGS. You'll go a long way with those assets on clay. The stronger the longer. This is always impressed on me when I play in Europe, especially Paris, where the slow clay courts dictate an entirely different game from the grass of Australia, Wimbledon and Forest Hills, or the pavement of other areas.

If there is a universal surface it is clay, found almost everywhere, and won on by those players who can control the ball and their impulses to overhit.

The defensive player has an edge because of the slower, higher bounce of the ball, giving him more time and a better chance to reach a forcing shot and make a good return.

Clay blunts the force of a powerful serve and favors those who can play steadily and accurately from the backcourt.

In their perceptive analysis of singles, Bill Talbert and Bruce Old discovered in charting matches between two big hitters, Lew Hoad and Pancho Gonzalez that Lew and Pancho won 75 percent of their points at the net on grass and 40 percent at the net on clay. Yes, they are different games.

Ability to keep the ball in play, move it around with changes of speed and spin, will pay dividends on clay. This doesn't mean that you should forget about attacking. Far from it. Against a persistent and sure baseliner whom you can't out-rally you have to get up to the net and break up his pattern with angled volleys. But you can't be impatient in going up there; your way must be well paved with a strong deep approach shot.

Most baseliners like it back there, and you've got to draw them up with soft shots and angles, make them play a few shots near the net where they're uncomfortable.

Since the huskiest serve in the business isn't going to be overly oppressive on clay, you'd better forget about blasting your serve and concentrate on placing the ball and getting the first one in. Naturally you'll let fly with a hard one just to keep the foe honest if he creeps closer on you.

Doubles on clay is about the same as doubles anywhere else—an attacking game. There will be more retrieving, longer points, but you have to get up to the net fast.

But in singles you may as well face the fact that you have to be fit and favorably inclined toward running. You're going to be on the court a while, most likely.

Bring your lunch.

THE SECOND LEG OF THE GRAND SLAM: THE FRENCH

PARIS IN THE SPRING MAY MEAN LOVE TO SOME, CHESTNUTS to others, but to me it signified the toughest two weeks of the year. The French Championships are where I, more often than not, got my spring cleaning.

But I'm a masochist, and I approve wholeheartedly of this great test. Rex Bellamy of *The Times* of London tells it better than anybody in these six paragraphs that headed one of his accounts of the 1969 tournament:

"The French championships are the game's finest advertisement. The surface, clay, is grueling to play on, yet provides the most exacting test of ability and the most satisfying spectacle. The entry is the best outside Wimbledon.

"All is grandeur and pathos. The grandeur is public—the protracted, absorbing exercises in tactics, technique, and physical and mental stamina. The pathos is private—the drained, exhausted bodies crumpled on the masseur's table or the dressing room benches.

"These are great but cruel championships. Nowhere else is the esthetic potential of the game so fully explored, or the physical cost of it so sadly apparent.

"The round of 16 in the men's singles summed it all up. We saw some superb tennis that day. But, at the end of it, the human wreckage of the men's dressing room was a pitiful sight. Manolo Santana, his head in his hands, was heaped on a bench. He was a broken man. John Newcombe, a superman at his physical peak, fell back onto the massage table like a crumbling pack of cards. He was so weary that he talked as if in some far-off dream.

"The bounding bundle of whipcord called Jan Kodes sat silently in a corner, looking as fragile as porcelain, hiding his pain behind an emotionless mask that told us nothing—but everything. There was hardly a murmur save for the birds outside, singing their evening chorus to the skies.

"All this after a day of crowded, colourful drama, booming applause, and smouldering heat . . . the contrast was as sharp as the thrust of a dagger."

By May of 1969, none of the "amateurs" or "players" or anybody of any other phony name were avoiding us pros and the big opens. The money was getting too good. Several had picked their spots in 1968, the year of the big mix, but anybody who meant anything in the game appeared at Roland Garros that spring for the second French Open.

This looked to be the roughest of the four Grand Slam legs. I'd squeaked by in 1962 as an amateur, with those clay court experts Rosewall and Gimeno outside the picture. Otherwise all I got from clay was grief and, literally, mud in my eye. Until I won in 1962, my won-lost record in Paris for five years was 6-5. Only once did I get past the second round.

Paris was relaxed, calm. No more riots. People were working again and the weather was bad, cold and chill. We pros played a small tournament in Amsterdam to get ready for the clay, but I was feeling pretty confident before that because I'd won the second biggest prize of the year, $15,000 in a Madison Square Garden Pro event two weeks before by beating Emmo on a slow, synthetic court, Uni-Turf. My groundstrokes were going well.

In my first days in Paris as a teen-ager, I didn't care for the clay and the low-pressure balls. I was less patient, but now I was beginning to savor the clay game. I had my shots well under control, and I was as fit as I'd ever been in my life, so that I could run and hit hard all day.

Everything went beautifully. For one day. That's about all I can expect in Paris. Then it becomes work. After a quick brush with a Japanese,

Koji Watanabe, I found myself looking up into a cheery Aussie face belonging to Dick Crealy. Dick is six feet five and loved to hit the hell out of the ball, especially with his forehand. I knew that, but I didn't think he could keep doing it as long as he did—which was long enough to win the first two sets. On clay, the ball bounces high, and my top-spinning shots bounce higher than most. This bothers a lot of people, trying to handle a groundstroke at shoulder level, but for a guy as big as Crealy it wasn't shoulder level. He was taking the ball right where he liked it, just above the waist and swinging through it with everything he had.

After the first set, I felt I was just chasing balls. I wasn't getting very many of them, and I was sliding all over the place. Usually the footing is good on those courts, but 1969 was not a vintage year. They were dry, dusty and slippery, more beige than the customary red. Much of the top dressing was blown away by the difficult, eddying winds. I didn't like it, but should I complain about the best French Championships I ever played?

After you had played Paris once you realized that the whole operation was casual. Matches never started on time—a distinct contrast to Wimbledon—and not unlike the way Forest Hills had been run in the past. But where the Americans were merely disorganized, erratic timing seemed to be a part of the French character. Don't worry—the matches will be played sometime, although it may not be the time you have in mind for producing your best tennis. Things have changed since then.

Crealy and I got started late in the afternoon, long after we were scheduled, and continued to play after dark under the lights. With Dick ahead two sets to one, a rainstorm stopped us for the night, a gloomy chilly night that matched my mood. He'd won the second set, 9-7, as I began to get into the match, and I took the third, 6-2. I felt I had him then, but the rain came and we had to sleep on it.

Sleeping is easy for me, luckily. It's meant a lot to my career, with our bloody wild traveling, that I can catch a nap anywhere and get some sleep no matter when I go to bed or what the circumstances. I was up at seven the next morning, because we were scheduled to resume at the silly hour of ten thirty. I hate morning matches. My reflexes are fuzzy at first, and I couldn't afford a bad start because here it would have been the finish. Some people can walk from bed to the court—and Crealy tried to. I couldn't. Emmo was up with me and we were at the courts a little before nine.

It was good of Emmo to help me out, but any Aussie would have done it. We stick together when we're away from home. When a bloke needs a hit, even at eight thirty in the bloody morning, he can find a compatriot who'll oblige. I wanted a long workout so I'd be good and warm. At most, I'd only have to play two sets, and I couldn't afford my usual slow start being down two sets to one.

When the 12,000 seats in the stadium are filled and people are hanging from odd ledges, railings and the scoreboard, as they were for the final with Rosewall, it's a very lively, warm, emotional place. Those people give you a transfusion of elan and it's great joy to play for them—at least if you're playing well. It's not quite the same sensation as a filled Wimbledon Centre Court. Sometimes the stillness of Wimbledon can drive you crazy. You keep waiting for a noise, an indication that they're alive. In Paris, there's no doubt. The buzz of humanity assures you this is combat as elemental to the people as a duel or a prizefight.

Although the better duels may have been held in the morning, when dueling was France's favorite sport, ten thirty is not really the French spectator's hour. I'll go along on that, and when you walk into that stadium and find yourself surrounded by nothing but cool, clammy concrete tiers, it is the coldest place in the world. The stadium wasn't quite empty. I think there were four people there: the umpire and three linesmen he dug up somewhere.

The enclosure is larger than Centre at Wimbledon and much deeper than Forest Hills, with great expanses behind the baselines. You feel very alone and small out there when the seats are vacant. Maybe Dick felt smaller than I did, cut down in size by seeming to play in a vacuum. I think it was much harder for him, but my experience in all sorts of situations held me up. As a pro, I'd gotten used to odd hours and playing at my best even though nobody showed up to watch, but the absence of people seemed to hurt a twenty-three-year-old on the verge of the upset of the year. No cheers would reward his good shots. People who could be counted on to holler for his every point were somewhere else at that hour. It probably seemed like a private practice match to him, and he may have wondered if the result would become known publicly even if he did win.

That's the way you can feel sometimes. He was a practically anonymous Aussie, who had been reading about me all his tennis life. Now he had a chance to make it all come true for himself, and nobody dropped by to appreciate it.

I appreciated, and that's why I went through such an unusually long pre-match workout, forty-five minutes. In contrast, Dick's was much briefer. I think he was afraid he'd leave something on the practice court. That was a mistake, a lesson for Dick.

Ready to get right into it, I won the fourth set 6-2 to pull up with him and took off on a 3-1 lead in the fifth. I'd won nine of eleven games, and that should have broken his spirit. But by that time some people were wandering in, and he was moving back into his form of the day before, blasting his forehand again.

Right back into the match he came to win three games to 4-3. I held serve for 4-4 and thought I'd better go all out to break him. The wind was tricky, and I didn't want to be serving a match game at 4-5 if I could help it.

Dick was thinking the same thing. "I'd like to have seen you serve at 4-5 with the match on it," he needled me later. It was his fault that I didn't, and only because he tried to make a shot too good. It's a temptation that even the best have trouble resisting.

He got to 40-30 and his next serve was a good one to my forehand, pulling me out of the court. I was lucky to get the ball back at all, but it didn't seem to matter. He was waiting at the net for it, ready to cream the ball and go to 5-4.

I shrugged mentally as he wound up, then watched resignedly as the ball streaked past me, crosscourt—and out. By two feet!

Deuce.

I had to keep the ball down, make this big guy bend over. Once again he was eating up my high-bouncing topspin. I decided I'd try to slice it, get under the ball to make low returns. I played two good ones at his feet, and he volleyed badly. I had the game, the serve, and the wind at my back. There was no way I was going to lose that last game.

I put more spin on my serve to make sure the first ball was in and that I'd have added time to get to the net. I roared up there behind the serve, my nose practically hanging on his side of the court. I had the edge and I was going to push it. With the wind behind me I could afford to get closer to the net than usual. A deep lob would be tough for him into the wind. The pressure was on him to hit his best returns with me right up there. He couldn't, and it was over in four points.

Playing in a swirling wind like that is tricky. I lower my service toss a bit so the ball won't be bobbing around. And I shorten the backswing on my strokes to get better control.

Crealy will think about that missed volley in the ninth game occasionally and wince. He had the entire court, and he made the mistake of trying to keep the ball as far away from me as possible. He hit for the sideline and was wide. No need for it. Take your time on the sure volley, the easy sitter. You have more time than you think. Dick didn't need anything but firmness. There was no reason to try to put it close to the line. I was out of the point—but maybe my speed was on his mind.

That's an added benefit from hustling all the time, which you can and should do if you're fit. Your opponent has watched you chase down a lot of balls, and he may try too hard to put the ball beyond your reach. I think that's what Dick did.

If you consistently hit the ball well inside the court you won't get into trouble. I realize that sounds insultingly easy, but that's the way I play. I'm not a stickler for accuracy, but I do want to hit the ball hard on my groundstrokes.

So the answer for me most of the time is topspin. I can hit for a general area without cutting it fine. Topspin prevents the ball from going too deep, even when I bash it, and carries the ball higher over the net, putting me in less trouble with that bothersome obstacle.

The tournament committee was anxious to keep everybody playing and reduce the size of the field to eight, the quarterfinals, by the end of the first week. After a bite of lunch, I returned to the court to fix an Italian, Pietro Marzano, in straight sets.

The next day, in the fourth round, I found tall Stan Smith to be a rapidly improving player. Stan was to give me a long, trying afternoon at Wimbledon a month later, but he still wasn't up to the clay court game. He's built like Crealy, six-four, and a hitter. Although 1969 began with America's highest hopes attached to Arthur Ashe, it was Smith, the less-publicized Californian, who became the No. 1 player in the U.S. for the year. He had a cold and it didn't help him that we finished the match at night in a drizzle. Stan couldn't get a set. I worked hard on that third set. I didn't want any more serialized matches continued to the morning after.

One match in the tournament that every player anticipated as eagerly as a tax refund was Andres Gimeno vs. Manolo Santana. It may have been only a fourth-round match, but this was for the spiritual championship of Spain. It was the prodigal (pro Gimeno) against the son who stayed home dutifully and did well ("amateur" Santana). It was Barcelona against Madrid, the outcast against the be-medaled national hero. Here were two men born to clay, artists whose strokes are pure brushwork, graceful, filled with duende, as the Spaniards say. They were old friends, once Davis Cup teammates. But a rivalry had been growing in their minds for nearly a decade, and in the minds of the rest of us who awaited the match so long.

At a formative stage, Andres, twenty-three, turned pro in 1960. He was Spain's best then, a shade ahead of Santana, but the game wasn't all that big in their homeland. Santana made it big in 1965 by spearheading Spain's 4-1 victory over the United States in the Davis Cup quarterfinal at Barcelona, getting even with the Americans for the Spanish-American War. Then he won the U.S. Championship, led Spain to the Cup final (where they lost toAustralia), and in 1966, he won Wimbledon. Generalissimo Franco awarded him the country's highest civilian decoration, the Medal of Isabella, and henceforth he might be addressed as "Ilustrissimo." Manolo became a wealthy amateur, one who could not afford to join Gimeno as a pro for both economic and patriotic reasons. Could he ever desert Espana's Davis Cup team?

Many of us felt that Andres was the better player, and it rankled Andres that with tennis' sudden popularity in Spain, he was virtually unknown, and certainly not considered by his countrymen to be in Manolo's class. The average Spaniard was convinced that nobody could beat Ilustrissimo Manolo, el Grande Campeon. That was that.

In a season and a half of open tennis, Santana played few opens, never encountering Gimeno. Now they would meet, and we all felt like Spaniards, wrought up—and festive, too—as though headed for a bullfight as we squeezed into the mobbed stadium.

I think we pros were for Gimeno to a man. Maybe we weren't too understanding—since all of us had been in Santana's position once—but we resented those who hadn't followed us into honest professionalism and still clung to the amateur make-believe. It isn't logical, admittedly, because every man has to make his way as best he can. For Santana, it was "amateurism."

Watching was awfully tough that day because Andres was awful. He was so nervous he could hardly hit a ball. Santana went through the first two sets with ease, hitting shots that would make me shout olé—if an Australian could shout olé unselfconsciously. Finally, Andres shook his jitters and crawled into the match to win the third set. They were straining for every shot as though this were an exhibition that would go on display at the Prado. One of those straining lunges of Manolo's pulled a groin muscle. Andres won the fourth set, and after the first game of the fifth, Manolo surrendered. He walked from the court, unable to continue, and he was saluted with everyone's heartfelt cheers like a gallant bull.

Victory for Andres was not altogether satisfactory, although he did fight until his opponent had to give in. It made Andres feel better, but it wasn't clear-cut.

Gimeno had to feel buoyed by the win, and it carried him through his first set with me, but I've always had the feeling that he's fatalistic about playing me. He doesn't believe he can win, but he's going to make a good showing. Winning that set was the showing. He could be pleased with himself. In the second set, I began slicing my backhand more to keep the ball low as I went into the net. This made it harder for him to hit passing shots, and I controlled the match from then on to win, 3-6, 6-3, 6-4, 6-3.

A slice is the best approach shot. While topspin speeds the flight of the ball, slice slows it, and you have more time to get to the net with the slice. Your opponent will have more trouble turning the low-bounding slice into a passing shot. This is not a hard-and-fast rule, because you should avoid stereotyped patterns. Of course, I approach with topspin shots at times, but the slice gets the best results overall.

When Ken Rosewall played Tom Okker in the semifinals of the U.S. Open in 1968, he must have had the uncomfortable sensation of encountering his own reincarnation. Both of them are short and unbelievably quick. They skitter around the court fascinatingly, like souped-up rats, getting everything back. Since they aren't hard hitters, that 1968 match wasn't dulled by patches of serve-and-volley. It was point and counterpoint with long, sensational exchanges that keep a crowd ecstatic.

You might say that Kenny, the elder by ten years, was an early-model Okker. Or that Okker was a late model Rosewall. Close, but not wholly accurate because Okker, though he's small, couldn't resist lashing out with colorful top-spinning forehands whereas Kenny was more conservative, and his forehand was flat.

Anyway, for the last two matches of the French, I was getting early Okker and late Rosewall in person. On clay you might be better off with double pneumonia. Either one can make you feel rundown fast.

Tom's phenomenal speed and reflexes would be enough to make him quite a good player even if his strokes weren't so sharp and his determination so firm. He was one of the best players to ever come out of Holland, faster than Hans Brinker on his silver skates, although he wouldn't know what I'm talking about. To Americans, Hans Brinker may be the most famous character to come out of the Netherlands, but he was created for American readers and the Dutch never heard of him.

Tom was like me in that he could hit a big-bounding topspin shot on the run for a winner, or pitch a topspin lob over the head of a man hanging at the net. He had these absolutely dazzling stretches, a wild man who made you want to cry because everything he did was so utterly beyond you. That's the way he was in our first set.

But I don't cry anymore when I lose the first set. It happens too often. I'm habitually slow to start, and even lightning wouldn't have saved that first set the way Tom was flying. "Well, you're going to be out here a while," I said to myself, which is what I generally say in Paris because there's no easy way through a match.

Ten games it took for him to win the first set, and by that time I was right. My anticipation was keen and I was picking off balls at my feet with slick half-volleys as I took the net away from him. The points began coming in an avalanche, and Okker wasn't winning any of them. "This is all right," I was grinning inside, and I just slid into magnificent form and began whacking everything and knocking them by him. He was fast but I was making the balls go faster. When somebody warned Sonny Liston that Floyd Patterson had very fast hands, Sonny answered haughtily: "Can he catch a bullet?" I was hitting bullets and Tom wasn't reaching them. The second set was a tennis version of Liston-Patterson: 6-0. Taking a love set from Tom Okker in the semifinal of a major tournament is almost inconceivable. You have to be doing more than something right; you have to be doing everything right, and I was. I was plugged in, comfortably and completely, to the clay game, and the struggle with gangling Dick Crealy seemed distant. Okker took only six games in the last two sets as I won, 4-6, 6-0, 6-2, 6-4.

Rosewall had been coming along nicely on his side of the tournament. No problems. Tony Roche, who had won the French in 1966 and knew how to behave on clay, went down in the semifinals fast after a difficult first set, 7-5, 6-2, 6-2, and here were Kenny and I again just where we'd been the year before.

LESSON · 11

The Serve and Spin

MOST OF THE TIME I use a sliced serve, and that seems to be the common delivery. I'm not tall enough to try many of the all-out cannon-ball flat serves. When I do, they usually wind up in the net, but with slice I can be more sure of getting my first serve into play and that it has something on it to move the ball around.

My slice (a left-hander's) will move to a right-hander's backhand, and that's convenient.

The kicker, or American twist, is useful when you want variety or you think you can bother your opponent by making him go for a shoulder-high ball. My kicker, from the first (or right) court will pull a right-hander wide to his right, opening up the entire court for me. If I slice from the second (or left) court I can do the same thing. It's pretty hard for him to make a crosscourt return when he's wide of the sidelines, but he has a good shot at a down-the-line return. Therefore, when I serve a man wide I edge that way to protect myself against the down-the-liners.

For a right-hander, to hit the slice you toss the ball slightly to the right of your head. The racket brushes across the right side of the ball and follows through across the body, putting a sidespin on the ball.

For the American twist, toss the ball slightly to the left. Hit the ball with a snap of the wrist as the arm moves from left to right with the follow-through finishing on the right side.

It's a good doubles serve because you have time to get to the net behind the high bounce. A sliced serve stays low.

The kicker is nice to have in your repertory. But as far as I'm concerned its use is confined to surprising an opponent—the high bound throws off his timing when he's been looking at a slice. Or for those rare occasions when you play on bad grass. Then a kicker is very important because it's liable to jump anywhere. It was a great help on the wet, rutted turf at Forest Hills in 1969.

One thing I've noticed about less experienced players is that they tend to practice their serves only from the first court where they'll be starting. Take practices from both right and left, and take plenty of them. It doesn't cost any extra.

THE FRENCH OPEN FINAL
AND KENNY ROSEWALL

I SUPPOSE KEN (MUSCLES) ROSEWALL IS THE LEAST APPRE-
ciated great player in the history of tennis. Those old-timers used to tell
me that Bill Tilden would cut us all down with his groundstrokes, but
there's no way I'll believe that Big Bill would have been able to bomb
out little Kenny from the baseline. I hope they get a chance to go at each
other on that great clay court in the sky. I'll be content to act as ball boy
and watch Rosewall's backhands go by. I've seen plenty of them, to my
discomfort, and I'd like to see what Tilden would do with them—even if
he got divine guidance.

Rosewall never got the credit he deserved because he spent his best
years with the vagabond rugbeaters, the pros, after signing his first contract with Jack Kramer at the close of 1956. He was twenty-one then,
had just wrecked Lew Hoad's bid for a Grand Slam by taking the title
at Forest Hills, and was about to be devoured by Pancho Gonzalez on a
head-to-head tour. Pancho beat him, and Pancho was at his prime then,
but Kenny, though devoured, was very tough to digest.

Eventually, he took over the leadership of the group, overcoming Gonzalez, but the public never knew or believed. To them, Gonzalez was the
once-and-forever king. Kenny was playing second racket to Pancho's
personality, just as he had to Hoad's as an amateur. Pancho and Hoadie
were stormy, handsome guys with terrific physiques. Kenny, like me, is
a runt, but has there ever been a quicker, steadier player in tennis? He

never said anything, he went to bed every night as soon as he could, sent his money home to his family. Somewhere in his home outside of Sydney, Kenny has his first five-dollar bill framed over the mantel. When Harry Hopman, the Australian Davis Cup captain, was his chaperone Kenny thought the largest bill minted was a five. Harry handed out the money. Jack Kramer let Rosewall in on a secret about those stirring portraits of Grover Cleveland on the thousand dollar bills issued at the time. You may enjoy the *Playboy* centerfold, but Grover Cleveland's picture is what really turned Kenny on. Nobody knows how many he had, but easily enough to paper his house.

So as a quiet, clean-living little guy who kept his money in a buttoned hip pocket, Rosewall was not quite the colorful type to be built up by the sportswriters. Unfortunately for him—and for Gonzalez—their best tennis was played before the game opened up in 1968 and we pros came out from under our rocks.

But some of Ken's and Pancho's best tennis was still evident when they should have been thinking about retirement. Every time I thought either one of them had decided to be sensible and graciously step aside like gallant elders, I got stung. It happened in 1972, when Ken beat me by two points at the close of a three-and-one-half-hour struggle for the world pro title and a $50,000 cash prize for the winner. I'll tell you the sad details later.

In 1967, we were playing the final of a pro tournament in Berkeley, California, best of three sets, and I was ahead in the third set, 5-4, 40-0—triple match point. My serve. Muscles wasn't rattled. I couldn't rattle him—ever. Three unbelievable backhand returns he hit to get himself to deuce, and then two more for the game. I was stunned, and by the time I got with it again it was time to shake hands. He'd won the next two games and the match. As it turned out that was the minor stunning. The major occurred when the tournament promoter told us our pay was applause. He hadn't collected enough at the box office to meet expenses. This was the big league?

Suddenly the loss hurt even more, with no runner-up money to console me.

I thought about that match and was glad Charlie Hollis, my old teacher, hadn't been there. He'd have been mad as hell. You shouldn't let anybody, not even Kenny Rosewall, out of a trap like that—triple match point on your own serve. In thinking it over I realized that I'd fallen into a foolish routine that grips us all. I served every one of those five balls to the same place, and Muscles got grooved. I didn't mix it up at all. I'd been having success that day with serves to his backhand corner. But also, I'd put enough on the other side and down the middle to keep Muscles honest. He couldn't set himself for the backhand. But in that 5-4 game I guess I got stubborn and wouldn't believe that he could just keep smacking winners. I should have known better. If you give anybody enough chances at the same kind of ball, he's going to begin eating it up. If the guy is Rosewall, he'll have you for supper—and maybe you'll end up paying double. He got the win, and he got the dinner. Since there was no prize money, Kenny was quite right in expecting me to pick up the dinner check.

Maybe it was easy for me to get a little careless like that, to get mesmerized playing against him because we had faced each other so often. Somebody said we could play our matches by phone. There's something to that, but it wouldn't be on Kenny's dime.

We're like those two old welterweight champions, Jack Britton and Ted (Kid) Lewis, who fought each other so frequently and evenly between 1915 and 1921. Kenny knew what was coming and so did I. The only way I beat him was to have a very good day. He anticipated my shots so uncannily that I simply had to hit them bloody well enough that his anticipation and his legs were no use. I didn't have too many days like that, but one of them was in that Paris final.

A year before, he handled my case quite nicely, 6-3, 6-1, 2-6, 6-2. I spent the match retrieving as he dominated. It was the same in the Hard Court final at Bournemouth, the first open. I was hitting the ball into the corners, fine shots, but Kenny was right there to put his shots smack on the lines. I was quite good, which earned me second place.

Because of those two matches on clay in 1968, I both dreaded and looked forward to finals day at Roland Garros. I knew how impossible

I avenged my loss to Kenny in the 1968 French Open final by beating him in the champion-ship match at Roland Garros the following year – earning me the second leg of the Grand Slam. I think Kenny is one of the most under-appreciated players in the history of tennis.

Rosewall could be on clay, but I also had something to prove. The Grand Slam would mean that much more to me if my Paris victory was over Rosewall, on his kind of court.

I think the subject of Rosewall is one that the other players and I agreed on: he was the player we all had the most trouble with.

"No, Laver doesn't worry me," Fred Stolle said at the time. "If the Rocket is hitting his shots there's no chance for me, true enough. But there's always the chance that he'll be a bit off and then you're right in the match. Rosewall was never off. The pressure was on you every second because you knew when you hit a bad shot he'll make you pay for it without fail.

"He's got you crazy serving because his return is so good. You knew if you missed the first serve you might as well forget the point because Muscles would murder the second ball. You were pressing so hard to serve well on the first ball that you would usually miss it and you were at the mercy of what he would do to the second. I'd rather play Laver any day than Rosewall."

Thanks, Fred. I don't think that shows the proper respect, does it?

But I know what Fred meant better than most because I played Kenny more than anybody else. Right after I'd turned pro in January of 1963, I played a series of matches in Australia against Lew Hoad and Rosewall. It was an inspiring indoctrination. Lew beat me seven out of seven. Kenny beat me four out of six, and he wasn't in very good shape at the time. I was two for thirteen in my first two weeks as a pro, and I felt like a midget batting against Vida Blue. I thought I would get him eventually, though, because we were sort of the same type. We were hitting big shots, and I thought I'd be able to keep it up longer than he would. He was getting past his peak.

But Rosewall, I could see, was going to be something else. He was closer with a point than a dollar, and he looked like he'd make about four mistakes a year, one for each season. That wasn't far off, although he began making more of them in 1969 because, I think, his nerves started to wear. He could still run as well and his reflexes stayed sharp, but the tensions seemed to eat at him a bit more, and he had some very sour patches, which wasn't like Kenny.

The first big win I had over him wasn't like Kenny either. It was in 1964 at the U.S. Pro Championships in Boston, the semifinal. Kenny was sick to his stomach, a bit of food poisoning. That is part of being a pro, of course. You play and nobody thinks anything about it, because we all go through these things. I had a very good day, and I was pleased to get through to the final where I beat Pancho Gonzalez and won the title for the first time. Kenny was mad. This was one of the first decent pro tournaments in America and first prize was $2,200, which was fantastic for us then.

As we came off the court, the reporters were all around me, and Kenny was off to one side, alone. A friend of his came up and asked him how he felt.

"Like a bastard on Father's Day," was Kenny's reply.

I suppose that says it nicely for everyone who has ever lost a tough match. I know the feeling, although in 1969 I kept it at such a distance that I almost forgot what it was like.

One or the other of us would know it that Saturday afternoon in Paris, though. No matter how many times I played the French Open, it was still startling to come into Stade Roland Garros. You walked down through a tunnel. It was so dark that you were practically feeling your way, and then suddenly you were in the arena with 12,000 people surrounding you, responding excitedly to your appearance. Maybe it's like being the girl who pops out of a cake at a stag party.

From the minute we began, I couldn't miss. Usually I was the one on the string as Kenny played me like a yo-yo. Not this time. I had perfect control, and everything I hit was going so deep that Kenny didn't have much chance to do anything but chase and scramble. I could get up to the net all the time, and I was moving quickly either way to cut off his passing shots. I don't know of any match I ever enjoyed more because I just kept getting better, and the points rolled in.

I never took Rosewall for granted. He never got his due. I thought about it before the match. He'd won this title in 1953, at the time I was deciding tennis would be my career. I was fifteen. Fifteen years later, he won it again. In 1971, he won the Australian title that he first won eighteen years earlier. In 1974, at the age of 39, he reached the final of both Wimbledon and the U.S. Open, losing both to Jimmy Connors. He even won a pro title at age 43 in 1977. There are no comparable feats of longevity in tennis history.

I wondered if, having won the French for the first time in 1962, I'd even be playing it in 1977. How many times would Kenny have won it if he hadn't turned pro, or if open tennis had come sooner?

Rosewall and Paris . . . they're linked forever in my mind like Sydney and oysters. In 1963 in the French Pro Indoor final, I played the finest tennis I believe I've ever produced—and he beat me. It was a magnificent match on a whizzing wood floor and we hit groundstrokes as though we were on slow clay. I led 4-1 in the fifth, and just ran out of gas. We had both gone all out, hitting a million shots, and I couldn't keep up with him.

Kenny and I have brought the very best out of each other, but the day of the 1969 French Open final was not one for sentimentality. Twelve thousand people wanted to see us do it again. After leading 3-1 in the first, I fell behind 3-4 as he won three games in a brisk streak. I held for 4–4 and broke him to take the first consequential step.

The first set was mine at 6–4 and my confidence was soaring. If I couldn't keep my shots near his baseline, I was in trouble with Kenny because he took anything short with his backhand, ramed it into a corner while he dashed to the net. He may not have been a heavy hitter, but when he got position at the net his volleys were crisp and well angled.

But my groundstrokes were working so well and landing so deeply that he was having trouble getting to the position he liked. He couldn't swoop in on the short balls simply because I wasn't offering him that many. I kept him pinned behind the baseline and you can't hit an approach from back there. Sometimes he tried, but he had too far to go to reach the net, and I was passing him.

My volleys were charmed, and I spent most of the afternoon finishing off points with them. My deep groundstrokes kept me at the net, and Kenny away.

Straight sets in a French final? I couldn't quite believe it when I completed the 6-4, 6-3, 6-4 victory. Monetarily it meant $7,000.

LESSON • 12

Forehand and Topspin

IT DOESN'T MATTER to me whether I hit a forehand or backhand because I reckon I can slap them with equal power and control. But for most people the forehand is the stronger, the stroke used for attacking and pressuring the opponent.

John Newcombe has developed a nice quick-shuffle to run around his backhand in order to smash a forehand return of serve. He showed it off handsomely in winning the 1970 and 1971 Wimbledons. His forehand return is unusually strong, and he uses it whenever he can. If he gets a second serve to the left court, aimed at his backhand, that isn't too deep or fast, he slides to his left quickly and smacks the return down the line. It's a good maneuver, but once you decide to do it—do it. Don't change your mind when the serve crosses the net. You should have your mind made up what you'll do with certain serves before they come to you, and then take that course.

It's pretty obvious when a player decides to hit a ball one way and suddenly changes his mind. He usually botches it. Of course, there are times when the shot coming at you is so good that you're trying bloody hard just to hit it.

In rallies from the baseline my forehand is almost always hit with topspin. It's reasonably easy to put top on the forehand, dropping the racket head below the level of the ball and coming over the ball with a snap of the wrist. With top your stroke will clear the net with plenty to spare, and the topspin will hold the ball in the court. You should work on strengthening your wrist if you intend to use much topspin. The topped forehand seems to be gaining in popularity. I can remember one of the original Australian greats, Jack Crawford, advising against top and recommending a flat forehand. But he conceded that Lew Hoad had something with his topspin. In my day, all the good ones, except for Rosewall, were using topspin on the forehand.

It's a nice feeling to hit the hell out of the ball and know it'll go way over the net—and not the backstop as well.

THIRTEEN STRAIGHT LOSING POINTS

I HAD A GOOD CHANCE FOR ANOTHER $1,000 IN THE DOUBLES at the 1969 French. Emmo and I had a relatively easy time moving to the final against the world's No. 1 pair, John Newcombe and Tony Roche.

Emmo is a great accomplice. Five different partners with whom he won the French title six times between 1960 and 1965 will testify to that. I was one of them. I've always marveled at those tremendous reflexes that allow him to make winning volleys time after time on balls that seem destined to go by him. He prowls the net, a panther, intercepting all but the absolutely best hit returns. He can flick the racket behind his back to cut off a ball shooting to his left when he has committed himself the other way. He did this twice during the same point against Chuck McKinley in a crucial Davis Cup match in 1963. A wooden Indian would come to life as Emmo's partner.

Since he'd lost in the singles, in the fourth round to Zeljko Franulovic, Emmo was especially keen in the doubles.

There was no reason why we shouldn't have repeated our victory of 1961, and we would have if I hadn't screwed up like an all-time hacker.

The ending of that final was such an abrupt reversal that I was completely blank on it until Newcombe brought it up a few weeks later.

"We really zapped you in Paris, Rocket, just when you had us, didn't we?" John was saying.

"I guess so, but I don't remember much about it."

"No wonder," Newc said. "It was enough to send anybody into a trance. I don't wonder that you've tried to blot it out of your mind. We won thirteen points so fast that you and Emmo didn't know where you were. Thirteen straight points. Never been in on anything like that myself."

It began to come back to me. Newc and Tony led two sets to one, but we won the fourth set, got an early service break in the fifth and were moving right along to the championship. It was good tennis with phenomenal volleying, good overheads, and every point a struggle.

At 4-3 for us, the serve came to me and we won the first three points for 40-0. That should have been that, to put us in excellent position, either with a chance to break and finish it, or for Emmo to wind it up on his serve.

We never got another point.

I don't know what the odds on that would be, but a million-to-one is close enough. Certainly the odds on my holding serve at 40-0 were very long. I mean my name is Rod Laver, isn't it? I wasn't so sure when it was over.

Those are the situations that drive us all mad, or at least to several beers more than we'd planned on after a match. It was pretty clear how I blew it, and anybody can do it. You don't need Newcombe and Roche on the other side of the net, either. It was a beautiful case of ignoring all the musts. You must get your first serve into play. I didn't put a single first serve in the court from 40-0. I succumbed to the great temptation of thinking 40-0 was the same thing as game. It's very close, but you still have to get that last point. I was thinking automatic 5-3, and I never got the next point. Nothing is automatic. Instead of spinning that first serve in at three-quarter speed, where all the pressure would have been on Newc and Roche to make good returns, I turned off my brain. I remember now I was going for big first serves, finish off the game with a bang. Looks splendid. Be a hero.

And I got just a trifle casual. You have to get into the net right behind your serve, but I wasn't snappy at all at 40-0, thinking one of those triple-game points would fall by itself.

With my second serve to look at constantly, Newc and Roche got a little edge. They could move up and hit with more confidence. Sometimes the pressure shifts subtly, sometimes dramatically. When they got to deuce, Newc and Roche knew they had a real chance. They were off the hook. They knew it . . . I knew it. I got fumbly. When that happened, so did Emmo. Hysteria was in season. Yes, even for players as experienced as us. With the match even at 4-4, Newc and Tony doubled their concentration, while I was still kicking myself mentally about that last game.

As the thought, "Forty-love, you idiot!" flashed over and over in my brain, they were taking us apart. There is just no use in replaying a game like that, until later—as I'm doing now—so you won't make the same mistake again. You've got to make yourself forget it and just say, "Okay, next point." One point at a time is the way you've got to discipline yourself.

It's a lesson everybody has to learn. It cost me a huge championship plus money, but I think it helped the rest of the year. I wasn't that careless again in a big one.

You can bet that Newc and Tony got their first serves in and were right up to that net. In a few minutes it was over. Thirteen straight points, just because I overlooked the first commandment of doubles. Put your first serve into play taking something off the ball to make sure. Forget that flat boomer and put spin on the ball. A man should cut his throat if he is as forgetful of the commandment as I was. If he doesn't his partner probably will cut it for him. Fortunately Emmo was as dazed by the turnabout as I was—and there wasn't a knife in the dressing room.

Doubles

ALTHOUGH I CAN TAKE CREDIT for almost singlehandedly losing that French Doubles, my doubles record hasn't been too bad. I did win the French with Emmo in 1961, the Australian three straight years with Bob Mark between 1959 and 1961, the Italian with Dr. John Fraser (Neale's brother) in 1962, and Wimbledon with Emmo in 1971.

I've made my money and my name on singles, and, like most players, that's my first consideration. But my greatest enjoyment has come from doubles because the action is so much faster with all the reflex volleying and the spectacular rallies during which you might attack and retreat several times before a point is won.

Doubles is an entirely different game from singles, and usually more exciting to watch. Despite this fact, tournament emphasis has been on singles. But I suspect that tennis would make a better impression on American TV if some doubles matches were covered.

Of course, doubles is the usual game for the vast majority of non-tournament types in clubs and on public courts. A few like the old French Davis Cup hero, Jean Borotra, continued playing singles into their seventies. "Never give the game up—never!"was Jean's cry. But doubles is a less strenuous way to keep on with the game till doomsday, and no reason you shouldn't. Frequently the older you get, the better doubles you play because it is a game of guile and control in which the sluggers can be baffled and browbeaten. An embarrassing example of that for Lew Hoad, 22, and Neale Fraser, 23, occurred in the Wimbledon final of 1957 when they were thoroughly outmaneuvered and beaten by Gar Mulloy, 42, and Budge Patty, 33.

It happens all the time, an older, less powerful team who understand the principles of doubles slickering a couple of youths who might be considerably superior in singles.

You don't need a big serve in doubles. It might, in fact be a handicap, since a cannonball doesn't give you as much time to get to the net. Better a spin serve that you can count on hitting into the court the first time all the time—as I didn't in Paris.

You aren't going to lose often if you and your partner keep the first serve going in, and moving it around to prevent your foes from zeroing in on it.

The volley is the shot on which most doubles points end, but probably more important is the return of serve. Sureness is preferable to speed as you try to keep the server off balance. A soft chip at his feet, a lob over his partner's head, even a lob to the server will keep them guessing. An occasional blast directly at the net man or down his alley will keep him honest, particularly if he shows signs of being the roving kind. Most often you will want to shorten your swing, just meeting the ball to make certain of a sure, low return.

The ideal in doubles is for you and your partner to get to the net and dominate, both when you're serving and returning. It doesn't always work that way. In winning the decisive match in the Federation Cup of 1969 (the worldwide women's team competition corresponding to the Davis Cup), Nancy Richey and Peaches Bartkowicz of the United States upset Margaret Smith Court and Judy Tegart Dalton of Australia. Hardly anybody who watched could believe it. Nancy and Peaches never advanced to the net. Incredibly, Peaches stayed on the baseline even when Nancy served.

The theory is that you can't beat a pair of strong volleyers like Margaret and Judy that way. Ninety-nine times out of a hundred, the theory is right. The exception comes when you can lob as well as Nancy and Peaches did that day. The overhead is the most tiring shot to hit, and Margaret and Judy were forced to swing at scores of lobs. They broke down—most players will.

Unusual formations and tactics can drive your opponents up the backstop. I remember vividly the job Americans Ham Richardson and Alex Olmedo did on Neale Fraser—an excellent doubles player—during the Davis Cup final of 1958 at Brisbane. Fraser, in the left court (as Mal Anderson's partner), had been returning brilliantly against the Americans. He was grooved with his troublesome cross-court return to the server. So they took this return away from Neale by stationing the net man directly in front of the server. The Americans call it the "Australian formation" while we call it the "tandem formation." Whatever, it made Fraser crumble.

With the net man in the way of his normal crosscourt return he had to go down the line, and he couldn't adapt himself to a new return. Naturally the server had to adapt, too, moving to his right to fill the hole vacated by his net man instead of charging ahead as usual. Neither Richardson nor Olmedo had any trouble adjusting as server. They were quick enough to deal with whatever weak returns Fraser could make in the new direction.

When his partner is serving, the net man must be a threat to "poach"—that is, move along the net quickly to intercept the normal crosscourt return. Sometimes a good team will poach all the time. Unless you and your partner are fast and well-mated this isn't a good idea. But you must poach once in a while just to let the enemy know that you aren't going to act like a statue and let them have half the court in which to hit their returns freely. You have to impose a mental hazard, making them wonder when you'll move.

This mental hazard weighed heavily on Aussies Hoad and Rosewall in the 1954 Davis Cup final when the Yanks Tony Trabert and Vic Seixas beat them in the decisive doubles match. Each time the Americans served, the net man turned his back to his opponents and made a hand signal to his partner, the server—like a catcher signaling a pitcher in baseball. The signal told the server whether the net man would cross in an attempt to poach. Often it was a bluff and the net man stayed put, but the signal system was a gimmick that disconcerted Hoad and Rosewall.

One of the rarest of disrupting ploys was pulled by the late Rafe Osuna, a marvelously swift and clever doubles player. In the U.S. Doubles of 1966, Osuna was paired with Ronnie Barnes in the quarterfinals against Wimbledon champions Newcombe and Roche, heavy favorites. When Barnes served, Osuna straddled the center line, crouching low, so that Ronnie's serve could clear him. I've never heard of this, before or since, the net man exactly in the center of the court, ready to dart either way to cut off the return. Rafe had the Aussies mystified, and he and Barnes, decidedly the weaker team, came close to winning the match in the fifth set. Only somebody who can anticipate and move as rapidly as Osuna could get away with that in the big league, but it is a neat concentration-shaker to file away for possible use.

As a left-hander, I've always played the left court. I feel that a lefty in the right court is at a disadvantage in trying to return crosscourt a serve wide to his backhand. Some players feel, however, that with a lefty in the right court (and a right-hander in the left) you'll have more volleying strength, since both forehands will be down the middle where most shots are hit in doubles. Also you have the court better covered for overheads, since you tend to smash better on your forehand side.

I've preferred the left side because I've been more comfortable there, and I've been lucky in recent years to have Emmo, a great right-court player, as my partner. That's the main thing: lining up the way you and your partner feel the surest.

And, of course, you want a partner you feel sure and easy with. There's no point to playing doubles with somebody you don't get along with (although I've noticed that in mixed doubles, getting along as roommates and courtmates may be two entirely different things. An otherwise happily married couple may turn a mixed doubles partnership into a scene from Who's Afraid of Virginia Woolf?)

You should have a "think-nothing-of-it-old-pal" air about you when your accomplice flubs a routine overhead on the big point. It isn't going to help your mood, his confidence, or the team's chances if you act injured by his mistakes. Compatibility and cool are the essence.

It should be understood that anytime either of you has a chance to make a point by picking off a ball that might have gone through to the other—do it. But make the point. This isn't hogging. It's just good sense to make the decisive move when you see the chance, particularly to hammer a forehand or shallow overhead. Teamwork and consistency win doubles matches. When your partner lunges in front of you to pounce for the kill, your move is to fill the hole he vacated.

If you can keep the ball low, your opponents will have to hit up to you, and you'll be able to put away a lot of balls. That's what you're after, ideally, the chance to murder a shoulder-high volley.

Until you have that opening, concentrate throughout on The Guiding Principle: keep the ball in play, avoiding temptation to overpower. Any ball hit over the net with care is worth two blasts that may well land in the bush.

14

PARADISE REGAINED—WIMBLEDON

WITH THE FRENCH MINE, THE GRAND SLAM BECAME AS REAL as that baby kicking in Mary's belly. The chances on this baby weren't nearly as favorable as Mary's. There were still two excellent chances for it to miscarry—Wimbledon and Forest Hills. But now it was definitely alive. When you win both the Australian and the French, then it's established you're shooting for the moon.

It was a fantastic coincidence that both my babies were programmed to make it on the same day. Mary's obstetrician calculated that she would give birth on September 7, the day scheduled for the final of the U.S. Open at Forest Hills. It didn't work out that way. Rick was nineteen days late, and I decided I'd never take an obstetrician's prediction too seriously again. Dr. Bob Woodruff is a fine guy. He did a wonderful job, but I wouldn't want to go to the race track with him.

After the Australian, I had no particular Grand Slam feeling, other than wanting it and knowing it was possible. Winning the Australian isn't that big a thing. It had the weakest field, and it's too early in the year to base anything on. But the French is altogether different. You've conquered the most demanding tournament physically, mastered the only clay test among the majors and you're halfway home.

In all tennis history, seven men and four women have won the Australian and French in succession to go into Wimbledon with a Grand Slam alive and quivering; Margaret Smith Court did it three times before her 1970 Grand Slam and went no farther, Emmo twice. Jack Crawford in 1933 and Lew Hoad in 1956 went around three turns before fading at the Forest Hills finish. Later, Mats Wilander in 1988, Jim Courier in 1992, Jennifer Capriati in 2001 got to Wimbledon and faltered. In 1984, when the Australian was the last of the four, Martina Navratilova crashed there. Don Budge, Maureen Connolly, Margaret Court, and I held up all the way. Steffi Graf would also do so in 1988.

The pressures of Wimbledon and Forest Hills are different during a Grand Slam, and it's hard to say which is more severe. Wimbledon pressure has to do with the event itself. This is the world championship, a sports event that everybody pays attention to. For two weeks of the year Wimbledon is a big story on all the world's sports pages, even in cities where tennis has little or no importance. There is no such thing at Wimbledon as an insignificant match because wherever you play, even on the most remote court, people will fill the spectator areas, whether there be grandstands or merely standing room.

The actor on Broadway, the singer at La Scala, the dancer at the Bolshoi Theatre understand what the tennis player at Wimbledon feels. So does the golfer at the Masters, the football player in the Super Bowl, and the baseball player in the World Series. It isn't the money. The connoisseurs are here. We play for ourselves, and we perform and play because it's in us and we must. We would do it whether or not anyone bothered to watch us. But we also play to be seen, to gain attention, to please and impress others. That's an important part of it. My love for tennis goes to my depths, but when the time comes that I can't play the Centre Court at Wimbledon, something vital will have gone out of that love.

The connoisseurs are the fans who pay to get in and the critics of the press, radio, and television who don't. At Wimbledon, they're the keenest in the world. We can feel the expertise of these people, even though they're the quietest spectators and the least intrusive critics.

No reporters are permitted in the dressing rooms or the players' dining room and lounge, so we have a privacy that doesn't exist elsewhere. We need it more because in London, as no place else, a tennis player is a celebrity. I could walk the streets of any American city for days without being recognized, but it couldn't happen in London. Tennis is so widely exposed in the press and on TV that even the minor players have followings. When the limousines carrying the players pull into the grounds, there's always a mob at the dressing room entrance anxious to gawk at whoever's arriving and to ask for autographs. Fortunately, the English are orderly and polite. Nobody tries to tear your clothes off or pound you on the back.

Limousine service in my day was one of the features of Wimbledon that made you feel like an extraordinary somebody. I doubt that any other sporting event takes such good and special care of its participants. You felt like a potentate when a limousine pulled up at your lodging every day to take you to the courts. It also took you home, if you wished. This service was standard for every one of the nearly 300 players, for the duration of the tournament. These days there is transportation, but cars furnished by sponsors rather than limousines.

England is the only country with what you could call a "tennis press," as America has a baseball press and Australia a cricket press. The writers concentrate on the game, and know what they're talking about — a good deal of the time. They write well, with grace, humor, and bite, too. During my playing days, David Gray of the *Guardian*, Lance Tingay of the *Telegraph*, Rex Bellamy of *The Times*, Peter Wilson of the *Mirror*, Frank Rostron of *The Express*, John Barrett of *The Financial Times*, and John Ballantine of *The Sunday Times* had millions of readers. I wonder if they ever tightened up at the typewriter during Wimbledon. Did they choke on a big match, and stress the wrong aspects, lose control of the verbs? Or try too hard and come up with botched prose? Did they strain and fail?

Peter Wilson, was probably the most widely read sportswriter in the world, a columnist covering every big sporting event. Boxing was one of his great loves, but he wouldn't leave home in 1969 to cover the Joe Frazier-Jerry Quarry heavyweight title fight in New York the first day of Wimbledon. It was the first heavyweight championship he'd missed in about thirty years, and boxing was very strong in England, too. But Peter wouldn't forsake Wimbledon even for a chance to play king-for-a-day in the Sultan of Kuwait's harem.

The British public is a captive audience for Wimbledon. There's little else on TV during the fortnight—live during the day, and a review of play in the evening. For many years, both of the only existing channels carried the tennis so there was absolutely nothing else to look at except the opposite wall. Regardless, even today tickets are nearly impossible to get, and people queue for standing room and sleep all night outside the gate for a chance at some general admission tickets. Scalpers used to do a big business. Attendance didn't vary much. They couldn't pack many more than 315,000 bodies onto the grounds over twelve days of play. In the days before television, people would buy tickets that entitled them merely to be on the grounds without a seat for any of the climactic matches on Centre Court or Court No. 1. They could keep track of the matches inside by watching the scoreboards. At least they got the feel of the place. These days, attendance has soared driven in part by the thousands of grounds passes sold.

That's part of the phenomenon of Wimbledon.

Wimbledon.

That's all you have to say. Everybody gets the idea. It's not really the name of the tournament, although by this time it might as well be. Actually this world championship, regarded as the British championship, has been called the Lawn Tennis Championships since it began in 1877. It could be called The Tournament, and everybody would understand.

The name Wimbledon comes from the London suburb where the All England Lawn Tennis and Croquet Club has its grounds. They are magnificent grounds, big league by any standard, dominated by a stadium that is Centre Court. When Centre Court is full, which is always, 15,000 spectators are there, 3,000 of them standing sometimes six and seven hours, packed like a cattle car (although that cozy custom has been abolished).

"When they faints, they faints standing up," an usher told me. "Somebody calls out to tell us there's been a fainting, otherwise we'd never know, and somehow we push through and get the person."

Nobody minds. You brought your lunch and entered the standing areas at noon. It stays light well into the evening in England, so that you might still be wedged into that fresh-air hole of Calcutta watching tennis at 9:15 p.m.

Faintings are not passed off casually at Wimbledon. Statistics are compiled and are announced every year by St. John Ambulance Brigade, the medical unit in attendance, and in 1969 the crowds obliged by setting an all-time Wimbledon fainting record. No fewer than 1,700 passed out during the twelve days.

A Grand Swoon, wouldn't you say, old chap? St. John Ambulance gave that figure to the press as proudly as a football press agent trumpeting a scoring record. One customer out of every 190 was treated to St. John smelling salts.

I have never keeled over at Wimbledon, but when I consider what a fashionable place it is to faint, and the efficiency of the care, I shall never fear when feeling queasy there.

Numerous changes have been made since I played there. A new Court 1 with 11,000 seats appeared in 1997. Copying the Australian Melbourne Park, Centre Court was fitted with a retractable roof in 2009 while the so-called "Graveyard" – intimate Court 2, burial ground of favorites – was rearranged. At the outside courts, it's still a standing, jamming proposition with herds pressing against the fences that enclose the courts. During the first week when all the courts are in use, the crowds are over 30,000 daily, and surely they could sell 50,000 seats in Centre Court if they were available.

Considering the incredible success of Wimbledon, the men like Herman David, who ran the place, emerged as extremely principled blokes in their determination to stage an open Wimbledon in 1968 in opposition to the wishes of the International Lawn Tennis Federation. Wimbledon has always sold out regardless of the quality of the tennis. The British love it and the game so much they'd turn out to watch Ma and Pa Kettle play mixed doubles against the champions of Spearfish, South Dakota.

But Wimbledon stood for the best, and insisted on being the best in more than name. Only the prestige of Wimbledon could break the status quo and force open tennis into existence in 1968. I really never thought I'd see it in my day as a player, and I was resigned to exclusion.

Our professional game was bumbling along, the money was good, and though we were always discussing and arguing open tennis, we weren't expecting it. There was no point in moaning about our exclusion; we'd chosen our way of life. We'd had the prestige part of tennis as amateurs. Now we were away from it but able to earn a decent living anyway.

So we bounced around on our one-nighters. We traveled to remote places like Khartoum, La Paz, and Reston, Virginia. There was never any time off to adjust to the changes in time zones after a long flight. That's still a problem, combating the punchiness you feel after flying, say, from New York to London. I found that taking a brisk workout as soon as possible after I landed—instead of going directly to bed—helped clear the fuzziness quicker. Either a practice session or a run. It could apply to anybody.

We'd play occasional eight and twelve-man tournaments in the summer in the U.S. Reston, a suburb of Washington, D.C., doesn't sound remote, but when we played there in 1965, they were just building the place. Our tournament was part of the promotion for this brand-new city, and everything was disorganized. You needed a guide to find the court. The area was so dusty we thought we were coming down with silicosis, and there were no dressing rooms. We dressed in our cars and showered some other time.

I thought about a lot of these times in my ragtag life when we heard that we'd be going back to Wimbledon like pardoned men. The time in Khartoum in 1965, when they'd been having serious rioting, there were soldiers and machine guns everywhere. We were scared to death, and we'd gone there for $1,000—to be split among four of us. We'd go anywhere for almost anything in those days. Because of the trouble there had been no newspapers or radio, no way of publicizing the matches. But the promoter wasn't giving up. He and a couple of his friends got on the phone and started calling people. It started a chain reaction, and there were about 1,000 people there for the matches. We couldn't believe it. We started in the late afternoon on grass courts and played until dark at six. Then everybody walked to a nearby hard court that was lighted and we resumed and played until the bug curfew. After a while, the lights attracted so many insects that it was impossible to go on, and that's where the matches ended. The crowd realized this was a natural conclusion, and went away quietly and happy, having enjoyed some good tennis.

La Paz was interesting, but I don't want to go back. Not to play tennis. In that altitude—something like 12,000 feet—the balls fly like pigeons and if you play hard you're liable to get a nosebleed. We played a four-man tournament, and first prize was a $600 watch. I laugh when I think how we killed ourselves to win a watch, blood streaming down our faces and the balls zooming everywhere.

Nobody but the spectators knew we were in Bolivia playing on top of a mountain. Personal pride pushed us, that's all. Everywhere. I tried as hard at La Paz and amidst all those bugs in Khartoum as I ever did at Wimbledon or Paris. They may have amounted to nothing more than exhibitions, but I seldom saw a pro give less than his best unless he was sick or injured. I'm certain I never saw anybody tank a match, or take it easy to make the other guy feel better. There were occasions, against the weaker players—we called them the donkeys—that I could practice certain shots, try to work on my weaknesses. That was possible and helpful—and could get me beat once in a while.

One of the things I experimented with was lobbing through the rafters. This isn't a tactic you'll find in any tennis text, and it may never come in handy again with the game growing up for us pros. But in the gypsy days, when we played in all sorts of odd buildings, low beams weren't infrequent, and you had to be able to adjust. I soon found out in pro tennis that you were dead without a good lob—by far the most underrated shot in the game. And you had to be able to lob over and through the rafters many nights. Pancho Segura was the leading practicioner of rafter-lobbing. His lobs always found their way through mazes of rafters and beams. I got pretty good at it and one night in Utica, I beat Gimeno with a beaut that wandered among the girders as though directed by radar.

You had to be able to laugh it off, even when you didn't get paid, or when the conditions were so ridiculous that a rhinoceros wouldn't have gone onto the court. The word was around about tennis pros: "Put up the money and they'll play barefoot on broken glass."

It was absolutely true. Gypsies don't make demands regarding playing conditions. We'd play if we suspected the money wasn't forthcoming. You can look at a crowd—or a non-crowd—and guess what's happening. But we liked to play tennis. It never seemed like a chore to me.

Maybe I thought about the perfect grass, the adulation and the limousines at Wimbledon as I inspected an armory in Utica for openings in the ceiling supports. But that was my life then.

These hardships we pros shared made us proud of our skills and perseverance. They were good for us. I think they helped our games, made us more determined. The five-year exile from Wimbledon and the rest of the places at the top made me appreciate open tennis more than the younger players who've moved right into it as a matter of course. They never had to risk their necks playing in a crummy ice rink like the one in Altringham, England, where Hoad and I almost broke our necks on the slick portable floor. Condensation dripped from the ceiling making the footing horrible. Neither one of us could do much. They should have taken up the flooring and given us skates. The score went to 20-20 and I did the splits going for a shot. Snap! I felt something go. A tendon? No—my jockstrap. With a face that matched my hair I called time and trotted to the dressing room for a replacement. "Emergency," I blurted to the umpire as the spectators guffawed. We had to quit at 27-27, the longest set I ever played, because we could hardly stand.

And there was another English rink in Nottingham where Frank Sedgman hit more passing shots by me than I'd ever seen. I was passing him pretty well, too. We suddenly got the idea the court might be too big. It was—a yard wider than regulation, and two feet longer. Somebody painted the lines wrong, and there was nothing to do but settle down at the baseline. No use rushing the net with all that extra room to cover.

The first pro match I played in the U.S., at Boston Garden, didn't do anything to help my state of mind. Instead of spreading the canvas court on the basketball floor, or the ice, as is the practice in large arenas, they put it on a rough floor of planking that covered the ice. Another mistake. You might as well have asked Minnesota Fats to shoot pool on a lumpy table.

That was the beginning of my first winter in the United States—my first real winter. I'd seen snow only once before, briefly during a tournament in New York the previous winter. This winter of 1963, there was to be no escaping it. One hopeful aspect of my pro debut in the U.S. was that I was playing big Barry MacKay. It was nice to get away from a menu of Hoad and Rosewall. It was like taking my head out of the cement mixer for a night, but I soon found out Barry could be worse on a court like that. He had one of the biggest serves going, and trying to return it on that bumpy court was like trying to swat jackrabbits with a broom. "Jesus," I thought, "so this is the pro tennis tour?"

Another beating. It took me a long time to get even, and by the time I did I was just pleased to be alive. That U.S. tour was sixty matches in eighty days. It seemed like around the world in eighty days. There were six of us—Rosewall, Gimeno, MacKay, Luis Ayala, Butch Buchholz, and me—and a couple of station wagons. We were on the run every minute, grabbing hotdogs, getting to bed about three every morning, driving, driving, driving.

One night in upper New York State, cold as a witch's mitt, snow all over the roads, we were on our way to Albany. The road was like grease. As we slid and swerved, I said to myself, "What am I doing here?"

The money was all right, but what was I doing freezing and skidding on my way to Albany when I could have been getting on nicely as an amateur, playing in Jamaica that week.

Of course, everybody has his doubts about his job once in a while. As I began to play better, I felt better. I wound up the tour second to Rosewall, and I collected more than $50,000 for the year, so I was sure I'd make my guarantee.

It was $110,000 over three years, although the word "guarantee" is a bit dreamy. All through 1962, the pros were after me to sign on with them. There weren't promoters backing the operation as Lamar Hunt would do. The players themselves were trying to hold pro tennis together, and they weren't doing very well—but how could they? They were trying to play and do everything else too.

They all talked to me about turning pro, but mostly Hoad and Rosewall, since they knew me better than the rest. They started with a $75,000 offer for three years, and I said to come back after Forest Hills. Then I'd won my first Grand Slam, and they knew they had to go higher: $85,000. I decided I wanted six figures, and finally we settled on $110,000. This was after I'd turned down a separate offer from Pancho Gonzalez of a $50,000 minimum and $100,000 maximum for a one year head-to-head tour. Pancho and I would have cut up the gate, and no doubt I could have made the maximum with the old champion coming out of retirement to face the Grand-Slammer. He had the biggest name, but I didn't know how I could face my Aussie friends if I did that, and I wasn't too keen on Pancho. I felt surer of a long-term contract with men I knew.

It was all on trust, actually, this figure of $110,000. There was nothing in escrow, no millionaire or experienced promoter to back it up. I was to get 25 percent of the gate on nights I won and 20 percent otherwise. Hoad and Rosewall pledged themselves to make up the difference if I didn't reach $110,000 in three years. They didn't have to, I'm glad to say, because I made $150,000 my first three years. I'm sure Lew and Kenny would have tried, but it was still a pretty shaky contract, and I doubt I'd have held them to it.

A financial gamble, maybe, but I wanted to get off on my own, and not have to haggle with every tournament as I did as an amateur. Even though I had earned a nice living as an amateur, I just wasn't a man to bargain and haggle over expense money like some of the fellows. I'm sure that several not as good as I extracted more money, and good luck to them. The most I ever asked for—and got—was $1,000 to play the National Indoors in New York in 1962. I thought I was being exorbitant, and purposely so, because I didn't want to leave home in February. When they complied, I reluctantly made the trip, and saw snow for the first time.

I hope it doesn't sound egotistical to say that in addition to trying to secure my own future, I was doing something for the future of professional tennis as well. The boys were desperate to get me. They needed new blood badly, a new face, the amateur with the big reputation. They hadn't signed one in a long time. Their most recent converts had been Ayala, who wasn't a big name, and MacKay, Alex Olmedo, Buchholz, and Gimeno, who were just beginning to make names when they signed pro contracts. No top star had turned pro in three years. Gonzalez hung out in one of his innumerable retirements, and the last tremendous name to sign on had been Hoad in 1957. They really needed me if there was going to be any kind of pro tennis at all, and that's why they were willing to give me such a large cut of the action. I'll admit that 25 percent of zero isn't always rewarding, but many nights the take was all right.

After five years like that, I could take any kind of playing conditions. Butch Buchholz, who'd been an outcast longer than I, felt the same. At the beginning of 1968, when Lamar Hunt began a badly organized tour with rookies Roger Taylor, John Newcombe, Tony Roche, and Niki Pilic, almost everybody was miserable but Butch, the old hand.

"As long as the building doesn't blow up, nothing can shake me," Butch said. "I'm a veteran of the Texas death march. My first year as a pro, 1961, somebody—and it must have been a fugitive from the Texas Rangers—scheduled us throughout the state on a tour that meant about five hundred miles a day driving. We were in towns that nobody has heard of yet, playing the worst buildings and courts, for short money. Every night I wanted to quit and go home, try to get reinstated as an amateur. I was only twenty. But I was a pro and I stuck it out. These kids now don't know what a tough tour is like."

They are less likely to know, and perhaps the opportunity is gone—if opportunity is the word. As the game continued its boom, a complete circuit of opens in the leading cities sprouted and the sport became genuinely a big league one. I'll never play Nottingham again, or Khartoum, or Accra, or La Paz. The kids who miss out on this seasoning just can't know the sensation of deliverance running through us old pros when we walked through the Doherty Gate into Wimbledon again on

June 24, 1968, a part of the act once more. Newcombe, Roche, Pilic, Taylor, had never been away. They were amateurs in 1967, pros in 1968. They couldn't know the elation of being recognized as respectable men again.

LESSON • 14

Court Conditions and Surfaces

THE SINGLES COURT is 78 by 27 feet, and that doesn't change, although on occasion I have played pro tour matches on courts that have been improperly laid out. But within that 78 by 27 you can find yourself in entirely different atmospheres.

I don't know how many different types of surface I've played on, from antbed—the first I tried at home—to a downtown thoroughfare in St. Louis where we played an exhibition in 1964 for a lunch hour crowd of shoppers. I've played on the bumpy deck of an aircraft carrier, on hard courts so glossy you thought they were mirrors, on grass that scrawny Masai cattle wouldn't have. My first years as a roaming pro, playing one-night stands, we stretched our canvas over any fairly level base—ice, boards, concrete— and that canvas was a quick, new, traumatic experience.

I learned to shorten my backswing, make it compact, which you must do on fast surfaces. No glorious windups like the kind I used to have for my forehand. On uncertain grass I'd use hardly any backswing at all, poising the racket as I would for a volley, waiting until the last instant to see which way the ball would jump and then slash at it.

One of the fastest courts I've played was at the Seventh Regiment Armory in New York where the U.S. Indoor used to be located. Polished wood was the footing, and the lighting wouldn't have done a cave justice. That ball would shoot through like a Japanese express train in the dark. Never mind the backswing. Just probe and hope.

On these fast surfaces, just try to meet the ball on return of serve; block it. The pace of your opponent's shot and the ball rocketing off the court will be sufficient without trying to add any more yourself. And think about getting to the net fast. You can't stand back on a fast court and let the ball bounce. If you don't become a volleyer in speedy circumstances you may as well take up chess.

Wind will change the situation within the 78 by 27 rectangle, too. Sometimes you think you'd be better off trading in your racket for a sailboat. Use more spin so you can control the ball, and a lower toss on serve so that the ball doesn't blow off course unnecessarily. Remember you can hit hard against the wind but a bare tap may be enough with the wind. Test your shots carefully before the match starts, and on a tricky windy day warm up from both sides of the court.

Not many people relish playing in the wind or under less than ideal conditions. But don't let yourself go sour. Conditions are the same for you and your opponent. He's bothered, too. Maybe more so—there's a good chance of that. He may not know as much as you do about making bad conditions work to your advantage: things like going to net as often as you can get there—even when receiving serve—if you've a strong wind at your back that will slow up his passing shots and make his lobs fall short.

Act like you love it. This is your kind of day and court. You grew up playing on furrowed fields in hailstorms, right? Isn't it glorious just being out here and working up a good sweat?

You can drive an opponent crazy by refusing to let anything bother you when obviously the situation is a mess.

RESPECTABILITY IS A CLUB TIE

THOSE OF US WHO HAD WON TITLES AT WIMBLEDON WERE
pretty obvious. We were permitted to wear the club tie again, the stylish
purple and green stripes of the All England Club.

It may be difficult for someone outside of tennis to believe, but a man
was actually stripped of his membership when he became a pro. It is
a Wimbledon custom, a nice and generous one, that a man or woman
who wins a title in the Championships becomes an honorary member
with club privileges and the right to wear the club colors.

But soon after that evil day when I signed a pro contract, I had the
same experience as other pros before me. A letter arrived from the All
England Club revoking my membership, instructing me that I must not
wear the tie. I suppose if I'd lived in England, a representative of the
club would have visited me, probably somebody looking like C. Aubrey
Smith, to slap my face, cut off the tie, and rebuke me for dishonorable
conduct.

I know it's laughable, but it also served to reinforce the fact that pro
was a dirty word in tennis, and that we had, in fact, lost our citizenship
in a supposedly decent world.

Miraculously, as if by papal decree, we were legitimized again when
Wimbledon decided to join the seventh decade of the twentieth century. Club ties sprouted like the first crocuses of spring on the many
great players who reappeared for that historic first open Wimbledon.

Frank Sedgman, who was forty and making a sentimental journey to play the tournament he won in 1952, had his tie on. So did Hoad, who was thirty-four and had won in 1956-57; and Don Budge, fifty-two, the original Grand Slammer, returned to enter the senior doubles for men over forty-five. Pancho Segura had no club necktie. He'd played only two Wimbledons back in 1946-47 before turning pro, but it wouldn't have seemed right to open up the world championship without Segoo. He was forty-seven, but he put his name in the record book by playing in the longest set in Wimbledon annals. For three hours, Segoo delighted the crowd with his shot-making and theatrics as he and Alex Olmedo downed the South Africans Gordon Forbes and Abe Segal, 32-30, 5-7, 6-4, 6-4. "I waited a long time for this day, so I had to stay on the court for a while to make up for those lost years," Segoo laughed. Everybody was glad he'd made it.

The fans were sorry when it was obvious that Gonzalez and Hoad were seeded too high, could be beaten by lesser names, younger and better conditioned opponents. Alex Metreveli, the Georgian from the USSR who wore down eighth-seeded Gonzalez, was nearly as dazed by his feat as old Pancho. "I read about him as a child," said Alex. "Gonzalez is the one tennis player whose name is known all over my country." Did we have to hear that from a Soviet guy, too?

There won't be a Wimbledon again like that in 1968. It was a reunion, an amnesty ceremony with all the pros coming out from their holes to glow once again in the sunshine of the All England Club's forgiving smile. Many of them were out of shape, playing on memories. Others, Andres Gimeno for one, were so nervous that they couldn't do a thing. Andres, seeded third, fell to the Wolfman, the hairy Ray Moore in the upset of the tournament. From the first day, the amateurs had great fun punching holes in the pros' reputations. The pros didn't know quite how to perform in respectable company, and I was the only one to uphold my seed, the first. Tony Roche, a pro rookie who'd never been away from Wimbledon, was seeded 15th, and he was my final-round opponent.

Amateurs Arthur Ashe and Clark Graebner got to the semifinals, although as I've said they were amateur in label only. Still it made for a wild, unpredictable tournament from the moment that Niki Pilic, seeded 16th, was beaten in the first round by a lightly considered American, Herbie Fitzgibbon. Fitzgibbon was reasonably amateur, while Pilic had been a quarterfinalist in 1967, his last year as an amateur. In playing American college tennis in the Northeast for Princeton, Herbie knew how to act in the wind. It was blowing a gale that day, and poor Pilic was outdoors for practically the first time of the year. Traveling with the pros and playing entirely in arenas, he'd forgotten the existence of wind.

Just before the end the tall Croat cried out in English, "Why we have to play in such weather this tennis—why?"

Outside of college players, fewer and fewer amateurs will appear in future Wimbledons. The professional tennis player is established. In 1968, the pros were in a minority, and although they won most of the titles, they briefly lost face in their many beatings by alleged amateurs. Then, as prize money grew, professionalism became thoroughly acceptable. It wouldn't have done so if Wimbledon hadn't stood up for progress and the game's integrity in 1968. We were back in the public eye. Wimbledon was open. We were permitted to visit the Lourdes of London and lose our leprosy.

Strangely, and amusingly, it was a bloke with almost no knowledge of tennis who became one of the tournament game's saviors by practically forcing opens into being. Without a frightening push from Dave Dixon of New Orleans — a man all but forgotten — Wimbledon probably wouldn't have been so determined to open up in 1968.

Dixon's sport is golf. He plays well enough to have qualified for the National Amateur. In 1967, he began taking a closer interest in other sports. As chairman of a proposed domed stadium for New Orleans, he was looking into any sport or activity that would keep the building busy. Football and baseball were obvious, but those wouldn't come close to filling the schedule of a year-round sporting palace.

"What about tennis?" Dave wondered. "Was there such a thing as a pro tennis circuit?" Like almost anybody else in the world at that time, he couldn't be sure. He had vague recollections of occasional odd paragraphs at the bottom of sports pages—tucked in among the truss ads—

relating to pro tennis. Wasn't Pancho Gonzalez still alive? Hadn't he seen something about Australians named Laver and Rosewall? He asked his secretary to check up on it, and then he went on to something else.

Sometime later, the secretary had discovered our flimsy organization, the International Professional Tennis Association, and learned of a tournament we were playing in Binghamton, New York. Dixon was going to be in New York City that week, so he decided to run up to Binghamton over the weekend and see for himself.

Nobody was ever hooked faster than Dave Dixon. "Where have these guys been? They're fantastic athletes," was his reaction. "And nobody knows about them. I got to Binghamton, and hardly anybody in the city could tell me where the tournament was. No posters, no publicity. Finally we found them hidden out at a private club, and we sat on uncomfortable wooden bleachers to watch."

Abruptly, Dixon was transformed from landlord to promoter. Instead of trying to fit tennis into the prospective stadium, he sought to fit himself into the tennis business and begin marketing the game, convinced that by modernizing it could be a smash.

He went home to convince his friend Lamar Hunt of Dallas that tennis could join the pro sports boom, and they became partners. Off Dave flew to London, where we were playing, to offer us contracts with World Championship Tennis. We would receive guarantees against prize money to play in tournaments that WCT promoted.

At the same time, George MacCall, the U.S. Davis Cup captain from 1965 through 1967, was forming his National Tennis League, and made us roughly the same proposition. Because it was obvious that Dixon, although a pleasant and smooth individual, didn't know his backside from a backhand, most of us signed with MacCall. We were wary of the novice. Dixon did grab three of our group — Butch Buchholz, Dennis Ralston, and Pierre Barthes —and he was undismayed.

Since he couldn't get the best pros, he would land the best amateurs. His idea wasn't new, but his approach and his ammunition were. Dave was backed with Lamar Hunt's money, which flowed no less reassuringly than Texas oil. The guarantees he offered John Newcombe, Tony

Roche, Cliff Drysdale, Roger Taylor, and Niki Pilic weren't based on wishes and good intentions as mine had been in 1963. The money was there, ranging from Wimbledon champ Newcombe's $50,000-per-year on down. Since MacCall had signed Roy Emerson, the amateur game within a month lost six of its top ten.

Amateurs had defected before, but never in such a rush of quantity and quality.

Newcombe, Pilic, and Taylor had been Wimbledon semifinalists in 1967. The men at the head of English tennis knew they had been offering a diluted world championship at Wimbledon, but the future loomed as ridiculous. They had been anxious to force open tennis, and now Dave Dixon's raid made it imperative.

Dave didn't last long in tennis, no more than a few months, not even until the first open Wimbledon at which he should have been introduced from Centre Court.

He bubbled with radical ideas. His troupe used the controversial VASSS (Van Alen Streamlined Scoring System) and wore different-colored shirts, either measure enough to send coronaries rippling through tennis' old guard. These innovations and variations were soon accepted. His principal difficulty was not tampering with tradition but failing to administer his first tour efficiently. World Championship Tennis lost nearly $100,000 in three months, and Hunt bought Dixon out and sent him to the sidelines. Hunt reorganized and did well since, multiplying the size of his roster considerably.

Professional tennis owes a great deal of gratitude to Dave Dixon.

LESSON • 15

Court Manners and Etiquette

SPORTSMANSHIP IS THE ESSENCE of the game, and yet you don't want to be too good a sport. Or what I call a false sportsman.

I will give you a couple of examples. In 1966 at Forest Hills, Clark Graebner, the American, and Jan Leschly, the Dane, were in the fifth set of an exciting semifinal. Leschly hit a ball that sailed over the baseline, apparently Graebner's point at a time when every point was golden. But Graebner said no. He called to the umpire that his racket had ticked the ball. Nobody noticed, nobody heard, but Clark knew it wasn't his point, and he wouldn't take it. In such a case the umpire accepts the player's refusal of the point and awards it to his opponent. Graebner won the match anyway, so maybe being a good sport pays off.

Now, in 1967, I was up against Andres Gimeno in the final of the U.S. Pro Championship in Boston. On set point for me in the second set, I knocked a ball just wide of the sideline. That should have made it deuce and kept Andres alive. Instead the linesman signaled that the ball had hit the line. Point, game, and set to Laver. Gimeno fussed. I asked the umpire to check with the linesman to make sure. I didn't want the point that way. I made it clear that I hoped the linesman would change his mind. He wouldn't.

I thought of a similar instance three years before on the same court. I was playing Pancho Gonzalez for the title and I hit a winner on an important point. The linesman called it out. Pancho wanted that point badly, but not on a bad call. He pointed to the spot where the ball had landed six inches inside the baseline, but he couldn't convince the linesman. In such situations, players benefitting from outrageous calls have been known to throw the next point or the next game to demonstrate their so-called sportsmanship.

Did I? Did Pancho? Not on your life. Once we had registered disapproval and asked the linesman to reconsider (they can change their calls, you know), we brushed that point out of our minds. On to the next point. In a tournament match, you must play the calls, as we say—accept what comes. There will be incorrect bad calls when humans are involved, but I think the supposedly noble gesture of giving away a point is a grandstand play. Further, it's an out-and-out insult to the officials.

In a match without linesmen and umpire, you're on the honor system. Make your calls quickly and fairly. If there's any doubt, give your opponent the benefit of that doubt. Don't let your opponent take advantage of you. If he's serving before you're ready, tell him politely. You don't have to get into a screaming match about quick-serving as Gonzalez and I once did.

In a club match, you can be pretty casual, but if your opponent cramps or injures himself and wants to resume three hours later, you may have to remind him about the play-is-continuous rule. You're not being a bastard by expecting a default if your opponent can't continue after a brief rest. Fitness is part of the game, and if a player breaks down physically, then he's the loser.

This rule is stretched badly, even at the top level. At the Philadelphia Indoor in 1970, Butch Buchholz was going at John Newcombe in a quarterfinal. One of Butch's shots skipped off the net and struck Newcombe in the eye. Newcombe was carted off to the dressing room for examination and treatment. A long delay ensued. Buchholz thought he was being a good sport by not demanding his rights: a default. By the time they returned to the court, Butch had gone cold, and he was in a mental stew about whether he should have insisted on the victory. He lost. It cost him money that night and possibly the $10,000 first prize.

Butch was wrong in not speaking up. The officials were wrong in allowing the delay. Newcombe was a bigger name than Buchholz. Everybody felt sympathetic, but it should have been Newc's tough luck, a break of the game.

It happens all the time, but don't accept it in a tournament. The rule says nothing about extenuating circumstances, only that play must be continuous.

Like Graebner, in that match with Leschly, you are expected to call infractions against yourself such as touching the net, double-hitting (a "carry"), or hitting the ball when it is "not up" (having bounced twice).

If you suspect someone of giving you the business consistently on bad calls, you can refuse to play him again. Or break his rackets over your knee. I never resort to the latter because I weigh only 147, and hardly anybody I play with is smaller.

A SHAKY BEGINNING

AS A BOY, MY PARTICULAR IDOL WAS LEW HOAD. LEW DIDN'T invent topspin by any means, or the all-out approach of hitting hard for winners in every situation. But from what I can learn, nobody in the game ever had stronger wrists and was quite so menacing with topspin off both backhand and forehand. I wanted to hit the ball that way, and Charlie Hollis encouraged me.

I got a great thrill from staying with the Hoads on a visit to Sydney for a junior tournament. Lew's parents often put up young players who came to town. He wasn't at home. His folks told me he was overseas playing Wimbledon, the greatest tournament in the world. It was then that Wimbledon began to register with me and the feeling began growing that I had to go there, to play there.

It would be a while yet, four years. The place was overwhelming when I first saw it in 1956. I wasn't too nervous, though, because I didn't expect to do much. Orlando Sirola, the giant Italian, saw that I didn't. It was David and Goliath in reverse as the big fellow, who stood fifteen inches over me at six feet seven, stoned me. He seemed to be serving out of a tree. The first set went to deuce, 5-5, and when he'd beaten me, 7-5, 6-4, 6-2, I didn't feel bad. I knew I'd be back, although not as quickly as I thought. I spent the 1957 season in the Australian Army, and couldn't go away from the country until 1958.

That year, I started to find out about Wimbledon nerves. I won my first two rounds and earned my competitive introduction to that shrine called Centre Court, against Jaroslav Drobny, one of England's favorites. In 1954, Drob, a Czechoslovakian refugee, had won the title at the unlikely age of thirty-two, interfering in the American-Australian postwar rule. He wasn't given much chance to become champion after he lost the 1949 and 1952 finals, so when he came through in 1954 against Rosewall, the British rejoiced.

To me, he looked like a brewer who'd been drinking the profits, a jolly fellow deceptive in appearance because he had surgical touch and control with his left hand.

It was an ordeal. First, I was worried about making an idiot of myself bowing. Unless you're Japanese or hang out with royalty, you probably don't know any more about bowing form than I did. The custom until 2002 when it bowed out, was that when you walked onto Centre Court, you and your opponent would turn toward the royal box, which is behind the near baseline, stop and bow. The women curtsyed. I didn't know a bow from a curtsy, but you know how terrified you can feel if you think you're going to foul up in front of 15,000 people.

If you blew the bow, there was nothing they could do to you. Nobody gets their head taken off for that sort of thing anymore. But it's something I worried about. I suppose I should give you a few hints on bowing in case you ever get as far as Centre Court. The main thing is not to bend too far, because you might fall on your face, which would be a bad show. A quick dip will do it, with something of a smile. The people watching know it's not your line, but I didn't know they knew.

Frankly, I don't remember my first bow, but by this time it's second nature. I was so nervous, my throat was dry and my hands were shaking. Then I looked at Drobny. Out of shape, I thought. His appearance should have given me confidence, except my hands wouldn't stop shaking. Everywhere I looked there were people, 15,000 of them. Half the population of Rockhampton. And they were all looking at me, expecting me to put up some sort of opposition, not waste their time.

Well, if you can't play well, play fast. It was fast. Drob served hard and flat and chipped the ball here and there so I was always bowing—

to him—bending and reaching and never coming up with much. He'd been around, a slick old bloke who, as a teen-ager two decades earlier, had played against Budge in Europe during Don's Grand Slam year. It was 6-1, 6-1 so fast that all I wanted to do was stay bowed and count the grassblades. But nobody had thrown a rock. It was only a tennis match. As I thought about that, I didn't feel weak any more. I was all right and I played a respectable third set, 6-4.

I wasn't going to lose many more matches here – winning 40 of my next 42 matches.

The next year, 1959, I would be in the final, losing to Alex Olmedo, and in 1960 in the final again, losing to Neale Fraser. I won in 1961-62 and then the opens of 1968-69.

In 1967, Wimbledon staged a pro tournament which I won, a test to see how the professionals might be accepted treading the sacred sod. The grass did not turn brown when touched by the outcasts' feet, nor did our presence precipitate a rerun of the Great Plague. We had played pro tournaments in London, of course, indoors at Wembley Pool every year. But crashing Wimbledon meant that we might be on the verge of the absolution which we received the following year.

Wimbledon is a tournament with a split personality, a vast garden party with hardened professional athletes in its midst breaking their humps for cash and recognition while the aficionados smell the flowers and eat strawberries and cream.

It began during the Victorian era, in 1877, as an amusement of upper-class sportsmen, a pitter-patter athletic diversion on the croquet lawns with all the proper touches. Tennis doesn't stop for tea, in the fashion of cricket, but nobody fails to stop some time for their tea. A tea garden expressly for that purpose is located outside of Centre Court where the famous strawberries and cream are sold, along with a concession to the present day such as Pimm's and Haagen Dazs ice cream. Aside from the hamburgers and the limousines, you might think you were walking into the nineteenth century as you enter the grounds. When you glance toward the royal box you expect to catch a glimpse of Victoria herself. That's one feeling Wimbledon gives you—an endless perpetuation of 1877.

Endless, maybe, but not mindless. Though the place is thick with tradition, there is life and vigor within the unchanging layer of stuffiness. Wimbledon, through its stature, made open tennis a reality. And Wimbledon is the paragon of operating efficiency. When it is stated that play will begin at two—they mean precisely. In 1968, when heavy rains stacked up the first week's program, it seemed reasonable to open play earlier on a couple of days, but deviating from the two p.m. starting time nearly took a special session of Parliament. After a long meeting of the management committee it was finally decided that it might be all right—as an emergency measure—to begin at one. Precisely.

Rigid custom and social frivolity are one side of Wimbledon. The other side—what it's all about to me, and I think most people—is the contests of athletes. Winning is everything, and Wimbledon is where we make our reputations. I suppose the crowds would still come if Wimbledon hadn't admitted us in 1968, and the tennis remained restricted and inferior. That's what tradition can do for an event. Now that the tennis is the ultimate, the finest ever played, the crowds can't increase much. There's only so much room. But the satisfaction of winning now is incomparable. The competition has never been so fierce. Money has something to do with it, but Wimbledon is one event we'd all play for nothing. First prize then—$7,200—was far from the biggest purse. The competitive atmosphere was, of course, what we pros had to get back into. There was just no way to change the public's feeling that our tour matches were meaningless exhibitions. Never mind the injuries and the agonies that went into those matches. We left one place and traveled to another so quickly that nobody ever knew. To the public, particularly the American public—for some reason I've never worked out—we were trained seals putting on a marvelous, well-drilled act. Of course, the English have always taken their tennis more seriously than anyone else. They feel the anguish and the drama of Wimbledon. To them any bloke who goes through a couple of rounds of the tournament becomes a hero, and the public soon knows all about him.

Wimbledon is as much the women's as the men's, and this is the only place where they enjoy complete equality— even since 2007, for the money. The British appreciate women's tennis, and at least twice I was overshadowed by the female champion: in 1961 when Ann Mortimer subdued national heroine Chris Truman in the first all-English final in forty-seven years, and in 1969 when Ann Haydon Jones, another Englishwoman, broke the three-year reign of Californian Billie Jean King.

Dressed by couturier Teddy Tinling—who made tennis dresses as handsome as ball gowns—some of the girls were indeed much better to look at than my finest topspin backhand. Despite their charm and chic, the girls were as combative as we men.

Because of Wimbledon's fervor for tennis, there has also been an aspect alien to tennis in the United States—although not to other sports. Wimbledon is the only tournament I know that is followed by bookmakers, who make a gambling line. There's a price on a large number of players. In 1969, I went off at 4-to-7. You put up 7 pounds to win 4, but even at that price I suppose quite a few shillings were made on me.

Then there are the scalpers who hang around the main gate-touts, or spivs, they're called in England. Scalping isn't against the law in England, although a tout can be pinched for blocking the sidewalk if he becomes annoying.

The top priced ticket at Wimbledon in my day, $3.80, might have been scalped for as high as $50, depending on the attraction. There used to be a colorful old guy named Dick Wymark, the dean of the scalpers. He was over seventy and had been working Wimbledon since just before World War I, from his "office," a shady spot in the parking lot. Dick handed out business cards and was able to get you a seat for anything, maybe even at the Queen's left for tea. If he knew you, or you had been recommended, he would mail you tickets and trust you to send him a check. "He was an honorable rogue" was the word around Wimbledon on Dick. Nowdays, gambling on the grounds, as well as scalping are not allowed.

Opening day of the 1969 Wimbledon was rained out. First time that had happened in maybe forty years. Sometimes the place has been a bloody rain forest during a tournament, but it hardly ever got rained out. There's an elaborate system of tarpaulins, and when you feel a drop, the tarps come billowing. Play is often delayed, but the day is long in London. It stays light enough for tennis until about nine thirty, so you reckon that if you're scheduled you're going to play. Part of your match anyway.

But that first day they never got started, so I was set back twenty-four hours in playing the first match on Centre Court against the Italian Nicki Pietrangeli. Nicki was always a master on clay, but he didn't have much heart for the grass game, and he was getting older and less interested. The match was fast. Too fast perhaps. I wanted to spend more time on Centre.

It didn't seem to matter whether I knew much about the Centre Court or not when I played Premjit Lall in the second round. We were out on Court 4, which was right across from Centre. No grandstand. Spectators stood in the aisles between the courts. The stuffed aisles alongside Court 4 looked like a run on a shaky bank. People were jammed against the fence six or seven deep, and the ones in the last row, pinned against the fences of adjoining courts had no chance of seeing anything. But they could hear the umpire calling the score. Once in a while they could see a racket above the mob if Prem or I went up for an overhead smash. "Laver's getting beat by an Indian" was the word that ran round the grounds.

"That's what's wrong with tennis," a friend of mine said later. He had come all the way from California to see his first Wimbledon, and had good seats for Centre Court. But when "Laver's getting beat!" flashed on the grapevine that operates at every tournament, he couldn't get near Court 4. No more than a couple of hundred people out of the crowd of 30,000 that afternoon could clearly see what was happening. "If they knew what they were doing," said my friend, "they would have put your match with Lall on the Centre when it became obvious you were fighting for your life. That's where the TV is. You have to let everyone in on it if Laver is going to lose."

As far as promoting tennis in the United States goes, he may have something. Golf has learned that the TV cameras must be where the greatest interest is. Is Arnold Palmer in trouble on the sixteenth green?

We'd better look in. If Laver is collapsing on a remote court, we'll find him a better place to come apart, if we can't get the cameras to his court. Move him into the big arena. It would never happen at Wimbledon. "Just wouldn't do, old chap," they'd tell you. But it's worth considering for U.S. tournaments.

Well, there I was, with my racket feeling like an old frying pan in my hand. Premjit Lall and I go back a long way together. He is a nice-looking, tall fellow, soft-spoken, a university man from Calcutta where he sometimes works as a cement salesman. Fortunately for me, some of his better cement lodged in his right elbow at a critical stage of the third set.

In 1959, the first year of Davis Cup for both of us, our countries met in Boston in the semifinal match to determine the final-round opponent for the U.S., which held the Cup. Both Neale Fraser and I beat Prem in singles, although his teammate Ramanathan Krishnan made it exciting by knocking me off on the opening day.

I had never lost to him, but he was clearly outplaying me as he won the first two sets. Prem was the kind of player who always made a good showing but hardly ever could sustain good play long enough to swing a really big win or take a tournament. I kept waiting for something to go wrong with his game, and when it didn't, I began to worry.

There wasn't any crispness in my volleys, and I tend to get more nervous in a match that I'm supposed to win easily. I think anybody does. You get behind and you try to make up the points too fast. This is when you should slow yourself down, and try to think about a few essentials. Watch the ball. Make sure your serve toss is high enough. Don't get helter-skelter. The pressure is all on you, but if you can just slow down—like a basketball team taking time out—then maybe you can win a few points and get the pressure shifted to the other fellow.

Prem didn't seem to be feeling any pressure though. We went to 2-2 in the third. He held for 3-2 and I won my serve for 3-3.

It was right here that I restated a very important truth about tennis to myself:

You can only lose a tennis match.

That's all.

That's the worst that can happen to you out there, and it's happened to everybody . . . Tilden, Budge, Laver, everybody. They ate as well the next day; the sun came up; they laughed again. It's good to remind yourself of this every once in a while. I don't think anybody who played a game ever wanted to win more than I do, but losing isn't the end of the world. They don't hang you by your thumbs from the backstop or revoke your passport. They don't even deny you your daily grog.

By this, I don't mean that you resign yourself to defeat as an unavoidable fact of life, and say, oh, well, tomorrow's another day. Hell no. But whenever I tell myself that all that can happen is losing, I also make sure that if I must lose it will be in my own way, the way I know best—hitting out. I'm not going to grope and puddle around and hope the other fellow comes apart. I'm going to whack the ball. I'm not very demonstrative but sometimes I shout at myself, "Hit the bloody ball!" I've got to get it through my thick head that it's the only way for me. With my topspin I can bang away without worrying about the ball carrying too far.

If I was going to lose to Premjit Lall, I was going to go out with everything blazing. Up to that moment, I had been gripped by a certain fear of losing, but after I'd gotten myself straight on that, the fear disappeared. I began hitting the ball better and stayed close to Prem in that game, 30-30. I felt I'd get him there for the break, but he hit a good forehand down the line that sent me into the corner on the enclosure and I had to lob. I'd been lobbing short all through the match, and I didn't alter my pattern here. He had an easy ball at the net, but the cement settled in his elbow. He knocked the ball past me and beyond the baseline. I had the ad, then the game with a good backhand, and I never stopped. That service break began a run of 15 games, as I won 3-6, 4-6, 6-3, 6-0, 6-0.

Since I was hitting again, and not pressing, I think I would have got him anyway. But one shot can change it all. Had he made good on that smash and held his serve, I'd still have been in a shaky position serving at 3-4 and two sets down.

LESSON • 16

The Crisp Volley

A GOOD PUNCH IN THE NOSE—that's the volley. A short, stiff jab with almost no backswing. You're blocking the ball, not stroking it.

The wrist is firm and below the racket when you punch, and you use the pace from your opponent's shot—if it's a good shot. Occasionally when a shot sits there weakly to be volleyed away you have to supply a little of your own power.

By keeping your eye on the ball intently and blocking it you can become a pretty good volleyer and a terror at an ordinary level. There is more to it than that as you progress. You will want to level the racket slightly so that you are hitting slightly under the ball to create a slice or underspin. This gives you more control.

Then there's footwork, without which you can't become a really fine volleyer. As you jab with your racket you're also taking a jab step into the ball. A right-hander steps in with his left foot for a forehand volley and with his right foot for a backhand. This insures that you're hitting the ball out front where a good volley must be hit.

That step is going to put more impact into your punch so that the volleys will gain length and fly to the corners and the baseline. Remember: you don't need backswing to give you depth. Meeting the ball out front with your body moving behind that jab step will do it.

To take the step you have to be side-on to the net. Not always possible in a fast match. Frequently you'll be caught head-on to the net. Then you pivot at the hips, like a baseball catcher who has to rush a throw to second base from his haunches.

"Wrong-footing" was a favorite tactic of Kenny Rosewall, and it's a good one for the volleyer once he feels he has control of the stroke. Wrong-footing is hitting to the place your opponent has just vacated, or will vacate to cover the next logical shot. He's gone to his left corner, say, to return your shot and then he dashes to his right to cover the wide opening. You wrong-foot him by volleying right back to that left corner, and if your timing is right he can't change directions to go back for the ball. But if you aren't accurate it will backfire because you may hit the ball right back at the fellow, not behind him.

Rosewall liked to do this especially with his backhand. You hit a crosscourt shot and he got his backhand volley on it, and rather than place it in the open corner he came straight back at you with the angle, and this beat an awful lot of good players. If they can spin around and get to the ball they won't do much with it and Kenny had a setup on the next shot.

When the ball is below the level of the net you're going to have to bend to get down to it. The ideal is still to keep the wrist below the racket. This will help you keep your volleys low, even the defensive volleys. If you don't bend and stay low you're going to pop your volleys up, and that's when the other guy gives you a punch in the nose with his volley.

17

A MAN NAMED GONZALEZ

WHILE I WAS GETTING STARTED ON MY EIGHTH WIMBLEDON, a good deal more attention was being devoted to Pancho Gonzalez's third. It had always been Pancho grabbing the headlines, for as long as I'd been a pro. He showed no signs of giving out, even though he periodically "retired." It was when he came out of one of those retirements in 1964 that I first began encountering him and his unpleasantness. When my son Rick was born, Mary asked me if I minded his crying. "I'm used to it," I said. "I've been listening to Pancho for five years."

He was actually a grandfather when he played in the final years of his career, but I don't think he would have stuck around if we were still gypsy pros. Open tennis gave him a new zest for the game, put him back in the great showcases like Wimbledon. As Pancho aged and mellowed, I don't think losing took so much out of him.

When I first played him in a pro tournament at College Park, Maryland, he was a very savage man. Toey at best. We Australians would say, "bit of a toey (edgy) bloke, Pancho," which was meant as understatement. He seemed to hate the rest of us, and himself as well when he lost. It absolutely killed him to lose. He fought you for everything, intimidated everybody in the place if he could—opponent, linesmen and umpires, ball-boys, spectators. Pancho had the air that says he's a champion. I remember sensing that in 1957 when I saw him first against Rosewall in a pro match at home. I never dreamed I'd be playing him. I was a teen-ager and he was getting near thirty.

If anything, he became more regal. When we played each other, the contrast was almost comical. Me with my bowlegs and 49,000 freckles, a little guy chasing about. Him with his dark forbidding face, crowned by the black hair tinged with gray, tall, graceful, gliding. The anger, the threat of an explosion, always near the surface. He was still capable of calling a line judge or umpire an idiot, of irresponsibly pitching his racket so that it could split a bystander's skull, of trying to strangle a photographer whose clicking irked him.

Gonzalez was the master gamesman, a badgerer and moaner. Yet his legs stayed stronger than the vitriol content in his system. He couldn't play the nearly forty-week schedule I covered in 1969, but he prepared himself mentally and physically for the prime occasions, and he seemed to be enjoying it more. Winning a big tournament was supposed to be beyond Pancho now, but didn't he beat Peter Curtis, Newcombe, Rosewall, Stan Smith, and Ashe in succession to win $12,500 and the Howard Hughes Open at Las Vegas at the close of 1969? Regardless of his capacity to conquer, there are dramas within a tournament that he would create and dominate.

One of those was his first round Wimbledon match against Charlie Pasarell, a twenty-five-year-old who had been the No. 1 player of the U.S. in 1967 and was able to beat anybody. He had Pancho beat when night came, stopping them, Charlie ahead by two sets. They had played the longest singles set in Wimbledon history, Charlie winning 24-22 and Pancho thought that was enough. Insufficient light. Pancho always worried more about seeing the ball than getting to it and hitting it. No light is ever good enough for him.

Mike Gibson, the Wimbledon referee, told Pancho to get on with it, he wasn't calling play off yet. "I realize it's difficult for the older man, but I must treat them as equals," Gibson said.

The Old Wolf howled, but Gibson wouldn't relent. The second set went to Charlie fast. Pancho gave up on it, and the gallery got on him for not trying and for bickering. Not the right spirit, old boy. And they booed him. Yes, a Wimbledon crowd booed Pancho Gonzalez. My God, you wouldn't think they'd boo Hitler in that place. The boo may be a part of sport, but not at Wimbledon. Yet they gave it to Pancho.

I've played there some days when I would have welcomed a shout, a boo, even a smoker's cough. It can be so quiet on that Centre Court that you wonder if the world has ended and nobody's bothered to tell you. But that first day closed riotously with Pancho stalking off the court steaming, enveloped in a massive scolding.

He was back the next day, though, to win three straight sets and the match. Pasarell had seven match points on Pancho but couldn't grab one of them, and there was the old man putting together eleven straight points at the end to complete a magnificent five-set triumph. It took them 112 games, Wimbledon's longest match then and the second longest singles ever played.

This time, Pancho strode from Centre behind a broad grin and applause that lasted for a half-minute. That's a lot of clapping for a British gallery.

Pancho knew the kind of applause none of the rest of us will ever get. He was just more appealing, and this seemed to increase as he aged. He got more sympathy. This made it difficult to play against him. Tony Roche found that out in 1968 when Pancho upset him at Forest Hills. The crowd was almost hostile to Tony, and they urged Pancho on with shouts and furious applause.

Ever a loner, he never made any attempt to be anything but antagonistic in my first days as a pro. He even sued me once, and that's still the most unsettling thing that ever happened to me.

In 1963, trying to put some semblance of order in the professional game, we players formed an organization called the IPTA: International Professional Tennis Association. We made a rule that nobody could play the tournaments unless he was a member. It seemed reasonable to us, and Pancho was the only one who refused to join. Pancho always got his own way. He insisted we had to let him play any time he wanted, and we refused.

Suddenly I was subpoenaed. So were Buchholz, Rosewall, Gimeno, and the others. Pancho was suing us for $250,000 for violation of antitrust laws. I'd never heard of antitrust. My respect for Pancho dropped to nil, although it didn't have far to drop. Here he was, slapping a suit on somebody trying to form a sound organization to help the game.

Maybe he was right, in a way, saying that we shouldn't keep him out of tournaments. But the point was it wouldn't have cost him much to join, and it was a time when pro tennis players needed solidarity to accomplish anything. They still do, but the situation isn't as precarious.

There I was in the wrong kind of court. Topspin wouldn't help me with that judge in Los Angeles, and I had to play it straight. I was a nervous wreck on the witness stand. You get so confused trying to remember things that happened long before and seemed of no importance at the time. When I now think of pressure in court, it's that trial—not Wimbledon. It took two days and cost us $7,000 in legal fees. We didn't have to pay Pancho any money, but he won, getting the right to negotiate his own deals with any tournament.

In a free enterprise system, he had a point, but there were times that he got paid and the rest of us didn't and that wasn't good for us or the game. But then the game was Gonzalez, as much as we hated to acknowledge it.

We knew he was mean and tough, but getting handed a subpoena one afternoon at the Los Angeles Tennis Club was a chilling thing. It happens to a lot of people, and I guess you can get sued by colleagues and even friends. But it was spooky being sued by a fellow player. Even if you didn't like him, you'd been through a lot together. And that sum of $250,000, it hit me tremendously. Where were we going to get $250,000 if Pancho won? I might work the next twenty years for my end. I suppose everybody who gets sued experiences that first moment of sweat and fear.

I could understand some of Pancho's bitterness because he felt he'd been taken advantage of in early financial dealings. He played a head-to-head tour against Tony Trabert in 1955-56 and made only about $15,000 while Trabert, the loser, had a contract that earned him around $100,000. Pancho wanted to make his own arrangements independent of any group, and he was still enough of a drawing card to deal for himself and demand guarantees exclusive of prize money at some tournaments.

It has been a Gonzalez characteristic that when he got mad he played better. If something bothered him and he began to rage—look out. This is unusual. Almost invariably the man who loses his temper loses his composure, his concentration, and his game crumbles. Not Pancho.

I hardly ever lose my temper, and almost never in a match. Nobody would put up with that sort of thing when I was a boy in Australia. Neither Charlie Hollis nor my folks would stand for any outbursts, which they considered poor sportsmanship. They also taught me that a show of temper is a great help to your opponent because it lets him know that you're disturbed and your confidence is letting down. That's generally true, except with Pancho.

Pancho liked you to lose your temper. He wanted to break down your concentration with his own fuming and fussing. That's what a lot of it was about. Most of us got used to it, and we accepted it as part of the game. We still didn't like it because no matter how ready we were for an explosion, we were apprehensive that the delay and his mad scene would pierce our concentration. That was the danger. While Pancho was screaming at a linesman or threatening to punch a spectator who made a noise, you were standing there trying to put it all out of your mind, hoping your rhythm had not been destroyed. Another reason for his fuming was to stall and gain a time-out for himself to rest. (Everybody has stalled at one time or another, though few as theatrically as Pancho. My method of taking a break was to "accidentally" step on one of my shoes in such a way that it came off. Then I had a few moments to make necessary adjustments.)

Most of the time you could do nothing but stand there and wait till the storm had passed. Sometimes you were the object of the storm. Either way, Pancho made me damned mad. That was his intention, of course, but we both found out something: I also played better when I was mad. I didn't care for the feeling, and it happened only against Gonzalez.

Once in New York, at the Seventh Regiment Armory, he accused me of quick-serving him. This was in the third set.

"Goddamn it, you served before I was ready," he screeched. "You've been doing it all afternoon!"

"Why have you waited till now to say anything?" I yelled, surprised to hear myself barking right back at him.

He had his racket upraised, as though he were Sitting Bull protecting the hunting ground from the white man. It wasn't a tomahawk, just a tennis racket but with Pancho enraged, would he know the difference? I wondered later if anybody had ever been scalped with a tennis racket.

"Do what you want, Pancho," I continued to yell. "You'll never upset me." My bristles were up. I got hostile and it helped. I finished off that set and won the fourth and the match, 6-1.

We had other run-ins. Once outside of Melbourne, we were screaming at each other about something or other, and the crowd was shocked because nobody had ever heard me say a word on court. Another time in Bogota, we were playing our hearts out in a match that meant $100 difference to the winner. In the dressing room afterward, he accused me of poor sportsmanship. I nearly fell over. "I've really given up on you, Pancho, after a statement like that," I growled.

We began shouting, and Dennis Ralston and Fred Stolle, who were in the room, took a look at each other and got out fast. They thought it was going to be a fight. I didn't know what would happen, but I was tired of all his crap.

I certainly didn't want to fight him, though. When I was a teen-ager in Brisbane, I spent my lunch hours at Snowy Hill's Gym, trying to build myself up. I'd hit the bags and do much of the same training the boxers did. "Discourage that kid," I remember hearing one of the hangers-on advise Snowy. "A scrawny mug with his awful coordination will get himself killed." I couldn't punch then, and I doubt if I can now, very effectively, but I thought I might get a chance to try. But Pancho and I just yelled, and we finished the day playing gin rummy together.

It's just as well nothing happened. I had seen Pancho punch steel lockers after losing a match, and tear up dressing rooms.

Pancho would never be one of the boys, but he got looser and more friendly. He could be very charming—women knew that for years. I don't think Richard Burton, Errol Flynn, or Giovanni Casanova ever did any better with the sheilas than Pancho.

I think his coolness toward the rest of us was partly a natural aloofness and partly a design to set us on edge and stoke himself up. It helped him to think he disliked us, to build up a hate for us—to think of us as the enemy. I can see how that could work once in a while—for a big game in a team sport or for a fight. But when you were playing somebody night after night, only a Pancho could keep it up.

I'd heard all about him from Hoad and Rosewall and the others. But I was brought up to regard everybody as a good guy. I was anxious to meet Pancho and get along with him. He didn't want to say hello. The first time I played him, I beat him. He was madder than a wet hen, so mad I thought he wasn't going to shake hands. He just brushed my hand with his and stormed off.

We played for the second time shortly after that at White Plains, New York. I won the first set, 6-0, and I'll wager that hasn't happened to Pancho more than a few times. I was ahead 3-1 in the second, a best-of-three match, and I figured the old boy was really over the hill.

That's the first time I made that mistake. Pancho not only beat me but he came back from two sets down to take Rosewall in the final.

A Philadelphia columnist, Jim Barniak, once lamented: "Laver doesn't have charisma. If you asked him what charisma was he'd think you were referring to the Romanian junior champion." Please, Mr. Barniak, everybody knows the Romanian junior champ is Marcu, not Charisma. Charisma won ten years ago.

I know I didn't have it. Pancho did. I understand that, and I'm glad for it. With it, Pancho helped to hold the game together. Pancho's personality put people in the seats.

When he came to town, a newspaperman could write about tantrums, sex appeal, flamboyance — and occasionally tennis.

I came to appreciate him more through the years. He amused me. There was depth to the man I didn't recognize before, and a generosity in advising younger players.

But on court he was still Pancho the bastard. I didn't mind Pancho having his show, and I think that 1969 was as much his Wimbledon as mine. I might have won the title, but I never was involved in a match as incredible as his triumph over Pasarell. Pancho always found a way to upstage you.

Playing Against Familiar Opponents

I GUESS ONE could perhaps say that when Kenny Rosewall and I played, it looked rehearsed. We had gone through it so often that there simply wasn't anything new we could introduce by way of a surprise. Maybe if he had started missing his backhands I would have been surprised—and pleased.

Principally, what I had to do was just play my own game, and try to play it better than he played his. I had to jump on a short ball and get to the net. If I got lulled into rallying from the baseline with him, I got killed.

It isn't likely that you'll run into somebody as often as I did Rosewall, and possibly there is something extra you can do to vary your pattern if you're having trouble with a certain opponent. You know each other very well, but is there a shot you haven't used that you can work on privately and spring on this guy—a drop shot, a lob, a chipped return? Something he's never seen from you that will complicate his estimate of you?

Try to analyze the pattern of your matches with this fellow. What is he murdering you with? Net rushing? Have you been lobbing enough? Or have you been trying too hard to hit perfect passing shots? Would blasts right at him, or soft shots at his feet be a different counter? Have you been trying to run him from one side to the other without much success—if so, how would he respond to a few drop shots to draw him in, followed by lobs?

If you think over your previous matches carefully, I'm pretty sure you'll see the need and place for something a little different.

But if you've been beating the guy, or playing him satisfactorily, well just keeping playing your game and enjoying it.

A FEW WORDS FROM MARY LAVER

MARY AND I WERE AMUSED BY AN OLD FRIEND FROM BOSTON named Jerome Scheuer, who was over for his first Wimbledon at the age of eighty. Jerry was a stern-looking, white-haired gentleman, bent over, always turned out immaculately in suit and tie whatever the weather. I'd been seeing him at tournaments ever since I started coming to the United States, and most of us had the vague idea he invented tennis. He knew as much about the game, the techniques, and the players as anybody I'd encountered. He knew our styles better than we do ourselves. Maybe that isn't unusual, because there are a lot of good players who haven't any idea what they're doing except hitting the ball. When you became acquainted with him you realized that Jerry had a fine sense of humor—except about one thing: the greatest player of all time. That was Bill Tilden. Jerry watched all the greats, and knew most of them, as a buff since 1905, when he fancied a bloke named Harold Hackett (one of America's most successful doubles players). We went through the argument at least once a year, and Jerry wouldn't budge on the subject of Tilden, the strongman of the 1920s, being the best. Neither did Allison Danzig, who was one of the supreme tennis writers during forty-five years with *The New York Times*.

"But, Jerry," Andres Gimeno would yip, "all modern athletes are better. Equipment is better. Competition is wider, conditions are tougher. The schedule is longer. They used to win with groundstrokes on grass.

You can't do that no more."

"Tilden would pass any of you big servers and volleyers," Scheuer answered "You never saw groundstrokes like his. He'd out-volley you, too, and whenever he needed an ace he'd serve it. On certain days, Don Budge may have been as good, but Tilden uniformly was the best."

It had been thirty years since Budge's prime. Although he didn't think anyone at the time had come along to rival Budge, much less Tilden, Jerry still savored the game, and he thought I played well. I'm grateful for that. He also regarded tennis players as artists.

Sometimes when I questioned what I did, spending my life chasing a little ball around—wondering if there was really any point to it—I felt better thinking of Jerry. I suppose at one time or another everybody has doubts about his occupation being worthwhile and his contributions to mankind.

Jerry scoffed at that. "Why, the pleasure you give people who watch is immeasurable. You can't imagine the service you render through entertainment. You do wonders for me, not to mention the young you inspire to take up this healthful game."

I liked that.

Jan Leschly, the Dane, had a nice way of saying things too. After I beat him in the third round, I said, "Hard luck, Jan."

He replied, "No, it was good to be out here, to be part of it." Jan's a lovely guy, a rarity, an excellent player whose greatest joy isn't winning but playing. Maybe it's something uniquely Danish. Torben Ulrich, fit and happy and finally turned professional at the age of forty, had that outlook. "Pancho gives great happiness," Torben said after losing the enchanting five-setter those antiques put on at Forest Hills. "It is good to watch the master."

Premjit Lall was good for me. That match showed me I wasn't concentrating fully. Wimbledon is a very tricky place because it lasts two weeks. So does the French, but there isn't as much importance attached to it. When you get to Wimbledon you want to go all out on every point. That's the feeling you have, but there's a danger of burning yourself out too early. There's a delicate balance between killing yourself and playing well enough to win. You have to save something for the long pull, pace yourself, build up for the tough ones. But what's the use of careful pacing if you lose to a Lall in the second round? You've got plenty left for next week, but you're spending next week on the practice court.

Once I won my first set from Lall, the rest of the match was relatively easy, but I became aware that it wasn't enough just to show up. I had to concentrate thoroughly and hit the shots.

Having Mary with me at the Dolphin Square helped immensely. We'd go out for dinner once in a while with a few friends, to a place we like called the Ponte Vecchio on the old Brompton Road. It was a gathering spot for pros when we were in London. But if we didn't feel like leaving the flat, she'd fix a steak and we'd watch television. Not the tennis, though, which came on every night in partial replay of the day's big matches. I didn't like to watch much tennis. I didn't want to have it on my mind all the time. Sometimes a reporter would come over for a few minutes, but I discouraged that during a big tournament. When I was not actually playing, I tried to guard my time. I wanted to rest, and spend it with Mary if she was around. I didn't like distractions, unless I created them myself to keep my mind off the tournament. Too many players lose matches by mulling them over beforehand.

Mary has observed me closer than anybody. She knows me better than I do, and I'm going to let her take over here for a few paragraphs to give her impressions:

"It was interesting the way Rod and I never talked about the Grand Slam in 1969. We knew he was going for this thing, that he had a goal, and it was good for his game to have a goal. It wasn't superstition, but we just didn't talk about it.

"I don't think athletes do dwell on something like this. That's the sportswriters' job. Each tournament is an individual matter, that's the way Rod feels. There was no sense lumping them together in his mind. Play them one at a time, to use the cliché.

"It's always amazed me how loose and easygoing he was, particularly when the pressure built. I thought he might show nerves a bit in 1968, the first time back at Wimbledon, and he had every reason to with all that went wrong. He had the bad wrist—eventually developing into the bad elbow—and halfway through the tournament his right foot became infected, the infection spreading up the leg.

"Nobody knew. That's the Aussie code—never let on. He was strapping his wrist before every match, but never in the dressing room where the word would get around. It wasn't only the show-must-go-on bit. He didn't want to give anybody he played a lift from knowing he wasn't completely right.

"So just before he was to play we'd go to a phone booth on the grounds and crowd inside while I wrapped the wrist. It looked like we were trying to revive the booth-stuffing fad of the late 1950s. The way we sneaked around to avoid being noticed we seemed like spies making a contact.

"The foot problem came from a blister. We were lucky that Dr. Norm Rudy, a friend from Los Angeles, was staying at the Dolphin Square, too. He came to our room in the middle of the night, lanced the blister and took care of everything. Rod was playing the next day.

"During a tournament as important as Wimbledon, you might share a bedroom and most of the day with Rod, but he was not really with you. I mean his mind is somewhere else. He got quiet. He would converse some, but never remembered what he had said. Most people think of him as a quiet person anyway, but this lapse into near silence was new for me when he took me to tournaments after we were married. Rod and I hit it off right away when we met, and we always had a million things to say to each other. I had to get used to the quietness of tournament time.

"But I don't mean he got moody. Nothing upset him. He's got the happiest attitude I've ever seen, the ideal temperament for what he was doing. He actually thrived on all the travel. He wanted to have his day filled with things to do, unlike Pancho Gonzalez, for instance, who wanted to be left alone. Some players get overloaded with business commitments. On the surface, Rod looked like one of them, always going here and there for commercial appearances and appointments. But the more things he did, and the tighter his schedule became, the faster his mind worked on whatever he was doing.

"He didn't like to just sit and think. He never worried about a match, or thought much about it until just a few minutes before he went onto the court. Then he wanted to be by himself and go over his plans and preparation.

"Until then, I doubt that it even crossed his mind who he was playing. Yet somewhere down there, below the consciousness, something got him revved up and is fixed his attention on the job without making him fluttery. I think that's what was going on when he was so detached: the automatic buildup within.

"Keeping busy was his way of consciously avoiding thinking too much about the day's match. He did the shopping when we were on the road, and the laundry and other errands. He had his favorite markets in London, and often at Dolphin Square he would do the cooking. He had to in 1969 because I pulled an abdominal muscle trying to open a stubborn window and was on the casualty list myself for a few days.

"That doesn't mean he's another Escoffier. He's an Australian —steak and eggs three times a day wouldn't seem odd to him. At least he fixes those well.

"Wimbledon in 1969 presented a folksy portrait of the champion that nobody saw but me. The Rocket bustling between his pots and pans, soaking his elbow with the hydroculator one minute and checking on the dinner the next . . . scooping up the soiled tennis clothes for a run to the laundromat . . . jollying up the pregnant wife and asking if the kid has kicked lately. The hero of Centre Court was also a behind-the-scenes domestic dynamo.

"Sometimes we took the limousine service to Wimbledon that's furnished to all the players. More often Rod drove himself. I liked the limousines. Rod drives the way he plays tennis: he keeps things spinning. They were hairy rides, but he knows London and he prided himself on taking a different route to the tournament every time we made the forty-five-minute drive. That was another of his little routines to put his mind on something else.

"People used to ask me about his ravaged fingernails that he chewed nearly to the elbow. They think he must have been awfully nervous. That was the only outward sign, and it was diminishing. I put him on a diet of thumbs. Chew those and let the other eight grow up normally. He said he was chewing less and enjoying it more.

"But what he seemed to be worrying about was somebody else. His heaviest chewing was done while he was watching a match. Or television, or a movie. Butch Cassidy came close to giving him the look of Venus de Milo. He loves cowboy flicks and must have seen Butch twenty times. If he's watching a Western on TV, I can hear his chomping over the gunfire.

"He had no business winning the U.S. Pro tournament in Boston right after Wimbledon. I was mad at him. He was due a mild slump; he'd come off grass to a very slow synthetic fiber court in the space of a couple of days. But nothing could discourage him more than momentarily.

"The worst thing that can happen to a tennis player is to lose his zest for the game. From what I've seen this is rather common. They get tired of playing so much. Or the traveling. They want to spend more time with families that are growing up. Maybe they're getting older and losing more.

"We hear a fellow say, 'You won't see me next year.' Then he'll be back on the circuit because it's still the only way he knows to make such a good living.

"I didn't want that to happen to Rod. I didn't see any sign of it at the time, but if he got tired of tennis I wanted him to quit. We tried to manage his money so that he wouldn't feel economic pressure or think he had to play to pay the mortgage. If he wanted to get out, he'd be able to.

"But I didn't see a man who loved it like Rod leaving for quite a while. It was life to him.

"If the pressure was a little heavier than usual in 1969 because of the Slam, the baby helped counteract it. Rod was really excited about becoming a father. He wanted a boy and got what he wanted: Rick Rodney Laver. He thought Paris was the hardest work of the Slam year—but that's only because he wasn't the one who had Rick.

"He delivered the Slam, and I delivered the heir. Neither of us could have improved on our performances and we didn't try. Rod decided not to enter the Australian Open in 1970 because the money was so low. One night he said, 'Guess I won't be trying for a repeat this year, Mary.'

"'Well, dear, neither will I,' I replied.

"We didn't want to be ostentatious."

LESSON • 18

The Care and Feeding of a Tennis Player

MARY SAID IT ALL IN THAT CHAPTER.

THE THIRD LEG OF THE GRAND SLAM: WIMBLEDON

ALTHOUGH ARTHUR ASHE HAD THE REPUTATION AND publicity, twenty-two-year-old Stan Smith was the best American of 1969. His dedication would keep him up there for a long time. He, Cliff Richey, and Marty Riessen were the only Americans to beat me during the year, and Stan pushed me harder than anybody else at Wimbledon. Maybe after beating him in straight sets in Paris I allowed my mind to wander in the third set of this match. I won the first two and I might have finished it in three, but Stan wouldn't let me.

He kept coming at me with more determination than ever. At six feet four inches, he's nearly as tall as the Italian Orlando Sirola, my first Wimbledon opponent back in 1956. But Stan is a lot more agile and competitive. As a boy in Pasadena, California, with his size 13 feet, he was so clumsy he was turned down as a ball-boy for the U.S.-Mexico Davis Cup series of 1963. Six years later, a star graduate of a self-imposed conditioning program, he was making me look like a ballboy in the third, fourth, and fifth sets.

He began attacking on return of serve as well as on his own booming serve that came out of the sky. He seemed to get to the net in one stride, towering there with a bleached head like the Matterhorn. His reach left no openings for passing shots, and lobs had to be dead perfect to clear him. When he won the third set, his confidence began climbing, and I could tell he now felt he could beat me. You shouldn't let a Stan Smith get into that mood.

He won the fourth set by simply outhitting me. I wasn't playing badly. My game was grooved now, and I had only brief, insignificant letdowns the rest of the way. But Stan had the scent of fricasseed Laver, and he kept coming to win his serve for 1-0 in the fifth and take the next two points to pin me at 0-30. That was a very uncomfortable set. Although I didn't lose my serve, I was behind in every service game.

Backhands pulled me out of it, plus very concentrated serving. I made sure to get the first ball into play. A couple of spinning backhands into the corners got me the service break, and I held for 3-1.

Smith became only more determined. A service break like that in the fifth set will usually make a young, relatively inexperienced player feel the weight of the situation, make it easier for him to rationalize and accept the impending "good loss," as it's called. Not Stan. He never stopped thinking he could win. He kept the power coming, his flat volleys zinging across the grass. Usually I countered power well and broke it down, but Stan kept me too rushed.

Each time I served, I was lucky to escape, but at 5-3, when I was serving for the match, he looked certain to pull even, cornering me at 0-40. He had three chances to break. I had to serve a little better, get to the net an instant quicker, volley a shade deeper. When I left the court, after doing just that to win five successive points, I thought if he had broken me it probably would have been my downfall. Stan was so tough and unrelenting when behind that a break would have put wings on his confidence. I don't think I could have fended him off.

Smith left the court dejected, but also knowing that he had it in him to beat me. It makes life that much harder when another good player has that revelation. I was in the business of thwarting and breaking confidence, not building it. It was built in Stan after this match. The next time we played, four months later, he did beat me.

In the U.S.'s first open, at Forest Hills in 1968, the prize money was $100,000 and first prize for men's singles was $14,000. Frankly, the thought of all that money petrified me. I kept thinking about how recently we pros had been pleased to play a week-long tournament for

$8,000 total. Now they were going to pay the winner $14,000, the biggest pot ever for a tennis player.

I could never get with it. I hadn't felt like that before or since, yet it seemed to be a foregone conclusion to everyone else that I'd win. I kept thinking the tenseness would leave me, but it didn't. My elbow bothered me a little, but that's not why Cliff Drysdale beat me in the fourth round. After all, I led two sets to one, and then he mopped me up, 6-1, 6-1. I could hardly put a serve in the court, and Cliff just knocked the ball by me with his tricky, baseball-swing backhand. Drysdale wasn't the first two-hander, but the best of the group that included Frew McMillan of South Africa, Mike Belkin of Canada, Jim McManus, Jimmy Connors, Harold Solomon, and Chris Evert of the U.S., and Ismail El Shafei of Egypt. Of course, Pancho Segura was the king of the two-fisted swingers – his a forehand.

A right-hander, Drysdale used his two-hander for the backhand. Some feel it was his weaker side, but I wonder. The strength of it was that you couldn't pick it. You didn't know where he was going to go with it. I was still having trouble solving him two weeks before Wimbledon when Cliff beat me in the West of England Open at Bristol. Bristol and the London Grass Court Open at Queen's Club were the prime tune-ups for Wimbledon, and I didn't take the results very seriously. I used them to re-accustom myself to grass, a surface the pros don't see much of, and to get ready for the big one.

But when Drysdale beat me at Bristol, he must have felt he had my number. I hadn't expected to play him in 1969 at Wimbledon because he needed to get by Roy Emerson. The porch off the players' lounge overlooked their court, and periodically I strolled out to check the score. It was a hard match, but as I suspected, Emmo took control and was serving for the victory at 7-6 in the fifth set. I left because Emmo never lets anybody out of that hole. Later, I was surprised to hear that Drysdale did get out, and would be in the quarterfinals with me.

Also in the quarters on our side were Arthur Ashe and Bob Lutz. If Pancho Gonzalez hadn't established himself as Wimbledon's most startling performer, the honor would have gone to Lutz, a brash, carefree

Southern Californian whose third-round victory over Ken Rosewall left the gallery uncertain of their feelings. Rosewall was a darling of the English. They—and he—greatly regret that Wimbledon was the only really big title to elude him. Kenny had trained himself fine for this one, and it appeared to be one of the last times he'd be capable of going all the way. Then Lutz, a twenty-two-year-old, stepped off a plane and into his first money tournament, and bashed fourth-seeded Rosewall in four sets.

In his last match as an amateur, Lutz had been beaten by somebody named Mike Estep in the National Intercollegiates at Princeton. "I got bored playing college kids," Lutz alibied that defeat. "But how can you get bored playing Ken Rosewall, when there's money on the line?"

I understood. Normally an upset by a bright new face is well received, but it was hard to enjoy the demise of Rosewall. Lutz might have had the greatest potential of any of the good young Americans, but he also had great talent for the dolce vita and might not have spared enough time for tennis or been as diligent as his doubles partner, Stan Smith.

The other half of the draw had narrowed to Tony Roche, whom I beat in the 1968 final, and Clark Graebner; John Newcombe and the Dutchman Okker.

I wasn't thinking about any of them. Actually when a tournament like Wimbledon began I didn't pay attention to the draw, trying to figure whom I'd meet as the tournament moved along. My feeling was I have to win seven matches. I have to be ready for seven good efforts. But now that it was Drysdale I felt that the championship hinged on that match. His was a strange style that bothered me, and although, except for Lutz, Cliff was the least formidable of the survivors, he might indeed have known the way to beat me, as he claimed the summer before at Forest Hills.

Cliff's a smoothy, tall and slim, a good-looking South African who could talk a Kreuger Park lion into becoming a vegetarian. After his big victory over me at Forest Hills, he described to the press how he had directed his shots at certain patches of grass on the court that were greener, thus slicker, so that I had more trouble coping with the skid. I don't think anybody is that accurate, and I don't know if it works anyway. The reason I lost was I served so miserably. But it was his hour, deservedly, and his theories gave the journalists a nice new twist.

There was no doubt that his style bothered me, and I decided I'd better do something to throw him off. You can't keep playing the same pattern against a man who's been beating you. My plan was to vary my net rushing. Sometimes I'd stay back when I served, which is almost unheard of in championship men's tennis on grass. This threw him off. His short, angled returns had been landing around my feet and were difficult to volley or half-volley. By staying back, I could move in on them easily and take the net with a strong approach shot. I began to attack against his serve, which isn't too strong, and put him on the defensive right away. I was wary of him and keen, and he didn't react quickly enough to my new tactics. I got the jump and beat him in the day's fastest match, 6-4, 6-2, 6-3.

The unexpected may throw your opponent way off. The simplest shot can bring the most astounding error if it's a shot he's not looking for. Drysdale couldn't believe it whenever I stayed back on my serve. He had the whole court to return to, and frequently missed it altogether.

Jaroslav Drobny risked all—and collected—with the unexpected shot on the biggest point of his life: match point in the 1954 Wimbledon final against Rosewall. Drobny led two sets to one and 8-7 in the fourth, his serve, but Kenny was wearing him down, killing him with passing shots off that rapier backhand. They went to deuce, and Drob got the ad. One more point. One more assault. If Drob had enough left he'd put it into one last charge, wouldn't he? He went to the baseline, and Kenny set himself to return the buzzing left-handed serve beyond Drob's net-rushing reach. But there was no buzzing serve, and no assault of the net. Drob just patted a soft one to Kenny's backhand and stood there and watched. For an instant Rosewall was startled. He'd begun his swing. He tried to change it to compensate, couldn't, and he knocked the ball meekly into the net.

It was almost insulting. But it was the unexpected in spades—and it worked.

LESSON • 19

The Backhand and Topspin

ONE OF THE GREAT MENTAL BLOCKS in tennis that shouldn't be there is the backhand. How many people do you hear moaning about their backhand? And avoiding the opportunity to hit it whenever they can?

Usually you learn the forehand first. I think you should start out with the backhand, and stop listening to those who say it's a hard shot.

Why should it be? It's the most natural shot there is—just letting your arm roll out to its full length. Try to think of it that way: unwinding.

Have you been ducking your backhand when you practice? That's what practice is for, you know, to work on the things you don't do well—not to keep tuning up your assets.

Not many players have a topspin backhand. The wrist has to be very strong, even specially built up. I strengthened mine by squeezing tennis balls and lifting pulley weights. I recommend that because in lifting weights you're even using the motion of turning the wrist over. A topspin backhand is nifty for me, Arthur, and a few others. It helped us make a nice living, but it wasn't a must by any means.

I'd say that 90 percent of the world's backhands back in the day were slices. Anybody who told you they were hitting a pure flat backhand wasn't entirely correct, I would have wagered. They were getting under the ball a shade anyway, slicing it a bit.

No reason why it shouldn't be that way. Slice keeps the ball low, helps you control the stroke, and is a good approach shot.

But I think you should experiment with your game. If you think you can topspin a ball—try it. If you want to really hit the ball hard on the backhand, you'll have to consider topspin. It's the only way, then.

At any level of play you have to get that lead shoulder all the way around—right shoulder for a right-hander. Get the shoulder around, hit the ball in front of the front foot, and let your arm unwind, and you've got it.

Repeat after me: the backhand is a cinch. Look at it that way, and you'll see I'm right.

THREE DOWN AND ONE TO GO

WE WERE IN THE SECOND WEEK NOW, WITH THE SINGLES well spaced to allow a day's rest after each. Within five days of the opening week I played four matches. All that remained in the last four days were the semifinal with Arthur Ashe and the final with John Newcombe.

The impact of Arthur Ashe on tennis is incredible. Probably the best thing that happened to the game in 1968 was that I didn't win the U.S. Open at Forest Hills and he did.

He had the right combination to make the world, especially the United States, notice: he was black, he was American, he was exciting—a big hitter—he was articulate and he knew his way around. He was new and different, and tennis needed that. His picture was on the cover of *Life* magazine, his face and voice on nationwide TV programs, and suddenly the public was fully conscious of a tennis player. No American had won at Forest Hills in thirteen years, and no black man had ever won a major championship. Arthur at once was an athletic-political figure, a champion considered a spokesman for blacks.

It was an awesome role. Sometimes Arthur seemed to act as though the world was on his shoulders. But the fact is that pressures on him from all sides must have been terrific. I can't imagine what it would have been like to walk in his shoes. I was pretty much content to hit tennis balls and mind my family. If that's all there was—and it was plenty for me—on Arthur's mind, he might have caught up with me. He never did, though, because he was going in so many different directions. That is what it must have been like to be a sensitive, concerned black celebrity in the United States in that day. Perhaps Arthur would have had a better chance to fulfill his tennis potential if there had been other blacks playing. He wouldn't be unique. He wouldn't have had to be all things. I imagine in baseball, basketball, and football the abundance of blacks makes it easier for all of them. Some are militant, some complacent, some confused, some sure of themselves. I don't know much about the problem, but in other sports you have a range of behavior and feeling among the blacks, just as you do among whites.

In Arthur's case, he was the breaker of barriers. Would Jackie Robinson have done so well if no other blacks had moved into baseball soon after his lead? I don't know. But every time I was impatient with Arthur for seeming to squander his tennis talent, or not working hard enough on his game, I would tell myself that I could not really fit into his sneakers.

Arthur's 1968 Forest Hills luster had tarnished and he was playing abominably. If you were an Ashe follower at Wimbledon, you had wall-to-stomach-wall ulcers by the time he came onto Centre with me for the semis. He'd lost the first two sets in the first round to an obscure South African, Terry Ryan, and twice the tiny Englishman, Graham Stilwell, had a chance to serve out their match in the fifth set.

But Wimbledon is the chance to make everything all right forever for a tennis player. Arthur had the firepower on that fast grass to blow me off the court and keep right on going to the world title. He was very capable of two hot matches now. He was like me—high for Wimbledon— and his best tennis burst forth in that first set, far above anything I had imagined for him. He played that set as well as a man can play. I was doing all right, but Arthur was knocking fireballs everywhere, and Centre Court was roaring.

I thought, if he keeps this up it's all over. There's not much to do about it except hope that he cools. Arthur's history told you he's streaky and he won't keep it up forever, but that isn't very comforting with balls shooting by. I was certain he couldn't maintain the pace for five sets, but the way he was going three might have been enough.

Arthur flew at the ball, and thrashed at it all-out. He was best on the backhand, and I started to pour my serve onto his forehand in the second set. The backhand had been burning me too much. His forehand was all right, too, but it wasn't so unbearable. The ball was staying in play and I began to whack a few winners, too.

I was feeling the kind of pressure I like, the challenge of a very good player in a very important match. I don't know exactly why I would respond so well in this kind of situation. I just played with feeling—if I felt the ball could be hit I just hit the damn thing.

We were bombing each other, taking great swipes like fighters throwing Sunday punches. Arthur had prepared carefully, practicing against three left-handers—Jim McManus, Torben Ulrich, and Niki Pilic—so that left-handed spin would be no mystery whatsoever.

But if you can't reach the ball it doesn't matter which way it's spinning. I needed to hit a few beyond Arthur's reach to edge my way into the match. He was hammering everything he could get to, but I connected with three beauts that outran those long legs of his to take his serve and go ahead 4-2 in the second set.

For the first time, I had the feeling that I was doing more than just hanging on. Before Arthur could check this surge I'd won six straight games and led 2-0 in the third.

Then he hit a few that ran from me like greyhounds—three magnificent backhands that broke my serve. We were both serving extremely well, and I was serving more aces than usual. We stayed neck-and-neck to 7-all.

I held for 8-7, and I could sense that his fine edge was wearing off just a bit. Arthur was having some trouble with his volleying. He didn't bend his knees enough to get down to the ball, and when his touch went off a shade it was his volleying that suffered most. I was trying to chip my returns low to make him reach for the volley, and he was reaching as though the ball was a cobra, sort of poking. He wouldn't get down to it, and his volleys were going into the net.

That's the way the third set ended, with him netting a volley, and I'd finally gotten on top of him. Now, I had to keep him down.

The ball was looking as big as a soccer ball to me. That's the way it is when you're dug in and knocking off everything. I had the first game with my serve, and I wanted the second.

I pushed him to 15-40, but he seemed to have the first breakpoint saved when he moved me out of position in the rear of the court so that he could baby a volley just over the net.

It was a good place for a drop volley because I was so far out of the play, about thirty feet from the ball when it bounced softly on my side of the court. I was running forward when he tapped the ball, figuring it for the logical shot.

The ball began to come down a second time, and nobody in the place thought I could get it. I wasn't thinking about the possibilities, just going for it in a mad dash like somebody trying to catch an egg rolling off a table across the room.

Later, after I'd won, 2-6, 6-2, 9-7, 6-0, Arthur said, "Speed is what Laver beats you with." And Fred Stolle remarked, "The reason Rocket gets balls like that drop volley is he plays every shot in practice just as hard. It's just second nature for him to go after every ball in practice, even the no-chance kind, and not let it bounce more than once. He's made himself want to hit every ball regardless of the circumstances. This attitude transfers to matches. He wasn't that quick as a kid. I think his work on the practice court gave him that extra step."

It had to be extra to get me within a shout of that ball. Moving so fast I wondered if I'd go through the net, I got my racket under the ball just before it touched down again and flicked it over Arthur's head.

He seemed transfixed by my sprint, certain with everyone else that I wouldn't make it. Now it was his turn to run. He pivoted and those giant strides of his got him to the ball, but he didn't have time to hit much of a shot. His backhand was in the net.

It was 2-0 and I wanted 3-0. Then it was 3-0 and I wanted 4-0. I guess this is the killer instinct. Whatever it is, I had no thought of relaxing. I had Arthur down and I was going to pound him. I never had any plan of trying for a love set, but each game I won made me want to win more. I was afraid of Arthur, afraid to let down for an instant until I had that sixth game. When it ended 6-0 I was stunned, but relieved that I'd been able to turn him off by turning myself on.

I was in my sixth straight Wimbledon final. Each time a different opponent: losing to Alex Olmedo in 1959 and Neale Fraser in 1960, beating Chuck McKinley in 1961, Marty Mulligan in 1962 and Tony Roche in 1968.

A couple of Englishmen did as well in the early days of the game. Willie Renshaw won seven titles between 1881 and 1889, and Laurie Doherty was in six finals between 1898 and 1906, winning five.

In those old days, in fact until 1922, Wimbledon used the challenge-round system. This meant that the champion didn't have to risk defeat by going through the tournament the following year. He was automatically placed in the final, and the survivor of the all-comers tournament challenged the champ for the title. Thus in winning a record six straight times (1881-86) Willie Renshaw played only one match per tournament in the years after he battled through the entire draw in 1881. Fred Perry, champion in 1934-36, had to play through, and it was his streak of 21 straight Wimbledon match wins that stood as a record until I completed the 1969 tournament with 28.

John Newcombe came into the final over Okker and Roche, and he came with the idea that he could beat me. He got that idea two weeks previously a few miles away at Queen's Club when he defeated me in the London Open. Just a trial match in my mind, but in the mind of the man who beats you it must have more meaning. His confidence increases.

Newcombe is muscular, strong, well-trained—and also bright. Although he made his name as a slugger, he can be thoughtful and patient, too. A quality he demonstrated earlier in the season by winning two of the biggest clay court events, the Italian and the British Hard Court.

In 1963, one began to hear of Newcombe as a surprise selection to play for Australia against the United States in the Davis Cup final. He was strictly a 19-year-old banger then, the son of a Sydney dentist who wisely cancelled his appointments for a few days after John was selected. Dr. Newcombe felt he'd be too nervous to take up his instruments during the matches, and his patients were grateful for his decision. John lost both his matches, to Dennis Ralston and Chuck McKinley, as the Yanks took the Cup. His game needed refining and he dropped out of sight for a while until he reached the Forest Hills final in 1966 and then became the last amateur champion of Wimbledon and the U.S. in 1967.

He had a pretty good plan, but I have to admit that once I'd gotten to the Wimbledon final, I never thought I'd lose. Centre Court is where I got the feeling I could beat anybody—Tilden's ghost, Budge thirty years ago, Pancho twenty years ago. Anybody. Bring them in. I don't mean to sound like Muhammad Ali, but the place made me feel important, bigger, stronger. I felt very tall walking out there. The atmosphere can bring out the best in a player, or it can ruin him. I've seen excellent players, not fellows you'd call chokers, destroyed by Centre Court nerves. The crowd can destroy a man, too, if they fall in love with his opponent.

When I was on Centre Court in the final, it is what my life had been about, a day I had worked for from the first swats on that antbed court in Langdale. Maybe more people watched me that day in 1969 than ever watched all the tennis matches ever played before because Tel-Star carried it around the world. It was something to think about before I hit a ball—You make sure your fly is zipped up before you walk into all those living rooms, and your hair is combed when you genuflect toward the royal box.

Centre Court is where I lived.

There's no electric chair waiting when you complete the tennis player's last mile, the walk from the dressing room to Centre, only a tall, green umpire's chair dominating the grassy chamber. You will get out of the place alive . . . you think . . . but you're not sure. Sometimes you don't care. A player can feel so mortified that he wishes they'd just turn on the juice and fry him right there. For me it would be death in the cathedral, and not a bad place to pass on.

After I beat him in the 1968 final, Tony Roche sighed, "I just wanted to find a hole out there and crawl in and cover myself up—but there was no place to get away from the Rocket."

Wimbledon nerves are worst just before an appearance on Centre. I saw blokes change clothes two or three times, check new socks for holes, pace the dressing room floor, do any number of little things that they thought might put off the walk to Centre. They were just kidding themselves, of course. When Peter Morgan came in and said it was time to go, we were always ready. We knew there was no deviation from punctuality in that place. We weren't dragged screaming, but sometimes our legs felt like silly putty.

It was always the same when you marched out for the final. E. G. Bulley, the locker attendant, carried your rackets and the referee, Mike Gibson, walked along to make sure you didn't get lost on the way, which is all of fifteen yards. Above the doorway to the court is that sign: "If you can treat those two impostors . . ." or some bloody thing. [The line, "If you can meet with Triumph and Disaster/And treat those two impostors just the same," from Kipling's poem "If," appears on that signboard as well as a similar one located back in the day above the marquee entrance to the stadium court at Forest Hills.]

You entered, bowed along with your opponent and then began the warm-up, which in England is called the knock-up. The expression is hilarious to Americans because it means something entirely different in their language.

Contrary to American custom, you are never introduced to the crowd by the umpire, a public address announcer, or anyone else. The English consider it superfluous, feeling that anybody in Centre who doesn't know Newcombe from Laver should be under surveillance by Scotland Yard.

By the time of the final, the court looked like a faded billiard table, the grass scuffed and worn. But it played like a new billiard table-fast, level, true. After the terrific pounding, the courts weren't the handsome lawns we began on two weeks before. But they never betrayed you. The bounce could still be depended on.

I looked up at Mary, lovely in a bright yellow dress and a matching ribbon in her dark hair. She'd gone into the tank for the Ashe match, but she wouldn't miss this one. When I played Arthur, Mary wasn't feeling well and she stayed at the flat and tried to watch on TV. Her answer to tension is the bathtub. She got so nervous that she took three baths

Centre Court at Wimbledon is where I got the feeling I could beat anybody. It made me feel important, bigger and stronger. The atmosphere can bring out the best in a player, or it can ruin him.

during the match, finishing the afternoon as the super-clean wife of a winner.

Newcombe was at home there, too. Any man who has won Wimbledon feels a kinship for Centre, and John had won there as often as I, considering his three doubles championships.

John knew I liked pace, and he wasn't going to give me any. Good thinking. He wanted to jerk me around, and he did it skillfully. He chipped his returns instead of hitting away in his usual fashion. When I came to the net, he tried to lob over me. I spent a lot of time looking at the sky. Hitting repeated overheads can be tiring. Though I won the first set, I began to miss my smashes in the second and he took that one.

The crowd liked it. The champion was in danger, and when Newcombe dashed ahead to 4-1 in the third they knew it would be a fight. Wonderful. Exciting finals weren't typically the rule at Wimbledon. Actually they were a bit rare. It seems true of most tournaments that the close, exciting matches occur everywhere but the final. Not always, fortunately, but too often. If Gonzalez and Pasarell's first-rounder had been the final it would have been an all-time sporting occasion. It seldom works out that way.

I was at 1-4, down a break with everybody hoping that the things would get even tougher for me. That was all right. The annoyance at taking Lall too lightly, the concern of getting into a fifth set with Smith, the apprehension about Drysdale, and the fear that Ashe wouldn't come down to earth were behind me. Now I was on my stage, one that I knew and loved, and it was up to me to strut like a proud player and do my act.

My serve, so good at the start of the match, had been going way off in the third set, culminating with a double fault at game point for the break that sent Newcombe ahead, 3-1. That was to be the low point in my serving, although I had no way of knowing.

After Newcombe won his serve for 4-1, he seemed certain to win the set and be in excellent position to go on to the championship. But that was the high point in his serving and within two minutes the momentum was to revert back to me.

I had to hold on to my serve now, and I did in a tight game for 2-4. On the last two swings of that game, I was certain my overhead game was in order again. At 30-all, Newcombe lifted one of his lobs and I smashed it away for 40-30. Then I stepped to the line and cracked an ace.

That felt fantastic. When my serve was right I knew I could do anything.

I was off on one of my streaks, a run of seven games that gave me the third set and a pleasant 2-0 lead in the fourth and what was to be the final set.

To my mind, the whole match was a backhand I hit past Newcombe in the seventh game of that third set. Even though my mental outlook had been reinforced by the smash and the ace that held my serve, Newcombe still was ahead 4-2 and serving.

After I won the first point for 0-15, we got into an exchange and he belted a forehand crosscourt wide to my right. As I lunged for it he pressed tight to the net ready to cut off anything. He edged a bit to his left, figuring logically that if I got to the ball all I could do was try and slap it down the line. I got there, barely ("Rocket beats you with his bloody legs, that's what," said Fred Stolle). A down-the-line backhand is my favorite in that situation. Everybody knew it, and I made up my mind I had to go the other way. (Pancho Gonzalez once said, "The dangerous thing about Laver is he hits the impossible shot when he's out of position—the time you least expect it.")

That was the time. I sliced like a man delivering a karate chop and sent a low under-spinning ball crosscourt. I still don't believe the angle—and neither did Newcombe. The shot was a clear contradiction of everything we'd seen and done. There was no way it could clear the net and still land inside the court, yet it kept fluttering along somehow almost parallel to the net, eluding Newcombe's frantic wave and landing just within the far sideline. You don't plan a shot like that, not unless you're on marijuana, and the only grass I'm partial to is Wimbledon's. I had the general direction in mind and the rest just happened. It was nice to watch.

But Newcombe was shocked. I reckon the shot value was worth a lot more points than just that one to 0-30. There was enough of a crack in his morale for me to pour through. Moments later, I had his service game as he double faulted the last point.

Newcombe was faltering and I was doing everything I could to help him. I won my serve quickly, then whacked two good forehands and a backhand to get another break for 5-4.

"Hit the ball," I kept reminding myself, but it was coming instinctively. On set point, the only bad bounce of the day saved Newcombe for a second. But I followed my next serve with a stiff backhand volley that gave me the set.

Now I was up 2-1 in sets, and I was determined to get him before he could recover.

He came in with the serve and I swatted a backhand down the line. All John could do was hurl himself after the ball, but it was well past him. He picked himself up and smiled despairingly. Everyone laughed good-naturedly, and a laugh is welcome in that place once in a while.

Two more backhands of mine pinched him at 0-40. Somewhere John found his serve for an instant, and he banged three good ones to pull himself to deuce. He was grunting as he served, tiring I could tell. I was peeved at not getting one of those serves back, then relieved when he missed by an inch with a lob that would have been trouble. My ad. He volleyed my return short, to the service line. For a long second it seemed the scene was frozen as we stood still facing each other at the net for this virtual match point. Which way would I hit the ball? He knew it didn't matter since I almost surely could pass him whichever route I took, but he readied himself for a stab. I waited for the ball to bounce, took it with my backhand, and drove it straight down the line.

One-love for me with serve. I kept right on going to the cup, the check, and the victory party. The score was 6-4, 5-7, 6-4, 6-4. On actual match point, I put away a smash of Newcombe's final lob. It was a satisfying ending.

They rolled out the green carpet to protect that hallowed sod from the street shoes of the Duke of Kent who came down to make the presentations.

After Newcombe won his Wimbledon in 1967, he told Princess Marina, then presenting the trophy, that he was going to go out and get drunk. Good, straightforward Aussie talk. Also expensive talk. It takes an awful lot of beer to get an Aussie full.

Fred Stolle likes to illustrate that point with a story concerning a national championship he won with Roy Emerson in the U.S. "We were playing the U.S. Doubles in Boston," said Fred, "and our pattern for that week was alternate sleeping. One of us would party one night while the other stayed home at the hotel. We'd reverse it the next night. One of us rested, we figured, was enough to win the championship.

"It was my night out before the semifinals when we were going to play the top American team, Clark Graebner and Marty Riessen. I was at this bash at a place on Beacon Hill when I got into conversation with a character they called the Baron of Hungary who hung around the tennis.

"The Baron wanted to make a little wager on the match the next day and asked me how much I liked myself and Emmo. Fivers, I said. 'Baron, I'll give you five-to-one and you can have Riessen and Graebner.' The Baron brightened noticeably. We had the icebox well flanked, and he never let me move a step. 'Have a beer, Fred' was just about the extent of his conversation as the hours went by. He kept reaching in and opening them for me. I kept drinking.

"As we moved through our second case I looked at my watch and it was about two thirty in the morning. 'Baron,' I said, I've got to leave, I don't want to be late for the match. It starts at noon, you know.'

"He wasn't in very good shape, but he said, 'Fred, don't you think you ought to let Emmo know about the bet? He ought to realize how important the match is.'

"'Right you are, Baron.' It struck me then as logical and I picked up the phone and rang Emmo, waking him from a sound sleep. He was not pleased. I believe he called me a bloody idiot while I was explaining the bet.

"I nodded to the Baron in the stands before the match. He looked like he might have a headache, but he seemed pleased about what he thought was a sure thing. I never played better and we killed Riessen and Graebner."

Beer is mother's milk for an Aussie. I don't know whether Newcombe could afford enough of it in his finest amateur hour to follow through on his statement to the Duchess of Kent. But I had won $7,200, and that will buy enough lager to do in even an Aussie.

We had some champagne Saturday evening to celebrate in our flat with George MacCall and his wife and my close friends from New Zealand, John McDonald and his wife. I struggled into my dress suit for the Wimbledon ball where I'd have the ceremonial first dance with the women's champion, Ann Jones. It was the first time two left-handers shared the opening fox trot which was "Fly Me to the Moon." I can't remember which of us led, but we didn't endanger the reputation of Marge and Gower Champion.

The last thing I recall about the evening was sitting in a discotheque called Raffles with the music and the beer flowing nicely. I was grinning a lot, and Aretha Franklin was wailing, "R-e-s-p-e-c-t . . ." Pat Stolle, Fred's wife, was talking with Mary about naming our baby.

"Well," Pat was saying, "I think Forest would be quite good if it's a boy. Since the baby is supposed to be born during Forest Hills, it would be a nice remembrance, wouldn't it?"

Mary didn't think so.

Nor did she like the proposal of Slamma for a girl. Or Slammer for a boy. She didn't seem to care for the tennis motif, and I assured her we wouldn't name the kid Drop Shot because we already had a dog by that name.

Everything began to run together. I forgot about Newcombe, the Slam, Forest Laver, Aretha Franklin, dancing with Ann Jones . . . and I woke up much later that morning in the bathtub, my tuxedo still on. I'd never been so well dressed for the tub.

At about 7:00 a.m., Mary tells me, the phone rang. It was a call from a newspaperman in Australia who wanted to talk to me about my victory.

"This is Mrs. Laver," she said.

"Well," said the reporter, "is your husband available now?"

"Uh," she mumbled, thinking of the body in the bath, "Rod's out." She didn't want to lie and she didn't want to tell the truth. I think that was a pretty good answer.

"Gone out at this hour?" the fellow persisted. "When will he be back?"

"In about five hours. Why don't you try him then."

The next time he rang I was ready to chat. I'd found my head behind the tub where it had rolled, and screwed it back on.

LESSON · 20

Returning Serve

MAKE UP YOUR MIND ON THIS: you're going to get that serve back over the net. Consistent returning puts pressure on the server. Usually you'll just block the first serve, since your opponent will probably have some pace on the ball.

Move in for the second serve and give that a good swat. Most people play too far back to return serve. You want to try to take the ball on the rise, and maybe you'll find yourself standing inside the baseline to do this. Try it.

Pancho Segura, one of the cleverest guys to play the game, used to move up to take the second serve, like most players, but frequently he would delay that move until his opponent was into the service motion. "Maybe my move will distract him and he'll double fault," was Pancho's reasoning.

Prepare.

May I repeat: prepare. Get that racket back as soon as you know whether the ball's coming to your forehand or backhand. Too many players are late in preparing to make the stroke and getting the racket back. Remind yourself to prepare as your opponent makes his service toss.

Even a broken-down-looking return gives the server a problem. Once you've put the ball over the net you've got an even chance of winning the point. Try to keep the ball low, especially against an opponent who follows his serve to the net. Use a lob occasionally against a net rusher. It will startle him.

Don't overhit. Nothing picks up your opponent more than ripping returns of serve—that slap harmlessly into the net.

Get that return over the net. Any way. Or go stand in the corner.

THE SPOILS OF VICTORY

MONDAY I WAS FINE AND LOOSE. I TOOK CARE OF A FEW business appointments before taking a cab to the airport with Mary. Business was better. Mark McCormack had been among the first to shake hands with me after my victory over Newcombe.

"This will do a lot for those contracts we talked about," Mark said. And it has. I never had any idea how the name Rod Laver could be exploited, but Mark McCormack, as business agent, had been making fortunes for sports page names since he began guiding one of the better known—Arnold Palmer. I was his first fling at tennis—a reluctant one. Having him and his aides, Jay Lafave and Dick Alford, minding my affairs meant a lot to my game, giving me a free mind and saving time so that my primary consideration could be playing. Endorsements do take a certain amount of time in appearances, conferences, and posing for promotional photos. I was not the free man I once was. But with Mark's IMG (International Management Group) handling the business, I wasn't burdened with the approach and negotiations to obtain the best deal. Frequently I was chiseled before IMG took over. I couldn't sell myself as well as somebody else could. That's not my line. Mary and I were going crazy trying to answer business mail, keeping track of endorsements, and merchandising me in the best manner. As a trained accountant, she was a great help, but still it was impossible to look after it all and really know what was best.

I realized that early in the game. Even though tennis hasn't always presented a new, booming market as it does now, there were certain commercial opportunities for the leading players, and I was taking advantage of every one I could. Some were for incredibly low money, considering what McCormack had done for me, but I took them all, figuring everything was gravy. I had no grasp of the possibilities, but I knew I had to get an agent of some sort. Every successful athlete reaches that point.

McCormack, then a young Cleveland lawyer, made his name handling the affairs of golfers Arnold Palmer, Jack Nicklaus, and Gary Player. He also represented big-name clients in the day such as like Jean-Claude Killy of skiing, Jackie Stewart of auto racing, Paul Warfield of football, John Havlicek of basketball, Stan Mikita of hockey, and Brooks Robinson of baseball. Other future clients included Roger Federer and Pete Sampras from tennis, Tiger Woods in golf, Derek Jeter in baseball, and, believe it or not, Pope John Paul II.

In the early days, I thought he might like a tennis player to join his stable, and I wrote him a letter about it in 1966. Mark replied negatively. There weren't enough opportunities to sell a tennis player to make it worth his while. That was more than a personal disappointment to me. It indicated that tennis was still in the backwater.

In 1968, I tried again. Tennis was now open, we pros were sprung from Siberia, and McCormack showed some interest. He sent Jay Lafave to talk to me. At about three o'clock one September morning in P.J. Clarke's saloon in New York (after I'd been beaten in the U.S. Open), Jay and I hammered out a tentative deal. Later I signed.

I was an experiment for IMG, their first tennis player. But, of course, I brought my $90,000 contract with National Tennis League into the deal, and that was a good start to build on.

Mark's management worked fabulously for me. Before he stepped into my affairs, my non-playing income was under $25,000 a year. For 1969, it just about doubled, and the probability was that winning the Grand Slam would eventually be worth several hundred thousand dollars in endorsements.

In reorganizing my business life, McCormack gave notice to the firms holding contracts with me that they would have to do a lot better when those contracts expired. He began looking for similar firms that might be interested in me when the time came to re-negotiate my contracts, and he found altogether new endorsements like a clothing line for Puritan, a tennis camp at the Mt. Washington Hotel in Bretton Woods, New Hampshire, the contract for this book, a movie—nearly twenty associations.

A bright example of how things changed was shoes. I had signed in 1966 with a small New England manufacturer who produced a line of Rod Laver tennis shoes. My deal was $1,000 plus 2.5 percent royalties. It was a bad deal and the shoe was inadequately promoted. I was getting royalty checks periodically for $7.80 or $25—figures like that. Beer money. When that contract was up, McCormack placed me with the German firm adidas, an arrangement that meant many times more.

Racket endorsements brought in more than $50,000 a year, and that is only for specific areas of the world. For instance, I endorsed a Chemold metal racket for the United States of America, a Dunlop wooden racket for Australia, and a Donnay wooden racket for Europe. In addition, Rod Laver Co., an export firm, bought rackets from Chemold and Donnay and marketed them separately in other countries.

Although metal rackets were starting to sell extremely well as many of the players switched from wood, I wasn't anxious to go mod. For one thing, I had a contract with Dunlop, who didn't get into metal until later in the rush. More important, I was comfortable with wood (with which I won the Grand Slam), feeling it was better for my game.

Clark Graebner, Gene Scott, Rosie Casals and Billie Jean King, turning to Wilson's steel racket, started the metal frames on their way in 1967. Changing over to steel abruptly at midseason, the four of them had great success in the U.S. Championships at Forest Hills, and flashed the message of the gleaming steelies across the country on TV.

Billie Jean won the women's title, Clark got to the men's final. More implausible was the caper of Scott, a lawyer and weekend player, who reached the semis and credited his steel racket. "The steelie helped me serve better and hit the ball harder with less effort, so I could keep up with the guys who were playing regularly and were sharper and in better condition," Scott said. He predicted, "Wood will be obsolete in ten years; wooden rackets will go the way of wooden golf clubs." Later Pancho Gonzalez switched to Spalding's aluminum, and his regeneration, whether due to the racket or not, had to be a recommendation.

The rush to metal was on. Sales spurted.

The established sporting goods firms all put out their own models, and some new companies got into the tennis racket business. One of the newcomers was Chemold in New York

It isn't quite true to say that I would endorse and play with a beer bottle if the price was right, although one of the first tennis professionals, Tom Pettit of the Newport Casino, actually swung a champagne bottle so deftly that he could beat a number of club players armed with rackets. Pettit, incidentally, played in the first open match, an exhibition he lost to the U.S. champion Dick Sears, at Newport in 1882.

No, I wouldn't have given up wood for aluminum just for money. However, the money was so attractive that I couldn't be stubborn in my conviction that wood remained superior. Some of those defectors, including Billie Jean King, returned to wood, feeling that touch and control with the old rackets meant more than the zip they got from steel. I said hesitantly that I would try the aluminum, as did Tony Roche, and would use it only if after a trial I believed it could improve my game. I wanted to be sure I had at least the same touch, and that I could serve better with less energy used.

I did concede that the latter would probably be true, but without touch I would feel like Andrew Wyeth using a gummy brush. I think most athletes care about what they endorse. They want it to be a quality product. I do. But endorsing, say, clothing and a racket are two different things. A pair of tennis shorts may make you look better, thus feel better, but I doubt that they will affect your game. But a racket is a special thing to me, and if I use it and recommend it I want to feel it's the best possible weapon for a tennis player. That's the way I felt about Chemold, although there were bugs at first as there have been in all the metal frames. I used it for quite a while, including my 13-win run dominating the Tennis Champions Classic and earning me $160,000 early in 1971. But for me (perhaps not for you) aluminum never quite gave one the "feel" I got from wood, so I gave it up and reverted to wood. There was an escape provision in my contract.

That's what I mean about the efficiency of the McCormack organization. Some tennis players, contemmporaries of mine, who followed me to Mark include John Newcombe, Roger Taylor, Margaret Court, and Evonne Goolagong.

Never did Mark, Jay Lafave, or Dick Alford talk about what a Grand Slam could do for me commercially. I guess they were afraid to jinx me. But I could tell they were thinking about it as soon as I won the Australian. After Wimbledon, they were as excited as I was. After all, a percentage of Laver on the verge of achieving the Grand Slam would tend to increase the excitement.

LESSON • 21

"Equipment"

WHILE STROKES AND EVEN STRATEGIES have changed considerably since my second Slam in 1969, the biggest changes are as a result of modern equipment.

Throughout my best years, I played with the Dunlop Maxply Fort wood racquet. I used natural gut strings (but was not that particular about string tension). My handle size was 4 5/8", and I used a natural leather grip (although I typically would carve the shape of my handle with a knife until it felt just right). The racquet weighed around 14 ounces.

This information will sound prehistoric to the modern player. They use racquets that are larger, stiffer, lighter, with relatively tiny handles (fellow lefty Rafael Nadal uses a grip that is a puny 4 ¼"), and nearly always with a synthetic overgrip to absorb sweat.

At the risk of sounding crotchety, it is easier to play with these modern racquets. I remember a remark made by Pancho Gonzalez, after he tried one of the latest-greatest models in the 1990s. "I would never, ever have missed a single volley if I had been able to play with this in my time," said Pancho. Already, one of the great volleyers of all-time, Pancho would have been even more fierce with a larger, lighter, stiffer model racquet.

Nearly all the top players from my generation used natural gut, which had a great feel to it. We would need to go to great lengths to keep our strings from getting moist though, otherwise it would compromise both the playability and durability of the gut (which was damn expensive). Today, nearly all the players use polyester strings. Some, like Roger Federer, use a hybrid of polyester and gut (on the main and cross strings respectively, or vice versa for other players). The advantage of these polyester strings is that players can haul off and really give the ball a poke, with little fear that the shot will carry long. That is reassuring.

One of my advantages was my reputation for swinging out at the ball. When the going got rough, I liked to let it rip. I reckon that I would have taken to these polyester strings. I believe that I could have gotten balls to really jump off the court, the way most players do routinely today. The polyester strings last longer too. I'd bet that Kenny Rosewall, who was pretty frugal with all of that prize money he earned, would not have to re-string his racquets but once during an entire year!

The biggest difference in playing styles has come from the advances in equipment. Television announcers always lament the lack of net rushers, but players today can play aggressive shots from all sorts of defensive positions, and this makes the net rusher more vulnerable than ever- even after hitting a perfect approach shot.

Also, the larger, lighter, stiffer racquets have particularly helped players return serve with more aggression and accuracy. It used to be that if you swung or kicked a serve deep into the box, then followed the delivery in to the net you would be at a great advantage. Back in the day, players would be forced to chip or block balls back when they were not in perfect position. Not so anymore. These days, players can take mighty cuts on most returns. Even when the returner is stretched and forced to block the ball back into play, it is done accurately and with interest. It makes the prospect of serving and volleying pretty damn hard in today's game.

The performance wear of today is remarkable. Modern shirts wick away perspiration, and keep you feeling fresh. I surely could have used some of these shirts and shorts during some of those broiling matches in the Aussie summer months. Roy Emerson used to cut the pockets out of his cotton Fred Perry shorts, to assure that they would weigh less as he perspired over the course of a long match. Rest assured that Emmo would not need to do this with today's clothing!

Do not underestimate the improvements in footwear. My old signature brand of sneakers, which are still made by adidas, remain hot sellers in stores today. However, they are sold with other vintage clothing for today's hipsters. Glad that I had some impact on the fashion scene! They are classic looking, and this is appealing to the fashion-conscious. They do not, however, provide the support, traction, durability, and comfort that the modern athlete has come to expect.

The quality of today's performance footwear is light years ahead of the canvas sneakers we wore in the 1960's. If you put those new top-of-the-line shoes on Kenny Rosewall, circa 1968, then he would have been even more efficient in covering the court. We used to wear two pairs of socks, a thin pair of cotton socks on the bottom and a thicker wool pair on top, to prevent blisters. I am not sure that is as necessary today. In fact, I doubt a single professional player has ever worn a pair of wool socks onto a tennis court.

If I were coming up in today's game, the equipment would likely have shaped the way I played. I would have likely used a more extreme grip on my forehands, to accommodate the higher bouncing balls. I would have hit bigger first serves more often, knowing that I could rely on applying tremendous spin to any second serve that I needed to hit. I would have been more aggressive with my approach shots most of the time. I love watching today's great players. There is a side of me that wonders what it would be like to give it a go against them with the modern equipment. It would be fun, that's for certain.

As I wrote earlier, the equipment has made the game easier to play- and to learn quickly for new players- and that is just terrific.

22

THE BEGINNING OF THE END

THE REST OF THE SUMMER WAS SOMETHING OF A MYSTERY to me because I didn't lose a match. Leaving London, I flew to Boston and Mary to Los Angeles, from where we alternately sympathized and sparred at long-distance rates during the U.S. Pro Championship. I've said I expected to lose there and, at the moment, would have welcomed defeat because it would have sent me right home to comfort Mary. But I didn't lose. And I didn't lose in pro tournaments in St. Louis, Bingham-ton, Ft. Worth, and Baltimore leading up to Forest Hills.

This not only surprised me; in fact it made me slightly edgy. Where was the letdown that you have to have? Except for the U.S. Pro Cham-pionship, those American tournaments didn't mean that much. A loss or two would have been a relief, and given me some time off. Instead I had to play right through the final each time. Nothing like this had ever happened to me. I know that Suzanne Lenglen and Helen Wills Moody used to go years without losing, and Budge, Alice Marble and Tilden had undefeated summers. But nobody is that dominant today. The op-position is tougher. Even in 1969, I got beat fairly frequently—16 times in 122 matches.

Nevertheless, I came into New York to finish the Slam with a streak of 23 straight match victories that began with Pietrangeli at Wimbledon. When I walked into the Forest Hills Stadium alongside a young Mexi-can, Luis Garcia, to launch the U.S. Open, my last defeat was nearly three months behind me—by Newcombe at Queen's.

Two things were on my mind when I arrived at the West Side Tennis Club in the borough of Queens: Mary and the Grand Slam. Mary came first, and this was a concern that hadn't existed in 1962. Then it was just tennis. Possibly the double concern was better for me. In worrying about Mary, I don't think the weight of going for the Slam got to me as it did in 1962. I was older, too, and I'd been through it before.

Mary's presence in my life made me more relaxed. Those tense phone calls between Bostonand California of July were forgotten, and now our calls buoyed each of us.

There were a couple of vital things I learned from the 1962 ordeal. Censor your newspaper reading. Stay in a quiet, secluded place during the tournament.

Billie Jean King's dad, Bill Moffitt, once gave her the best advice an athlete can get: "Don't read anything that's written about you," he told her. "It will be either overly complimentary or overly critical, and neither will do you any good."

Billie Jean could be glad she didn't read the London paper that suggested she had cancer when she became ill just before Wimbledon of 1968. But so many reporters asked her about it that she found out. She was merely run down, but the newspapers can blow these things up. An athlete is better off not to take the press to heart.

You have to talk to reporters. I like most of them, and they've been good to me. But you don't have to read what they write. They're all looking for a different angle, and that angle could spoil your digestion or your sleep.

Certainly they were going to ask about the Slam and I was going to discuss it. But as long as I didn't see it in black and white I didn't have to build up additional pressure on myself. You can contribute to the pressure yourself.

I did that in 1962 by reading everything that was written, and by being more available to the reporters and well-wishers than I should have. This time I didn't stay in a hotel where I could be tracked down, and I didn't go out much to eat.

Chuck Heston was very helpful. Chuck, who impersonated Moses, Michelangelo, Andrew Jackson, Ben Hur—and also did a good impersonation of a tennis player when he could escape filming—loaned me his Manhattan apartment on the East River. John McDonald, my friend of many years since I first played in his native New Zealand, kindly came over from London to act as confidant, cook, practice partner, and buffer.

We moved into Heston's spacious, high-ceilinged penthouse with a tape recorder for musical company, a supply of eggs and steak, and settled into a quiet routine, spending as little time as possible at the West Side Club, then only to play or practice. Unlike Wimbledon, there's no privacy for the players, no place to relax away from the press or the crowds. At one time, I imagine Forest Hills was a very pleasant place, well out from Manhattan, an enclave of its own. Now Queens is crowded, unattractive. The club is hard to get to through the traffic; parking is impossible. It always amazes me how the English, jammed into that little island, have managed to preserve their greenery so that Wimbledon is such a countrified place within a huge city, while Queens has become a depressing jumble.

Financially, the U.S. Open is No. 1. Prize money at Forest Hills added up to $137,000 in 1969, with $16,000 for the winner of the men's singles. In prestige, it's No. 2, behind Wimbledon. But in playing conditions in the day, it was a far-down bush league all its own. The courts are grass, and American grass is for cows and lovers—not tennis players. In fact, American grass courts are so uncertain underfoot that an unwary cow might break a leg strolling from baseline to net. Or starve. There isn't much grass left on an American court by the time a tournament reaches its climax.

Uncertainties of American grass made tennis at Forest Hills comparable to driving theIndianapolis 500 on cobblestones. The 1969 Open, practically ruined by record New York rains, made it clear that grass must be replaced by a level, all-weather surface, which it eventually did by moving to clay in 1975 and then to hard courts in 1978.

But grass is tradition, and tradition was the grass-stained enemy of the growth of spectator tennis in America. Because the most important tournaments were on grass, it is a sad fact that few Americans at the time knew how thrilling it was to watch excellent tennis. There wasn't much of it in a grass tournament in the States.

When you say that Wimbledon is a grass court tournament and Forest Hills is a grass court tournament—and isn't grass, after all, grass?—you may as well say that Raquel Welch is a woman and Twiggy is a woman, and what's the difference? Wimbledon is so alluring and appealing because it is cuddled and cared for more than King Farouk ever was. No American club has the grass-growing climate or the resources to duplicate Wimbledon. Even so, Wimbledon doesn't produce as exciting tennis as the slower surfaces. But at least at Wimbledon you know where the ball will bounce—and that it will bounce.

Because grass makes for a low, skidding bounce, points are normally over very quickly. An ordinary serve can become impossible when it begins darting this way and that off bad grass, and an ordinary player can keep a good one on the court for hours without either accomplishing very much other than the promotion of tedium. The longest three-set match in history was played at Newport, Rhode Island, on a grass court in 1967. Dick Leach and Dick Dell hung in for more than six hours—spread over two days—to outlast Len Schloss and Tom Mozur, 3-6, 49-47, 22-20: 147 games. Fortunately it wasn't a best-of-five-sets match. It's also fortunate that Leach made a lucky shot on match point, or they might still be playing.

Of the sixteen matches in tennis history reaching or exceeding 100 games, nine were played on American grass, another on British grass at Wimbledon. One was indoors on canvas at Salisbury, Maryland, also a very fast surface, and two were on American concrete, just about as fast. The other three were indoors on boards, very fast.

A match like that one at Newport is dreadful. You can imagine where it would drive a television producer who was covering it. Right up the antenna. Though I love tennis, I would find it more boring than watching a week of "I Love Lucy."

Of course, that is why tennis didn't succeed very well on TV in America in the early days. Limited television coverage was for years mostly devoted to Forest Hills and the National Indoors at Salisbury, Maryland (on a fast canvas). Frankly, the tennis has been deadly dull serve-and-volley stuff. Wham-bam . . . the point's over. Bad to play; bad to watch.

The theory in America has seemed to be that since Dick Sears—the first champion in 1881—did his thing on grass, it would be a sacrilege to change. Tennis was a warm-up for a tea party in those days, and grass was lovely. It still is for club players. You can play barefoot, luxurious exercise. But when your livelihood depends on it, you feel like Rudy Nureyev trying to dance in a rockgarden.

I hope this isn't taken as a knock at the groundskeepers—Owen Sheridan at Forest Hills, Walter Chambers at Longwood, or Joe Leandra at Newport—who were all splendid, hardworking men who kept their courts so nice for the members. But labor problems and the climate are insuperable. American grass just doesn't hold up long beneath a thundering herd of tournament players. All the groundskeepers would be as happy as us pros to roll up the grass and ship it to neighborhoods that need parks.

Grass is becoming deader for athletes than God for atheists. Writing back in the day in *Sports Illustrated*, Dan Jenkins said God goofed when He invented grass instead of Astro-Turf. Jenkins was referring to football fields, but tennis fitted, too, although Astro-Turf has been too fast for tennis. Uni-Turf has been slower and better, but perhaps I'm not a neutral witness. I used to represent the company.

Today, there is only one remaining grass court tournament in the United States – the International Tennis Hall of Fame Championships in Newport, R.I. The grass court season as a whole only consists of two weeks of pre-Wimbledon grass court events, The Championships, followed by the festivities in Newport in the week after Wimbledon.

In the day, I'd have played Forest Hills if the surface were macaroni and cheese. I'm a professional. The money was there along with a big title. I've played much worse conditions for a lot less money, or none at all. You adapt. The game I played at Forest Hills—or on any other American grass—was entirely different from how I played on Wimbledon's firm and true grass. Junk brought results at Forest Hills. I serve my kicker (American twist) a lot more because it took erratic bounces, whereas at Wimbledon it would stand up too high and I used it only to vary my serving pattern. I chipped the ball around a lot, hooked and sliced, even chopped, trying to produce skips and annoying hops to throw off the other fellow. You improvised at Forest Hills.

LESSON • 22

Know Yourself

IT'S FINE AND DANDY to read about how Rod Laver and Ken Rosewall and Pancho Gonzalez did it, useful and worthwhile, I hope. There are shots that I may be able to help you with in this book. That's why you're reading it.

Nevertheless, there is one overriding fact of the matter when you get into a match: you are you. You have progressed to a certain ability in tennis, and you must be aware of this when you play.

It does no good to try to whack a topspin backhand in a difficult spot if you haven't practiced it, or you are unable to make it work. The fact that I can escape with it doesn't help you. You may be better off lobbing.

What I'm getting at is this: don't try to play beyond yourself. You win tennis matches on the other guy's errors and by keeping the ball going. You're just aiding and abetting the enemy by trying to pull off the impractical or impossible shot in certain situations. If you're pushed wide of the court, you'd better hit down the line or lob rather than trying a slick crosscourt that has only a slight chance of succeeding.

Wait for the opportunity to put your best shots into use, until you have the edge and the chances of success are high. Until then, work for that opening by getting the ball back to your opponent's weaknesses.

Cut down on your mistakes. If you're up against a strong server, don't try to overpower him with your returns. Go all out against his weaknesses, not his strengths.

Take stock of your physical limitations. Don't take unnecessary steps or run for balls on which you have little chance. If you don't have a roaring serve and good volleys, don't play a net rushing game.

Know what you can hit well, and when to use it. A little thought on the matter will tell you.

Sometimes you'll be inspired. That's the joy of the game. You'll be hitting away like mad and everything will work. Fine. It's most likely to happen when you start out solidly with the things you can do well, not trying to play above yourself. When you win some points and games that way, your confidence will expand.

Talk to any really good professional player and ask him how he plays me. "Keep the ball in play and let Laver make the mistakes," the guy will say. "Laver does make mistakes."

So, I reckon, will your opponent.

23

THE LAST LEG OF THE GRAND SLAM: FOREST HILLS

JOHN MCDONALD WAS GOOD COMPANY. HE'S A LITTLE OLDER than I and played Davis Cup for New Zealand. He could give me good practice, and he squeezed the orange juice and poached the eggs beautifully. We know one another's families and habits, have much in common. He lost in the qualifying round and wasn't concerned about his own game. The common goal was my rest and tennis, and I appreciated his part in my winning. At night we'd watch the telly or listen to tapes— Aretha Franklin, Dave Brubeck, Jose Feliciano. Sometimes we'd have a few Australian friends in, and one evening we threw a birthday party for an Aussie living in New York, Mike Irving. Both he and his wife, Veronica, were top models in America.

My chief preoccupation was my racket handles. Arnold Palmer fussed with his clubs and shaped them to his own liking, and I did the same with my rackets. I was always unwinding the leather grips, changing them around and rewinding them, experimenting to get the best feel. I sat around like an old maid with her knitting, the rackets in my lap as I fiddled with the grips. It was a sure sign of staleness for me if I was not rearranging the grips. Pancho Gonzalez was the same, and he also worked on his aluminum frame, grinding it down here and there, or drilling holes to change the weight ever so slightly and bring about just the right balance.

In the first three rounds of the U.S. Open, it seemed as though I—a

U.S. resident—was trying to destroy the Good Neighbor policy as I went through Luis Garcia of Mexico and Jaime Pinto-Bravo and Jaime Fillol, both of Chile. I picked up a little Spanish in that stretch of straight-set victories, although I don't think any of the words need repeating. None of the Latins was comfortable on grass, although Fillol gave me a spirited first set. He was a good prospect who would become the leading South American.

Dennis Ralston had been the forgotten man of American tennis. People tended to think of him, if at all, as over the hill because he went back so far. He was a Wimbledon champion before I was, winning the doubles with Rafe Osuna in 1960. But he was only eighteen then, but people had the tendency to write him off in the late 1960s. Memories of Ralston were mainly of Davis Cup disasters, one of them—a defeat by Brazil's Edison Mandarino—ended his amateur career in 1966. But as a pro, he had done quite well, often extending me, notably in my only five-set match of Wimbledon in 1968.

He usually extended me, but he didn't beat me. I think this was in the back of both our minds when we played. When we got to the critical point, he was the one who was going to crack.

But when he led me two sets to one on a lovely sunny afternoon with the Forest Hills stadium nearly full, that critical point was some ways off. Dennis was playing beautifully, returning my serve damagingly with his good-looking net skimmers.

The crowd of about 10,000 had forgotten all their disappointments with Ralston in the past and were rumbling exuberantly for him. The opportunities for an American crowd to push one of their own to a victory over an Australian were infrequent at Forest Hills in those days, and they let Ralston and me hear their approval—of him.

A crowd like that can grind their opponent down. You find yourself getting smaller and smaller if you're not careful to do something to counteract it. When we changed ends of the court, I was toweling off quicker than Dennis at the umpire's chair and moving to position a little sooner. As I walked to the baseline . . . silence. No boos, mind you; nobody throwing anything. But the silence told me that I was in enemy country. Then Ralston would begin his walk to the line and the place spilled over with cheering. I felt like a Communist at a John Birch Society meeting. A little of that and you can really be shaken.

I remembered playing Davis Cup in Mexico in 1959, against Rafe Osuna, and the same thing happened. He was lingering during the change, and letting me walk on first. I got the glares and he got the great morale-lifting explosion. Harry Hopman, our captain, straightened it out quickly. I was not to move until Osuna did. That's what I had to do with Ralston, and later in the semifinals with Ashe.

I'm all for cheers, but I'm going to share them whenever possible. So when Ralston walked out and the cheering started I walked, too, and let it fall on me as well.

As a pro, I hadn't encountered such nationalism much, although it was strong for Pancho Gonzalez, especially in his hometown, Los Angeles, where I had to time my moves to coincide with his.

Ralston was playing very well, but his game didn't vary much. He had little flair, and as I started serving better and hitting all my shots better, I knew I'd get him. I won the fourth set without much trouble and he became vulnerable. At 2-3 in the fifth, he could have saved a break point against his serve by making an easy backhand volley. My return was high, and he should have put it away. Instead I think he was trying to make it a shade too good, as you will when you're pressing, and he dumped it into the net. I had the break for 4-2, and I could tell by that hangdog look he got that he was through. And I was into the quarterfinals. I keep finding out one shot can make the difference, in this case Denny's bad volley at the critical point.

To be fair, Denny turned the tables on me the following year, and I had to revise my estimate of him. (That story is told later.)

I'm the rainmaker. Forest Hills confirmed it. Everywhere I went and won, the tournament suffered washouts—Brisbane, Paris, Johannesburg, London, Boston, and now Forest Hills. Within 48 hours, 6½ inches of rain struck New York, a 25-year record there for wetness. In South Africa, where it hadn't rained all year, a three-day deluge interrupted the open, and the agricultural officials wanted to hire me and keep me there. Maybe there was something about my crazy, spinning shots that upset the atmosphere, but while South African farmers hailed the rain, New Yorkers were less than ecstatic. Sections of the city were flooded, including the West Side Tennis Club, whose antiquated protective facilities did little good. The tarps in the stadium and grandstand were inadequate, and coverings don't exist for the other courts.

Forest Hills became a morass, and the tournament closed down to wait two and a half days for the sun. The coverings were simple canvas laid on the grass. If they were left on very long the grass smothered. At Wimbledon, canvas tents, run up on pulleys and cables, were spread above Centre Court, allowing the grass to breathe. You can play there whenever the rain stops [The new retractable roof will keep the show going, whatever the downfalls.] Admittedly, it hardly stopped pouring in New York, but when it did, the courts were unplayable.

We played anyway, slopping about like rice farmers and ripping chunks of sod from the courts. Any athlete knows that waiting to play is the worst part. We tried to keep busy during the delay, driving to indoor courts in Englewood, New Jersey, to practice, working out in the New York Athletic Club's gym.

It helped to fill the time, although I got stiff running on an indoor track. The pounding affected my legs after playing on grass, and I hustled myself into a hot bath with epsom salts. This is always the thing, anyway, after a hard workout or match. A good tub. I don't think enough American athletes realize this, especially the ones who don't have whirlpool baths available to them. A weekend player, who may have gone a little too hard, can bring himself back for the next day by moving right from the court to a tub. It does a lot more for you than just a long, hot shower.

When the rain finally stopped, my edge was gone. I could feel it immediately as Roy Emerson won the first set and broke me for a lead in the second. I was always in trouble on my serve as we sloshed about the grandstand court. The balls were soggy and heavy, like hitting cantaloupes.

And there was my old buddy Emmo, my friend and rival for a dozen years, with a good chance to finally ruin a Slam for me. Three times I beat him in finals during the 1962 Slam, completing it with a four-set win here.

I had been so nervous during that 1962 match that I lost the feel of the racket completely. I actually held it wrong and hit a volley straight into the ground once. It was so comical that I laughed myself, and that helped break the tension.

I think I've learned to overcome that kind of panic, although I did suffer it once long enough to lose the match at Madison Square Garden earlier in the year to Cliff Richey.

It's what I call "whisky wrists." Your grips don't feel right and your shots are jerky. You're not necessarily choking, but you're so rattled you don't know where you are. You're rushing, you want to get it all over— yet you're not anxious to lose.

You have to slow yourself down. Take a little more time. Release your grip between points. Put your racket in the other hand for a moment, and let your racket hand relax. Stop yourself before you serve, and get in mind what you want to do. You've probably been snatching at the ball instead of watching it closely and hitting through it. Make sure the first serve goes in, even if you have to take something off it. Placement is more important than speed. When you've been going badly and your opponent is gaining confidence, he's going to step in on your second serve and take advantage of it.

Get the first one in. If the situation is reversed, step in on his second serve. It appears to me that most club players stand too far back to receive the second serve, thus reducing the opponent's disadvantage. Move up on the second ball and you can almost always return well enough to follow your return to the net. If your opponent stands far back to receive, bloop your serve short—catch him off balance.

When you've got those whisky wrists, pause and try to think about a couple of key things. Keep your eye on the ball. Forget where your opponent is, and try to see the ball hit your racket. And bend your knees. That'll help loosen you up. Take a deep breath.

Tell yourself to hit the ball. I mean by that to hit through it. You can only lose, and that's not the worst thing that can happen.

There weren't going to be any nerves for me the rest of the way. Emmo had the lead, and he might beat me, but I felt confident that if I took special care with my serve and kept hitting through the ball that I'd find my form. I had all through the Grand Slam, and this wasn't any different. Emmo had slowed himself down, too. (After all, he knows as much about what's happening as I do, maybe more.) He realized he couldn't clout those heavy balls the way he likes, so he contented himself with taking the pace off his returns. We were slipping and sliding, but I made up my mind I was going to get to the net quicker to knock off those slow returns before they bounced on my side of the court. You're crazy to let a ball land on a grass court most of the time, and at Forest Hills it's like dropping a baby out of a window: It may bounce nicely, but it isn't likely. My legs have won me as many matches as my strokes or my opponents' mistakes, and they won this one. I was quicker on that wet court than Emmo, who swears there's a duckbilled platypus lurking in my family tree. Maybe so. I must have had webbed feet to pull out the second set. He lost the third, 11–13, it turned out, on a forehand passing shot that we both watched anxiously. Roy thought it was good; I couldn't honestly tell; the linesman shouted, "Out!" You get all the calls when you win a Grand Slam.

Rather than game for him it was deuce. Then I hit a pair of passing forehands that he narrowly missed to take the set.

Now he knew he had to go five sets to win, and that has to take something out of any man, even Roy Emerson, especially on that marsh. He had to climb a slippery mountain, and I'd known him so long I could sense something leaving him. He never stopped battling. He didn't get the feeling he was beaten the way Ralston did. A man with one of the greatest records in tennis history still felt he could win. Yet just a smidgin of something was gone, and it made me that much tougher. Roy is two years older than I and that started to hurt him.

Emmo dragged his rear foot when he served, and he ripped up the baseline area horribly. In cleaning up after himself, he built a pile of sod chunks next to the fence that separates the court from the grandstand.

Soon he'd dug a trench behind the line, and couldn't find any clear patches to serve from. This bothered his motion because he was catching his drag foot in the trench. But since I don't drag I was able to serve reasonably well in the mess he'd created. I went to 4-1 in the fourth, and he caught me. I served to 5-4 and felt very certain when Emmo lost the first three points and was down 0-40—triple match point. Two of them he brushed off, but on the third I caught him with my first topspin lob of the match. He was coming in, and there was no way he could reverse himself quickly to pursue it in the muck. He didn't turn to look, just kept coming to the net and reached for my hand. My old friend had plagued my every step to make this the hardest match of the tournament, 4-6, 8-6, 13-11, 6-4.

LESSON • 23

Hitting Through the Ball

ONE OF THE FINEST MATCHES I've ever seen was on my first trip to Forest Hills in 1956: Dick Savitt, the big, strong American, against Kenny Rosewall, who went on to win the title. They battled it out fantastically on a bad grass court with groundstrokes. Savitt's were booming, and until he tired he had Rosewall in trouble. I was impressed with the way Savitt hit through the ball, getting his body into it and producing a heavy ball.

He prepared well, getting his racket back in plenty of time as soon as he knew whether he'd be hitting a backhand or forehand. Then he got down to the ball, bending his knees, and when he hit the ball he kept his stroke coming with a long follow-through toward the net.

That's hitting through the ball, as opposed to slapping at it or coming across it. Don't stop the groundstroke on impact, but keep following toward the net.

Stay down as you follow through. By coming up (unbending your knees) too soon you raise your chances of hitting the ball long.

Even if you're not too strong, hitting through the ball will give you more power than you thought you had because you're getting your body into the ball. Savitt did it, and into his forties he was still tough for any player in the world for a set or two.

I was cheering for Rosewall that day, my countryman, but I had to salute Savitt, who was twenty-nine, semi-retired from the circuit then, for making Kenny sweat for five sets. Savitt really showed me something about hitting the ball with pace.

He also showed me the value of firm, decisive thinking. Savitt stayed back most of the time, and as I said, the groundstroking was wonderful. Kenny tried to come in when he thought he could, and he was usually frustrated because it was clear that Savitt made up his mind what to do as he approached the ball. If he decided to hit down the line, he held to this and didn't try to suddenly switch if he sensed that Rosewall had it covered.

You see, you must hit your shot, and not worry about the netman. Savitt had played enough so that he wouldn't be ruffled by the sight of his opponent crowding the net. Frequently, at a lower level, you can shake your opponent into errors by merely hurrying to the net.

Conversely, you mustn't take your eye off the ball in order to pay attention to your opponent. Don't let his movements distract you. Decide quickly what you are going to do with the ball, and then hit that shot as though the other court was empty. You're better off to hit the ball well, regardless of where your opponent is, than trying to switch the direction of your shot at the last instant. Even if he smells out the direction and is there, any opponent will have trouble volleying a ball that you hit through. Rosewall had his problems with Savitt.

SEMIFINAL

I BRUSHED MY TEETH BEFORE GOING OUT TO PLAY ARTHUR
Ashe in the semifinals. This isn't a ritual, but I do it more often than
not before a big match. I shave and spend a little more time than usual
combing my hair, whitening my shoes and making sure I look my best.
Feeling fresh in every way and looking good adds to your general confidence and may help you play a little bit better. It doesn't hurt you. The
first good players I knew were Roy Emerson and Mal Anderson, both
Queenslanders. I looked up to them, and one thing I noticed was that
they were so well groomed when they went out to play. I guess I copied
them.

There have been times when tight scheduling made it necessary for
me to go immediately from one match to another, with no time in between to change and freshen up. I'd feel grubby and ill at ease, not in the
right mood to play. I'm sure that in the heat of a match this is soon forgotten, but if my mood is wrong at the outset, it might cost me a couple
of points that I may not get back.

I don't think this is vanity, just a feeling that the right appearance is as
much a part of being prepared as good equipment. I would have made
a lousy hippie.

Ashe remarked that the first match he ever played at Forest Hills was
against me. I didn't remember it, ten years before when he was sixteen
and I was a Wimbledon finalist. He had been extremely nervous, vom-

ited before we started, and recalled the feeling that Forest Hills seemed so huge to him then. I had similar recollections of my introduction to the big league, but it was different for Arthur in that he sensed he was in truly alien territory.

That has changed for him, but in 1959 he must have felt very alone when he edged through the crowd on his way from the clubhouse to the grandstand court to play me. Maybe he felt better when he saw that I wasn't too impressive physically and he could look down on me. The score in 1959 was 6-2, 7-5, 6-2. I guess he got over his nerves after a while and played a good second set.

Newcombe and Roche were in the other semifinal as they had been at Wimbledon. They've been playing each other close for nearly ten years since they were kids in Sydney tournaments; and this time the match would go to Roche in five sets as Newc's serve disintegrated at the climax.

Ashe hadn't won anything since I'd played him at Wimbledon, although his sore elbow was all right again and he had corrected a faulty motion so that he was humming that serve again. It was a tremendous serve, but often that was all there was to Arthur. He was bang-bang, thrash-thrash, and the points came in clusters. Unhappily for him, there were too many stretches of clunk-clunk.

But he had been serving beautifully to blow Manolo Santana and Ken Rosewall off the court on the way to the semis. I knew the crowd would be backing him up noisily, and I hoped I could keep him from getting into the match. Frankly I was up for this more than usual because I was annoyed with Arthur. Some of his statements had gotten to me. He kept saying that his generation—Newc, Roche, Tom Okker, and himself— were catching up with the older generation—me—and would soon be passing. I suppose I shouldn't let that generation talk bother me, but after all Arthur wasn't a kid. Only five years younger than I; and despite all his publicity he hadn't accomplished much, aside from his hot spell in 1968 when he won the U.S. Amateur and U.S. Open in succession.

He should have won the first and third sets. Instead I won in straight sets over two days, 8-6, 6-3, 14-12. Darkness closed us down at 12-12 in the third set, and it took me only two games the next day to finish it.

When I say he should have won those sets, I mean the opportunity was there for a guy who could fasten his mind on the right approach and lock out everything else. Arthur didn't do that—he admitted it —and it took a while before he became a great player, winning Wimbledon in 1975, and winding up in the International Tennis Hall of Fame.

He served for the first set at 5-4 and tried to blast me with big first serves. They didn't go in, and he was left with his second which made me feel better. I was determined to make the returns somehow, leaving the pressure of hitting winners to him. I chipped the ball down the middle. I used a middle-approach against Arthur to take away the angles. Let him hit it as hard as he wants, I thought, and we'll see how far it goes. He'll kill you for a while, but he can't keep it up.

Arthur didn't come close to winning his serve for the set. Four games later I broke him with a neat lob—that most useful and too often neglected shot—and had the set, 8-6.

The second went pretty fast and I was feeling good, keeping aware that Arthur could flare up and become a forest fire. He jumped to a 3-0 lead in the third set. I got it back and we hung together as the games on the stadium scoreboard increased and daylight decreased. I thought I had the break in the seventeenth game, but he slashed a good forehand volley past me. In the next, with me serving at 8-9, Arthur backed me up and had a set point at 30-40. I steadied myself, leaned on the first serve and knocked it into his backhand corner. He couldn't return it. That got me to deuce, and we stayed even to 12-12 when Mike Gibson, the referee, said "enough for today." It was nearly dark.

It was going to be a battle of nerves to see who cracked first. Arthur couldn't afford to, though, or the match was over. I was in a comfortable spot. If I lost the set I was still up 2 to 1. Another strong argument for a revision of the scoring system: These long deuce sets fouled up a tournament and made it more difficult to get the game on television.

Jimmy Van Alen had the answer: the tie-breaker. As the blue-blooded Bolshevik of tennis from the gilded ghetto of Newport, he had been lobbying for a new scoring system—his own VASSS (Van Alen Streamlined Scoring System)—for years. "Down with deuce sets!" was Jimmy's cry.

He was plotting, thinking, an act often considered blasphemous in tennis circles.

I think Jimmy's tie-breaker has merit, and it was installed at the U.S. Open of 1970. It was a best-of-nine-point sequence, called Sudden Death, used at 6-games-all. We players first decided to try tie-breakers during the 1970 Philadelphia Indoor Open with a slight change proposed by me. I felt the tie-breaker should be best-of-12 points, but with a margin of two points. Laver's variation on a theme by Van Alen? Something close to that was eventually approved world-wide.

Of course in 1969, we were on the conventional scoring at Forest Hills, and Ashe had an overnight reprieve. He still had hopes of winning that third set and carrying me into a fifth. He was the last American in the place, and he was the one to be worried. He looked it. Sleeping can come a bit hard when a match is dangling like that.

I didn't want to hang around the apartment thinking about it. We went out for dinner, had a steak and a couple of beers at the Press Box with some friends. We stayed out till eleven and I felt pleasantly tired when we got home. The beers relaxed me and I went right to sleep. I slept only six hours, but my mind hadn't raced because I was relaxed when I went to bed. I felt rested and ready.

The situation further favored me in that Arthur would be serving first. Seldom is anybody completely warmed up to serve an opening game. That's why I frequently chose to receive when I won the toss before a match began. You see this all the time with the pros. Let your opponent serve first, and if he's cold or the least bit shaky, you have the chance to break him right away and jar his confidence.

There was no toss now, we just continued the same order of serving, and it happened that Arthur was first. Arthur had good chances, leading 30-15 on his serve, and 15-30 in the next game on mine. Those are very special points, of course—the points that can take you to game point. These points must be played correctly. By that I mean getting the first serve into play, and hitting your strokes surely—not pushing them and not taking chances either. You have to hit firmly so as not to give your opponent anything too good to work with, but you don't go blasting away.

You hear the expressions "big points" and "big games," and certainly some points and games are bigger than others. Depends on the situation. Sometimes 0-40 is tragic, and other times—if you have a good lead in the match—you might not struggle at 0-40 because you might be tired and figure it would take too much energy to squirm out of that hole.

But if the match is close and you're down on your serve 15-40 or 0-40 you're going to have to make sure of that first serve and not throw away any points. On the other hand, if your opponent is way down on his serve, then you can go for the winner and get that break of serve. To me the first point of every game is very important—it seems to decide which way the game will go most of the time. The first game of the second set is extremely vital. You have to really screw in your concentration here. If you've won the first set, it's common to have a letdown as the second begins. If you've lost the first set, you've got to charge back into the match. In an even match the eighth game is very big. If you're serving at 4-3 you play consistently—you must hold. No fancy stuff. If your opponent serves at 3-4, here's where you dig in to break, so that you'll be serving for the set. You must return serve, cut down on your backswing, block the ball back-do anything to keep it in play.

Naturally when you're in a deuce set the same tactics apply. But Arthur didn't serve well when he should have held from 30-15. He double faulted by stepping on the baseline for a foot fault, and it was 30-all. He flubbed easy volleys and within a minute his opportunity to go up 13-12 vanished.

I now had the serve at 13-12, and I made certain the first serve went in. Plenty of spin, medium speed. Even though I got behind 15-30, I held to my philosophy: let him hit winners if he can. It was up to him and he couldn't.

One champion was dead and a new champion was in the final.

More rain. It was Monday, overseen by a bleak sky whose lavender clouds were popping. We were twenty-four hours past the day set for Mary and me to collaborate on a coast-to-coast double. The baby was late. Rain delayed my final. God wasn't cooperating.

LESSON • 24

Chipping and the Middle Approach

A CHIP IS NOT A CHOP, and a chop isn't seen much anymore, although the champions of days before my era like George Lott (one of the great doubles players) insisted that players overlooked a useful stroke. A chop is just that—a sort of karate chop, a hard straight-down slice. It puts back-spin on the ball and can give lesser players problems if hit well. The last two people I remember using it were Margaret duPont and Shirley Fry when I was just coming up. It seemed to trouble some of their female opponents.

But a chip—there's a shot you need, a gliding kind of slice that is quite a good return against a man who charges the net. This is because the ball skims the net and drops at the net-rusher's feet. It is a softly hit shot, a slice just meeting the ball, sending it sliding nicely crosscourt and making your opponent bend low for the ball. Tough to volley a ball like that. You can direct a chip well, but I don't think there's much accuracy to a chop. (Wallace Johnson, another old-timer who nearly beat Tilden with chops, would disagree.)

To chip, you just meet the ball with the racket beveled below the ball. There's hardly any follow-through. A good return for doubles, of course, when the server is generally always coming to the net.

Now, if your opponent is gobbling up your crosscourt chips, or any crosscourt shots, you can remove that possibility by using the middle theory: hitting the ball down the center of the court. This can disturb a player who likes to hit balls wide to either side of him. If you can keep the ball deep when you hit it down the center, your opponent can't hit down the lines or angle the ball off the way he might with crosscourts.

It's not a bad idea to approach the net behind a shot down the middle, as long as it's deep. You're taking away the angle with this approach.

If the guy keeps beating you to death, you might try lobbing—which is the next lesson.

25

GRAND SLAM

TONY ROCHE AND I HAD COME A LONG WAY OUT OF THE
Outback to play for the U.S. Open Championship and the biggest prize
in tennis, $16,000.

"You could buy your hometown for sixteen grand and put it in a mu-
seum as the Roche birthplace," a reporter said to Tony.

"Might need a bit more," replied Tony, whose background was so
much like mine. Tarcutta, the sheep town, wasn't any livelier than Marlborough, the cattle town where I spent my early days. My Dad had been
the town butcher for a while - as was Tony's.

We were sitting around the locker room, talking to the writers because the start of our match was put off by the rain. Didn't look like
we'd play that day, but there were 4,000 hardy people under umbrellas
and ponchos waiting for us in the stadium. Not much of a crowd for a
national final, but considering the day, we were pleased that many had
come on this waterlogged Monday.

Even worse from the customers' point of view was the scheduling of
the women's doubles final to precede Tony and me. Much loud complaining emanated from the seats, especially when a patchwork team
of Francoise Durr and the seemingly used-up Darlene Hard ineptly
lost the first eight games to highly favored Margaret Court and Virginia Wade. "Get 'em out of here!" was the sentiment. But instead of
more rain, lightning struck in the form of a phenomenal recovery.

Hard, 33, once a U.S. champ and wondrous doubles player, but by then a teaching pro, reached back a decade to show why she became a Hall of Famer. Durr, also a Hall of Famer-to-be, had never met Hard before, but they suddenly blended like ice cream and cake to win 0-6, 6-4, 6-4. A nice bit of trimming on my day.

On the wall behind the couch where Tony and I sat were photos of the men who had won the U.S. Championship since 1915 when the tournament broke away from its status as a society diversion in Newport and moved to New York to become a major sporting event. My picture was there, from 1962. Tony wanted to be on that wall.

Tony was saying to a reporter, "Laver played me in one of his last amateur matches in 1962 when I was just a kid coming up; I gave him a good go in Melbourne, but he had other things on his mind. The Davis Cup was coming up and he was turning pro. He was a hero of mine, left-handed, you know, and a country boy like me.

"I had been hoping he'd win the Grand Slam. I heard about it on the TV that comes out of Wagga Wagga. Then I read about it a couple of days later. The Sydney papers took a while to get to Tarcutta.

"It's a bit different between us now. I had one chance to stop him, and I might have done it in Brisbane except for a bad call. I'll never forget that one."

No reason why Tony should; neither will I.

For the hundredth or so time we were asked to figure out how our rivalry stood. Tony kept better track of it than I did—probably because he was leading. Overall he was ahead six wins to four. He had a good edge for the year (5-3), but apart from the New Zealand Open, he hadn't beaten me in a big one. Three of his wins had come in small pro tournaments. My wins over him had been in the Australian and Philadelphia Opens.

I talked to Mary on the phone. She felt fine, but was puzzled that the baby hadn't come, saying, "Now, it'll be just my luck to go into labor while your match is on TV."

It didn't happen. I was the only one in the family laboring that afternoon when the rain let up long enough to allow us to get started. The court was greasy, but somehow slow, which favored me because Tony's slice didn't take. Movement was tough, and this was a break for me because Tony decided not to put on spikes. He figured his strained thigh muscles would be jarred by the quick stops you make in spikes, possibly bringing on a cramp.

That first set was one of the strangest I've ever played. I should have won it and deserved to lose it. I got what I deserved and Tony took it 9-7, just took it right away from me after I'd been serving for the set at 5-3. He did it with beautiful backhands. I was sloshing and slipping around, and a couple of times I had asked referee Mike Gibson for permission to put on my spiked shoes. I'd wanted to begin the match in them, but he'd refused. After that game, Mike said all right. It meant all the difference to me.

Tony immediately won his serve in four points, but I felt surer on my feet and I knew I'd get going. Especially when I stopped him two points short of the set to keep even at 6-6.

But I wasn't so sure when I lost that first set anyway. I'd had a lot of luck during the year, and I wondered if it had run out at last.

Although I'd worn spikes here and there throughout my career, the occasions were so rare during my professional days that they took some getting used to. You consciously changed your movements at first. Picked up your feet. No sliding. It was a new sensation until you were re-accustomed to them.

The slight uncertainty of moving in spikes was gone for good in the first game of the second set when I came through with a big serve at the crucial point of the match. With the first set his, and the pressure on me, Tony got me down 30-40 on my serve. One more point and he'd be up a set and a break, a pretty good edge in that mush.

We both knew this was a huge point. He took his time getting ready to return, and I did the same lining up—not overly so, maybe not even noticeable to the crowd, but we had to be right for this one. I was righter. I threw myself into the serve, and sliced it wide to his forehand. It didn't come back. He barely touched it, and I could tell it pained him to miss the opportunity. You don't get too many break-point chances on grass—

215

It was a soggy – but satisfying – win at the 1969 U.S. Open, which clinched the Grand Slam. Wearing spikes on the wet grass court gave me an advantage over Tony Roche, who was afraid to use them and was unable to counter my better shots in his sneakers.

and he didn't have another.

It wouldn't be apparent for a while, but the match turned upside down right there. I won the game and began hitting harder and harder as I got surer of my footing. Then I won the next and the next—five straight. From that break-point chance in the first game, Tony managed to win only five of the last 23 games. He came all apart as I wrapped him up, 7-9, 6-1, 6-2, 6-2. Not even a rain delay of a half-hour at the beginning of the third set could rust my concentration or help him pull his together.

Unlike 1962, I had control of myself all through the final match of the Grand Slam. I was never dazed as I had been against Emmo seven years before during a brief case of nerves down the stretch.

Serving match game, I opened with an ace. I knew what I was about, and wasn't going to let Tony breathe. It was 40-0 when I did try to end with a grand-slamming flourish on a forehand volley. I blew it. A minor disappointment not to be able to score with a put-away as I had on the championship point at Wimbledon.

It fell to Tony to lose it with a forehand that he hit long. Both of us were glad it was over. Afraid to use spikes, he'd been victimized in sneakers, unable to counteract my better shots, including a number of very good lobs. It was one of my best days with the lob, always a useful shot, but even more damaging that day when running was tough.

Not enough ordinary players realize the value of the lob, and I guess I didn't until I became a seasoned pro. It's much more than a desperation measure. As an amateur, even if the odds were against my making a shot, I'd usually let fly anyway. When I became a pro, I couldn't risk throwing away points like that because the opposition was equal or better. This meant I had to be realistic. If my chances of making a shot from a difficult position were doubtful, I found you seldom get hurt with a lob.

But there were no more lobs to be hit. Not one more stroke on a chase that began God knows how many strokes ago in Brisbane when I hit the first serve to a fellow I wouldn't know if he walked into the room, Massimo di Domenico. The others I knew pretty well . . . Andres . . . Arthur . . . Emmo . . . Tony . . . Newc . . . Dennis . . . Kenny . . . Okker . . . Smith.

There were 1,005 games in 26 Grand Slam matches, and now it was all over.

I had won 30 straight matches since losing to Newcombe in June, the week before Wimbledon, the longest I'd ever gone without a defeat. Here it was September 9—and no letdown yet. It would come soon, in the second round of the Pacific Southwest Open in Los Angeles, Ray Moore ending the streak at 31. I hardly noticed.

Now the applause was coming through to me as I loped toward the net and Tony. Everything was coming through. My concentration burst, flooding my mind with a hundred things.

How was Mary? I wanted to call and see, and ask if she'd watched the match on TV, and wasn't it wonderful to have made the Grand Slam— and the $16,000? During the phone conversation she would say, "You know, Rod, that's the first time you've mentioned the Grand Slam all year. I'm glad there was something about it in the papers to alert me." Then we laughed.

Yes, I'd have to find a phone, but first there would be the TV interview and the press conference.

I was thinking about the evening ahead, too. John McDonald would be inviting people to the victory party. Mustn't overlook anyone, or fail to put in enough beer and champagne. And some food, too.

I'd be on the first plane tomorrow, but we should have a glass or two tonight to reflect on this thing properly. I was very thirsty.

I thought about the party they gave me in Brisbane when I got home after the first Grand Slam. Two-pint mugs were the weapons and they kept loading them endlessly. It's an Aussie custom at those affairs that the guest of honor drains his mug at every toast. For the toasts they go through the alphabet, one toast for every letter—A to Z. They may have got to Z, but I'm still waiting to hear it. Or L for that matter.

I wasn't that thirsty.

Tony and I were at the net and he was holding out his hand. Suddenly I was in the air. What's this? I was leaping the net in the classic fashion. I must have gotten high just thinking about that party in Brisbane.

This wasn't me. I hadn't jumped a net in a dozen years. I thought it a bit show-offish for one thing. I feel humble about beating a man; I don't want to be one of those bloody gloating high-jumpers who can't control his emotions. And possibly I've always been self-conscious, afraid to look the fool as I had that 1957 afternoon in Adelaide after I beat Herbie Flam. I was nineteen, giddy at my first victory over a world class player, a U.S. Davis Cupper, who ranked No. 4 in the amateur game. I really didn't know where I was that day. In mid leap I caught my foot on the net and went on my face. Flam thought I'd fractured my skull—a minute too late for him—and the giggles came rolling down from the grandstand. I felt like the fighter who takes off his robe to discover he's forgotten his trunks.

Never again, I promised myself. I would be a dignified winner and loser.

But here I was bounding about like a kangaroo with spring fever, making it over the net to shake with Tony. Something inside me had released the built-in restrainers and said the hell with poise.

Where was dignity? Oh, well, where was the check for sixteen grand?

And where was the phone? This would be a very pleasant call to the West Coast. I went through the interviews and then found a pay phone behind the press stand. At that moment, I also found out something vital to twentieth-century man: you may have the Grand Slam; you may have just come from a televised appearance in millions of homes; and you may even be clutching $16,000 in your omnipotent left hand. But none of this will get you a dial tone if you don't have a dime.

I had everything I wanted but to hear my wife's voice, and I couldn't have that without ten cents. Sixteen thousand dollars—but not a dime in hand. For the first time all afternoon, I panicked. Only for a couple of seconds, until a newspaperman nearby loaned me a dime. He looked at the check and figured I was good for it.

LESSON • 25

The Lob and the Answer

IN THE U.S. DOUBLES of 1967 at Boston, my usual doubles partner Roy Emerson was in a bad way. (He might have been worse off if I'd been there, but I was a pro by then and he was still an amateur.) The grass courts were mucky, the ball wouldn't bounce; Roy had a bad back, and he was playing with an unfamiliar partner, Ronnie Barnes. "You're going to see more lobs in this match than you've seen in a lifetime," Emmo told a reporter.

And that's the way the tournament went for him: he kept lobbing, and he and Barnes kept winning, until finally Emmo broke down in a 105-game quarterfinal. Because of the low bounce and his back, Emmo couldn't get down to the ball to make the stroke he wanted, so he lifted everything much of the time, and it was pretty effective, even against those topflight players.

This was an odd case, but it is a fact that none of us good players, myself included, use the lob often enough. It can wreak havoc, in singles as well as doubles.

You have the defensive lob and the attacking lob. Kenny Rosewall was probably the most effective with the attacking lob, which is a shot with low trajectory. You're actually wrong-footing the person who's coming to net. He's approaching, and at the last second you hit under the ball and lift it. It doesn't have to be too high, but if you can pitch it just over his head, you'll catch him off balance and he won't be able to do much with it. That opens the court for your next shot. Rosewall still caught me with it, even though I'd seen it often. He disguised it so well, and the element of surprise was as important as how well you hit the shot.

Hit the attacking lob over to the backhand side. Nobody handles a high backhand very well, and if the fellow runs around it to hit a proper smash then the court is really opened up.

When you're out of position and need time to get straightened around, the defensive lob is the shot: up high, 50 or 60 feet.

Strangely, a lot of club players omit the lob from their repertory. They seem to be embarrassed by it, as though it's some sort of soft blooper that isn't quite manly. Rubbish. A lob not only gives you time to get into position, it poses a "think" ball for your opponent. He has time to think too much as that ball rises slowly and then descends on him during a tight match. Nobody hits overheads well for too long if the lobs are deep and well placed.

Fellows like Ion Tiriac and Ilie Nastase, the Romanians, made themselves one of the world's finest doubles teams by tossing up lob after maddening lob. In doubles, you can break down your opponents' teamwork with lobs.

One of the most deadly lobs is the topspin lob, and Spain's Manolo Santana was the first player I ever saw hit this ball well and attack with it. When the ball strikes the court it runs away. It's a difficult shot to make. You cock your wrist, as for other topspin shots, and hit up and over the ball with a snap of the wrist. Try it out in practice, and see if it comes to you. It's terrific if you can get it working. Your opponent will come to realize that he can't afford to let it drop. And a top-spinning ball is tougher to hit out of the air, so you have an additional psychological edge if you can perfect this shot.

You can fight lobs with lobs, and see whose patience erodes first. Or you can discourage them with sound smashing. If the lob is extremely high, or it's a windy day and the ball is bobbing, you may want to let the ball bounce before smashing it.

Obviously, if you allow the ball to bounce, you're permitting your opponent more time to deal with your smash.

It's best to smash the ball out of the air. Get side on to the net, and hum to yourself that folk tune, "If I had a hammer . . ."

Seriously, that's the stroke you want—hammering a nail into the wall. Not too much backswing. Imagine the ball is a nail at the highest point you can reach. And pound it with a hard, downward stroke. I like to leave my feet to throw my body behind the stroke. That takes good timing. Put away a few smashes and you'll dishearten the lobber. I hope.

LIFE AFTER TWO GRAND SLAMS

WHEN YOU HAVE TO WALK THROUGH ANKLE-DEEP SLUSH to get from your hotel to the court, you know you're in the wrong place. I knew it even more the next morning when I paid my hotel bill. It was one of those rare occasions that I hadn't made enough playing to cover the bill. I opened the 1970 season on January 23 a loser, dropping a five-set match in New York's Madison Square Garden to Pancho Gonzalez. It hurt for a lot of reasons. This was a winner-take-all match for $10,000, and the crowd, 14,671, was the largest I'd ever played for in the United States. Since I held a 2-1 lead in sets and should have won in the fourth, I couldn't be too pleased, especially losing that way to Pancho, 7-5, 3-6, 2-6, 6-3, 6-2. And it was the first five-set match I could remember losing.

However, how can I begrudge anything to the aged the miracle worker Pancho? He stayed in the big league as a factor longer than anyone else. Three months before his 44th birthday in 1972, he beat 24-year-old French Davis Cupper, Georges Goven from two sets down, 3-6, 4-6, 6-3, 6-4, 6-2, to win Des Moines, Iowa. That year – four years after his anointing for the Hall of Fame -- he was No. 9 in the U.S., the oldest (or should I say the most mature?) to rank so loftily. Losing all those years (1950 – 1967) of jousting for major titles, banned as a renegade pro, he still managed to fit into the world top ten two decades after his first entries: Nos. 3 and 1, 1948-49, and Nos. 10 and 6 in 1968-69.

Was my early loss to Gonzalez a bad omen for the year that lay ahead, a year in which I would lose both my Wimbledon and Forest Hills titles? Some people might think so, but I don't think that way.

There were a couple of bad moments for me in 1970—the fourth-round defeat by Roger Taylor at Wimbledon, and the fourth-round loss to Dennis Ralston at Forest Hills. But I couldn't consider it a bad year. After all I won fourteen tournaments, and nobody else came close to that. My prize money was $201,453, a financial record for the game, raising me to $714,230 for eight years as a pro.

But there were no regrets. I had a good run at Wimbledon—an unprecedented 31-straight match wins before Roger Taylor caught me. It was a sour afternoon for me, but Roger deserved full credit. He lost the first set and kept plugging. When he had his chances he made the most of them and got better. He kept the pressure on me so that I couldn't recover. At match point I was serving. Clunk-clunk . . . two balls into the net. What a way to go, but it does tell you that it can happen even at Wimbledon. You may have even done it yourself, friend.

I hadn't been put out of Wimbledon so early since 1958. "Now we could go out and enjoy ourselves," Mary told the newspapermen. It was a nice chins-up line.

The U.S. Open at Forest Hills was different. I played better than I had against Taylor, but Ralston played what several critics described as "the match of his life."

He won the first two sets. I struggled to win the next two. It was then that I confronted a changed Ralston, a cool character. In other years, he folded when he and I reached the crisis. Not this time. Nothing stays the same, I guess, and I've had to revise my estimate of Ralston. I had my opportunities. On a break-point against him in the fifth set, I hit a forehand return as well as I can, right on his toes. Miraculously, he scooped out a backhand half-volley that won him the point.

That shot was the match, we agreed. In 1969, I doubt that he would have made that shot.

Afterward, Denny was pleased but gracious. He didn't gloat, "See! How about that one!" at the several reporters and columnists whose standard line had been: "Ralston doesn't win the big ones." He said some nice things about me that seemed to sum up the 1970 season as well.

"I don't think losing Wimbledon and here means the Rocket has slipped," Denny said. "But I don't think he or anybody else can dominate the world the way he did in 1969. It was improbable that he would win the Grand Slam again. With everybody playing for money and the number of good players increasing, it's a whole new world."

I had no thought of another Grand Slam in 1970, simply because our pro group (Lamar Hunt's World Championship Tennis, which took over the MacCall-Podesta operation) did not enter the Australian or French Opens. The deal wasn't right. There were in 1970 what I consider the Top 15 tournaments, and they were won by nine different men: Australian (Arthur Ashe); Philadelphia Indoor Open (Laver); U.S. Indoor Open (Ilie Nastase); Dunlop Open, Sydney (Laver); South African Open (Laver); Italian Open (Nastase); French Open (Jan Kodes); Wimbledon (John Newcombe); U.S. Pro (Tony Roche); West German Open (Tom Okker); U.S. Open (Ken Rosewall); Pacific Southwest Open (Laver); Paris Indoor Open (Ashe); Embassy Indoor Open, London (Laver); Stockholm Indoor Open (Stan Smith).

I entered eleven, won six. The variety of winners was good for tennis, and showed how strong the men's field had become. Maybe no man will make a Grand Slam again, but the very fact that some people think it's out of the question makes it more alluring. The Grand Slam goal put a zest and drive into me for 1969, and still warms me.

While Forest Hills eluded me in 1970, I'm sure everybody was pleased with the outcome: Kenny Rosewall winning his biggest prize at age thirty-five. He played in such a rejuvenated way that it's clear he would be tough into his forties, like Pancho. And that made me still just a kid, right?

Another youngster, Roy Emerson, and I got to the doubles final at Forest Hills, and I was sure I'd salvage one title. We were up against Niki Pilic, the Croat, and Pierre Barthes, the Frenchman, who had never won anything together. They beat us. I guess that figured, the way things had gone at Wimbledon and Forest Hills. I was a little annoyed. I wanted to win something in that place. We walked over to the platform where

Charlie Tucker, president of the West Side Tennis Club, was awarding the prizes. First he handed Pilic and Barthes their checks for $1,500 apiece and little gold balls, the latter emblematic of a U.S. championship. Then he handed us the silver balls that the runners-up get, along with checks for $1,000. I guess I didn't look too happy, and Emmo looked over at me and gave me one of his golden grins—enhanced by all the gold in his front teeth.

"Well, Rocket," he said, "at least they didn't give us a kick in the ass."

I had to laugh. Emmo was so right. As long as you could swing your racket and play this game, win or lose, you didn't have much kick coming.

The kicks aimed at me continued to come, annoyingly, from light-footed Kenny Rosewall. As our rivalry ran into the 1970s and began to get more and more attention, it became known as "The Rod and Kenny Show," and the ending was almost always happy for me. We played a lot of terrific matches, most of them tournament finals, and during 1970-71-72 Kenny managed to win only three of fourteen.

Only? Damn him, two he came through in what were only the biggest, financially, that any tennis players had ever been involved in. And they came within six months of each other: the finals of a new competition called the World Championship of Tennis, staged in playrooms selected by promoter Lamar Hunt in his hometown, Dallas, and arranged by his director, Mike Davies.

Big D meant Bigger Dollars than we could imagine: $50,000 to the winner of the first-place match and $20,000 to the runner-up. Eight players came to Dallas for the $100,000 shootout, and both times Rosewall took the fifty grand and ran to Sydney, leaving me feeling mugged and morose.

Near the close of the 1970 season, at Forest Hills, Lamar Hunt, Al Hill, Jr., and Davies—the triumvirate atop World Championship Tennis—announced their new scheme for pro tennis, which would be called the World Championship of Tennis. WCT was ready to pull the game together professionally after many false starts by many promoters, including the most recent by George MacCall with my old outfit, National Tennis League, and Dave Dixon, Hunt's first partner in WCT. Hunt and his nephew, Hill, had bought out MacCall and hired as executive director Welshman Davies, an ex-British Davis Cupper and colleague of mine during earlier helter-skelter touring days. Little Al Hill (as distinguished from Big Al, his father, a good senior player) had been a regular on the tennis varsity at powerhouse Trinity University in San Antonio, and of course Davies had been in tennis all his life. While Lamar's critics within the hostile ILTF (International Lawn Tennis Federation) kept feeling—and hoping—he'd lose interest in tennis and fade away to his other sporting interests, his zest for our game and WCT increased. He had a house in Dallas that made Versailles look like a tenement, and working hard on the backyard court, he had become a decent hacker. There was a time when Dixon was floundering with WCT and the game hadn't really hooked Lamar, that he might have backed off and forgotten it. But Lamar's wasn't a quitter. He was determined to make something of pro tennis, as he did of the American Football League, and to my mind, his presence had been the single most important factor in the incredible advance of the game.

In presenting WCT's World Championship of Tennis format, Lamar felt that pro tennis needed a logical progression toward a world championship, a season of clearly defined competitions that would lead to a title playoff embracing the leaders over the season. This wasn't an original idea for tennis. Jack Kramer had devised the Grand Prix, which started in 1970, administered by the ILTF and injecting a good deal of the sponsor's (Pepsi Cola) money into the game. You were awarded points on the basis of results in Grand Prix tournaments, and the leading points winners gathered for a Masters Playoff which that year was a six-man round robin in Tokyo. Although Stan Smith and I finished the playoff with identical 4-1 records, I was accorded second place because my loss was to him.

The trouble with the Grand Prix was its unwieldiness and inequities. There were too many tournaments, and the value of points varied from tournament to tournament, often incomprehensibly. It was chaotically operated, and clearly it was being used by the anti-Hunt ILTF as a means of trying to drive WCT out of business. The ILTF theory was that if Grand Prix events could provide enough prize money, then players wouldn't be tempted to sign contracts with the enemy, Hunt. To me, the political struggle had come down to professionalism vs. amateurism.

Anyway, it was obvious that WCT couldn't promote a meaningful pro circuit while shackled by ILTF regulations and ineptness. Hunt, Hill and Davies decided to set up the World Championship of Tennis entirely apart from the ILTF, manned by 32 players who, ideally, would be the top 32 in the world. A poll of tennis writers around the world selected the 32, with me at No. 1. A few of the 32 chose not to sign with WCT—Stan Smith couldn't because he was serving in the U.S. Army— but the majority did, and the roster was filled by those who came next in the balloting.

WCT scheduled this troupe to play twenty $50,000 tournaments in America and eight other countries around the world. Prize money and points would be awarded uniformly. "We're building an entirely new million-dollar competition, strictly professional, to determine the professional champion of the world," said Lamar. So it was.

We opened in Philadelphia in 1971 at the Spectrum where John Newcombe beat me in the final for the $10,000 first prize that was standard in the WCT tourneys. Everywhere we went the crowds were gratifyingly large and the publicity splendid. The schedule covered ten months, and we were playing other tournaments, too, like Wimbledon, where I lost in the quarters to a sizzling Tom Gorman. One tournament in the WC of T was rained out, so we had nineteen in all and nine different winners, pretty good balance. Newcombe, Rosewall and I won four apiece, and by the time I beat Arthur Ashe to win the Italian Indoor, the last leg at Bologna in November, I was at the head of the class.

Following me in the standings were Tom Okker, Rosewall, Cliff Drysdale, Ashe, Newcombe, Marty Riessen and Bob Lutz—the eight who qualified for the $100,000 playoff. The first two rounds were played at Houston, where I beat Lutz and Ashe, and Kenny stunned Newcombe and wiped out Okker.

Ashe and I had a good four-set match, but it was the same old result: going into the 1973 season, Arthur still hadn't beaten me. The victory was worth $20,000 to me by assuring me of at least second place and raising my prize money for 1971 to a record of $292,717. I had been the first tennis player to earn over $200,000 on the court; if I could beat Kenny I'd be the first over $300,000. Meanwhile, as Arthur and I were shaking hands, the WCT press agent Ron Bookman was announcing to the press at Hofheinz Pavilion: "Rod Laver has become the first millionaire in tennis history. With today's win his prize money for nine years as a pro is $1,006,947."

Mary, who'd been sitting in the row in front of the press, turned around and smiled at Bookman: "Ron, would you read those figures again? There's a very nice ring to them."

Bookman obliged, "One - oh - oh - six - nine - four - seven."

It had a lilt to it, all right, and was good for publicity purposes. But the figure hardly made me a millionaire. I'm sure you're aware of taxes and the fact that it has cost something to live in the years between 1963 and today. I hope this doesn't sound too materialistic—still, those figures let me know I've been successful at what I set out to do.

Nobody would rather deflate a millionaire and steal some of his money than Kenny Rosewall (who crossed the million mark himself during the summer of '72, in his sixteenth professional season).

Neil Armstrong, the moon-tripping astronaut, was among the 8,700 spectators in the Dallas Memorial Auditorium in 1971. He showed up to present the huge trophy, and I wondered if Armstrong ever got as high in his rocket as Rosewall sometimes does on a tennis court. It was one of those stratospheric days for Kenny as he whipped me, 6-4, 1-6, 7-6 (7-3), 7-6 (7-4). As you can tell by the score, I had a good shot at it, losing two tie-breakers. But Kenny was way up emotionally, and he played those tense tie-breakers particularly well. I think I lost it in the third set as he served at 3–3. It was a five-deuce game with five break points for me. I played it a little too safe. Maybe $50,000 on a match put a few more twitches in there and restrained me a little. When he escaped from that game he seemed to get looser, and his backhand and half-volleys got sharper.

He came down long enough to hug the trophy, pocket the check plus a diamond ring that annually goes to the champ, a sports car thrown in by a TV sponsor and a diamond bracelet for his wife, Wilma. I had $20,000 and—if it was possible—added respect for the little nuisance.

Thus ended a season that began with the brightest tournament concept yet for pro tennis as well as an event I called "The Rod Laver Benefit." That's not what Fred Podesta, the promoter, called it, but he might as well have because Laver was the only one who made any money out of it. The "Benefit" was a $210,000 series of one-night stands across the U.S. actually named the Tennis Champions Classic. Rosewall and I launched the series at Madison Square Garden in New York, and the idea was that the winner would take $10,000, the loser nothing, and at the next stop another pro would appear to challenge the winner. I loved it. I don't think I ever sent Podesta a thank-you note, but, Fred, here's a capitalized Thank You in print. Thirteen matches I played and thirteen matches I won, extracting $160,000 of Podesta's $210,000.

Getting myself into fantastic shape before the trek began, I found myself back in the old days of one-nighters in varying arenas. I had a good night right away to take care of Rosewall, and then I had a lineup of guys who weren't quite used to this sort of bouncing: Newcombe, Roche, Emerson, Ashe, Okker, Ashe, again, Taylor, Okker again, Ralston and Emerson again. Eleven matches—$110,000. Like plucking mangos from the trees at home in Queensland. Nobody was quite sure how Podesta decided who the next opponent would be, but we wound up with a four-man lineup for a semifinal and final at Madison Square Garden. I beat Ralston for $15,000 in one semi and Okker took Emerson in the other. Finally, I overwhelmed Tiny Tom, 6-5, 6–2, 6–1 for $35,000 more.

The year had hardly begun and I had won more than any other player up to that time except Laver. I guess you think I was greedy in playing out the rest of the season. Only Roche had a real chance at me, holding a match point in grimy Boston Garden where I'd made my U.S. pro debut, losing to Barry MacKay eight years before.

That crowd in Boston told me something: the Tennis Champions Classic was a mistake. Just as when I'd faced MacKay and pro tennis was a zero, there were about 2,000 customers in a building holding 13,000. They looked like the same people, left over from 1963—the hard core you could expect to show up at any tennis event. Tennis was appealing to a wider audience than that hard core, but for the one-nighters only the core corps bothered to stop by. One-nighters were dead, and the Classic couldn't revive them or anything but my savings account. Regardless of the money involved, the Classic seemed an exhibition. The customers wanted tournaments.

For the fourth straight year, I was over $100,000 in prize money for 1972. Barely ($100,200). It was an extraordinary year—for me, for our game—and each year improved on the one before. This may sound strange when you consider that I didn't win a major championship, was excluded from Wimbledon, and for the first time in nearly a decade, wasn't generally regarded as the No. 1 player in this world.

Yet it was exhilarating because so many positive things happened: American network TV at last discovered tennis; WCT and the ILTF made peace, and WCT expanded; after numerous failures we formed a players union, ATP (Association of Tennis Professionals) that could mean as much to tennis as the PGA has meant to golfers. And at the end of the year Dr. Omar Fareed diagnosed my back trouble that had knocked me out for three-and-a-half months after my Forest Hills loss to Cliff Richey, as a spinal inflammation. The pill Omar gave me might get me blacklisted at Churchill Downs since it contained butazolydin (allegedly the drug that cost Dancer's Image his Derby triumph in 1968). But I didn't want to win the Kentucky Derby, just half a dozen or so tennis tournaments a year.

I'd better not overlook the progress made by the women in 1972, led by the Czarina, Gladys Heldman, head of their hastily-concocted union (the Women's International Tennis Federation), and by fiery Billie Jean King. I was astounded by the money that poured into their side of the game. Billie Jean made $117,000 in 1971 and $113,200 in 1972. Did I think I'd live long enough to be out-earned by a woman in my line of work? It would have been too preposterous to even think about. The women did an admirable job in opening up new territories for the game.

They settled on a new union in 1973 that has lasted, the WTA (Women's Tennis Association), the year that Billie Jean stood up for the so-called weaker sex by making pork chops out of His Piggishness, Bobby Riggs, at Houston. Although no title was in the balance, the "Battle of the Sexes" caught on, luring 30,472 to the Astrodome, resounding to this day. Bobby, 55, was an old guy baiting young women in gender warfare. Having beaten a nerves-paralyzed Margaret Court in the "Mother's Day Massacre," he threw a challenge at Wimbledon champ King, 29, who batted it right back with her racket, 6-4, 6-3, 6-3. Suddenly, he looked like a guy whose foremost triumph, Wimbledon, 1939, was 34 years in the past. Womankind was saved.

The biggest disappointment of my career came in 1972: another defeat by Rosewall in the WC of T final in May. Nevertheless, in retrospect, it had its positive aspects, too. Gene Ward in his column in the *New York Daily News* appraised that three-hour-and-thirty-four-minute installment of "The Rod and Kenny Show" as the greatest tennis match ever played. Takes in a few tennis matches, and, though I'm grateful for that opinion of a writer who has watched top tennis for forty years, I'm not sure I'd agree with Gene. I even feel Kenny and I had played some that were better. But, did anyone else but Kenny and I know?

The occasion, in assigning greatness, is all-important. Don Budge probably played better matches than his five-set epic triumph over Gottfried von Cramm in the Davis Cup semifinal of 1937, but the situation and the stakes, the attention paid by the press and public, set that one above the others. You couldn't beat the setting: Wimbledon's Centre Court.

Well, Kenny and I had never played for so many people. There were 8,500 filling chummy Moody Coliseum at Dallas, but there were countless millions of living-room types freeloading at their screens. On that Sunday afternoon, May 14, somebody who did try to count the watchers (a TV ratings maker) stated that our match outdrew the pro basketball playoffs on another channel and the pro hockey playoffs on yet another. The estimate was 21.3 million viewers for "The R & K Show," which ran well over its allotted time on 170 NBC stations and yet they almost missed the climax.

As the match wound through the tense fifth set, hotter and tighter, Jim Simpson and Bud, the babblers in the NBC-TV booth, got a discouraging message from director Ted Nathanson. Orders from network headquarters in New York. They were to be prepared to apologize to viewers just before the broadcast was cut off at 6 PM eastern time. It was clearly going to run into the 6 o'clock news, and the Sunday 6 o'clock news was sancrosanct at NBC. Untouchable. How could they do that to Kenny and me – and the audience? Easily.

Jim and Bud, working their first season as NBC's tennis commentary team, were dismayed at the thought of deserting this lalapalooza. But the next time they heard from Nathanson through their headphones, at 5:55, his voice had gone from sour to sprightly. 'Keep going fellows – we're on to the end. No apology necessary.'

Whoever the genius-in-charge was at 30 Rock that evening, he wasn't going to abandon something this good and compelling. Kenny and I not only beat up on each other but also the mighty 6 o'clock news. Close call, but to hell with the news and the sponsors -- our show went on.

The greatness of this match was that it had everything: a huge title, comebacks by both of us, spectacular shotmaking, tension, heavy money, a steady buildup to an unbelievable finish. I had to save a match point to take myself to a winning position . . . and when the match was on my racket, Kenny snatched it off. Dead on his feet, he somehow won the last four points to take the second tie-breaker, the title, the $50,000 and the other baubles again, 4-6, 6-0, 6-3, 6-7 (3-7), 7-6 (7-5)

It was as competitive as a sporting contest can be as we ran miles and hit thousands of shots, and I guess that's what held hordes of viewers who knew nothing about tennis.

I think if one match can be said to have made tennis in the United States, this was it. I know it made me more well known than I could imagine, and I don't think the full impact in promoting the game has been felt. It was a chunk of sporting history, and I was part of it, helped make it. That much makes me glow when I think about it. Then I have to think about those two supernatural Rosewall backhands that beat me—made me a loser by just two points—and I know it was The Disappointment of my career.

In talking to the networks, Barry Frank, the TV agent for WCT, confirmed what he suspected: the pros would have to alter their year to get on camera. The 1971 final had been televised on a limited scale but was lost in November football coverage, just as the U.S. Open is swamped by baseball and football in September. If WCT could conclude its year in May, the networks would take a chance. NBC took a package deal of eight live tournaments, and CBS put on a taped series of fifteen tournaments called the CBS Classic, which ran in the spring and summer.

In order to stage a WC of T for 1972, Mike Davies made up a winter-spring schedule of ten tournaments plus the $100,000 playoffs in May. Eight of those were televised. Davies wanted a twenty-tournament basis for deciding which eight would play for the most serious money, as in 1971. To arrange that, he stipulated that points for the last ten tournaments of 1971 would count in a 1971–72 season. When we resumed playing in February 1972 we already had a half season on our records. From 1973 on, the WCT season is to be only eleven tournaments in length, from January through May, but there would be two groups of 32, with four to qualify from each group for the playoffs.

I was off to a fine start, winning the first three tournaments, five of the ten, and finishing on top of the points standings once more. Next came Rosewall, Okker, Drysdale, Riessen, Ashe, Lutz and Newcombe – the same faces as 1971 though in different order. After I beat Newc and Riessen, and Kenny took Lutz and Ashe, it was our show once more.

All I can say about that incredible final was it took so many twists that I still can't understand how I lost. Two points. I never came so close and lost. But I had my chances and that's all you can ask. I had the serve at 5 points to 4 in the decisive tie-breaker. The odds had switched dramatically to me. I had to win it. I looked at him and he couldn't stand up. Nobody was going to beat me now, after I'd been down 0-3 in the fifth, after I'd saved four break points in the next game to avoid 0-4, and after I'd zinged an ace on match point against me at 4-5. I couldn't lose it now. I wouldn't.

And I did. Or, rather, he beat me, that bloody thief Rosewall.

It had been a shotmaking feast throughout, for more than three and a half hours, but after all the sprints and swings and skids I had him. I can tell you the three swings of mine I regret the most. They came in the tie-breaker with me ahead, 3-1. I jerked him out of position and whacked a forehand down the line that nobody could have touched. The tape interfered, and the ball dropped back on my side. Just a fraction higher, and it'd been 4-1. Then I double-faulted. Instead of maybe 5-1, it was 3-3.

Never mind, I told myself, and I got two of the next three to 5-4 with serve. Two points to the championship—and my serve. Great. Concentrate. I was going to go for his backhand corner. Yes, don't tell me—I know all about that backhand. But this time I'd slice it wide and clean him out of the court. He just couldn't move anymore to get back in position.

Surprise. He didn't have to move. Terrific serve . . . only the return was even terrificker, a cross-court angle that I'd never seen even from Kenny. I probed to make the half-volley, reached the ball but couldn't control it. Anything over the net would have got me the point with him sagging so badly, but my half-volley went long. It's 5-5.

One more serve, and I still knew I could outlast him, even if he could carry me to 6-6. He was absolutely dead, and I felt great. Another serve to the backhand corner, and this was Kenny's last stab. Zoom, the ball went down the line and I was passed with plenty to spare. My edge was gone, just like that.

His serve at 6-5—match point. Could he lift the ball to serve it? Didn't much matter. I was glassy over those backhands, and I hardly noticed that he floated a serve over the net. I waved at it with a backhand and tapped it into the net. "I can't lose," registered in my mind. "How . . ."

Kenny was so bushed he didn't make sense in the TV interview. Not so bushed that he didn't make sure the check for fifty grand was signed by Lamar.

They say he was cold and emotionless, but in the dressing room, Kenny broke down and cried. I wanted to, but I still couldn't believe it. A reporter asked him to think back to 1962 and try to imagine what he thought then that he'd be doing in 1972. "Selling insurance in Sydney,

I guess," said Kenny. "Certainly not playing tennis. Certainly not for $50,000 in one afternoon."

Was there any place I could buy a policy insuring me against Kenny Rosewall?

It's our match forever—his win, but our match—and I feel people will keep talking about it. I won't discourage them.

1973 WIMBLEDON BOYCOTT/ DAVIS CUP

PROBABLY MY LAST CHANCES TO WIN WIMBLEDON WERE 1972 and 1973. They were slim (at ages 34 and 35), but I wanted at least to take a shot. It never happened. Out of my hands.

In 1972, we pros under contract to Lamar Hunt's WCT were barred from the majors by the ITF, one of those silly anti-Hunt disputes. So "open" tennis got closed from time to time to the Hunt gang. Stan Smith beat the "Bucharest Buffoon," Ilie Nastase, for the title. They were pros, of course, but the right kind: unattached to Hunt. So-called independent pros could play. The U.S. Open didn't support the ban, but Nastase had a splendid fortnight, beating Arthur Ashe in the final.

This kind of absurdity, OK-ing some pros but not others, was interfering with the livelihood of many, and made us pros realize we needed protection from the ILTF. It all led to the 1973 formation of the ATP (Association of Tennis Professionals) and the absence from Wimbledon of numerous upper class pros – me included – for the second straight year.

This was the year of the ATP's Wimbledon boycott, also known as the Pilic Affair. Named for the Croat, Niki Pilic, whose homeland was a chunk of Yugoslavia in those days, it is a tangled tale that kept us out of Wimbledon, but had a happy ending for the players – and the game itself.

Pilic, a Wimbledon semifinalist in 1967, and later, uniquely the Davis Cup captain of two different countries (Germany, 1988-89, 93, and Croatia, 2005), was one of Hunt's original troupe, the "Handsome Eight," in

1968. Although he was expected to play Davis Cup for Yugoslavia, and did it well, Niki chose not to go to New Zealand for an early round.

His refusal, enraging Yugoslavia's tennis federation, got him suspended, and the ILTF expected its members to honor that suspension. Although the French, where he was finalist to Nastase, and the Italians ignored the penalty, Wimbledon surprisingly upheld it.

The newly-formed ATP declared that if Pilic didn't play, his lodge brothers would walk. However, the All England Club wouldn't budge. No Pilic. After all, we were the hired help.

Nobody believed we would vote to boycott, but 59 of us did, all the marquee names but Nastase. Included as strikers were John Newcombe, champion in 1970-71, and defending champ Stan Smith. It was a principaled stand by men who felt we had to control our own destiny.

Nevertheless, the press, the public and Wimbledon management were against us. How dare we defy the Big W, commit sacrilege in the temple?

To me it was disappointing that Herman David, the head man who had been so strongly influential in bringing about open tennis in 1968, had turned his back on the players in 1972 and 1973. Pilic is a left-hander, and I guess the tournament committee thought we were just a bunch of radical lefties.

Nastase, leading a largely anonymous pack, seemed ready to cakewalk to the title, but he got sabotaged early by an American college kid, Sandy Mayer. Instead, Wimbledon was served an Iron Curtain final, Czech Jan Kodes over Soviet Alex Metreveli, who said their federations wouldn't allow them to belong to the ATP or take part in a strike.

I have no idea if the players today, far better compensated than us, would support such a cause. I'd like to think they would. The Pilic Affair wasn't really all about him and his unfair treatment, but more to make sure that we were no longer beholden to our national associations.

We became free agents. Animosities were soon forgotten, and the ILTF [now the ITF or International Tennis Federation] broadened to promote development programs throughout the world, and, among other things, oversee the four majors.

I didn't return to Wimbledon until 1977, a sentimental journey to be part of the Centenary Celebration that drew many of the old champions. It was very emotional, ending as we held hands in a large circle on Centre Court and sang "Auld Lang Syne." Elizabeth (Bunny) Ryan, 85, whom I'd never seen, was cheered wholeheartedly. Winner of 19 titles between 1914 and 1934, the tournament record until Billie Jean King and Martina Navratilova topped it, Miss Ryan slowly, painfully but determinedly, walked on two canes to receive her commemorative medal.

I was glad to accept mine, too, but wanted more – to play a last time on Centre Court. Fortunately I did. Though I lost a second rounder to a good young American, Dick Stockton, in four sets, it felt so good to be on that wonderful patch of grass. It brought out the best in me for four championships. I always felt the importance of playing on Centre, and paid close attention.

Ah, but I was intruding on a new generation. I was two years beyond by last ranking in the Top Ten, and Stockton, No. 10, was paying attention too closely.

Despite the show of player strength in the Wimbledon boycott, a lot of screwy things were still going on regarding what and where the Hunt pros could play. Take Davis Cup. Even though tennis was supposedly open in 1968, not all pros were permitted to play Davis Cup.

Namely we Australians: John Newcombe, Kenny Rosewall, Tony Roche and me. We would have made up a pretty fair team. Except that we were, in the eyes of the ITF, with the bad guys, Lamar Hunt's WCT. We had lived for Davis Cup as amateurs, but it was off limits now.

Meanwhile the Americans Arthur Ashe, Clark Graebner, Stan Smith and Bob Lutz – no less pros than us – captained by purposeful Donald Dell, had broken a five-year drought and regained the Cup from a weak Australian team at Adelaide in 1968. That was the end of the line for the brilliant motivator Harry Hopman, who had captained 16 winning teams, four of them embracing me. Hop would move to the U.S. as a coach to inspire numerous excellent players (John McEnroe and Vitas Gerulatis among them), and open his own tennis academy in Florida.

The Yanks took over, grabbing five straight Cups. The only times we had a shot at them were in an annual, strictly Yanks vs. Aussies show-down called the World Team Cup. It started in Boston in 1970 as a benefit for the inner city youth program, the Sportsmen's Tennis Club, and moved later to Hartford for some glorious clashes before fading away.

Our playing captain was my old Queensland mate Roy Emerson, and -- this always amuses us – we were unaware of his stature in tennis history. Sure, we knew he'd played on eight winning Davis Cup sides, the record. But we didn't know that he also held the record for major singles titles, 12 – six Australian, two each of the other three. We didn't really care or find out until Pete Sampras began stalking Emmo, getting closer and closer.

"People had forgotten me until Pete got nearer," laughed Emmo years later. "Nobody knew I had such a record – including me. People didn't pay attention to that stuff. I have to thank Pete for getting me a lot of publicity"

American Big Bill Tilden, the giant of the 1920s, won seven U.S. and three Wimbledons, and that stood for 37 years until Emmo won the Australian and French, for 12, in 1967. That lasted 33 years before Sampras beat another Queenslander, Patrick Rafter, in the Wimbledon final of 2000 to reach 13. Pete added a 14th in the U.S. final of 2002.

I won 11 major singles titles – equaled by Bjorn Borg with his win at the 1981 French. In saluting Emmo, I must add his 16 majors in doubles for a 28 total that nobody will ever beat.

I was having a pretty good 1973, ranking No. 8, but there was no Dallas WCT reprise for Kenny Rosewall and me. Both of us lost in the semis, Stan Smith, the champ, beating me. But in the third place match, that rascal, Rosewall, got me, 6-3, 6-2. For me, Kenny and Dallas go together like camel riding in the Sahara.

Still, we oft-banished Aussies got some good news. The ITF, in a rare burst of sense and forgiveness, announced in 1973 that all pros were now eligible for Davis Cup. She'll be apples! That's an old Aussie expression for good days ahead.

And I got the Davis Cup itch again after years of feeling it was no longer for me. Why not? But, realistically, I was 35, not at my very best, and for a very long time hadn't been involved in the most stifling of tennis pressure, Davis Cup – yes, greater than a Wimbledon final. Especially in Australia where so much success had raised expectations to the clouds.

I hadn't been on the team for 11 years, a lark, overrunning Mexico in 1962. But I was getting itchy to prove myself since the 1960-61 Cups were also romps, over Italy. The lone tough encounter of my four winning teams was the U.S. in 1959, and I lost both singles, to Barry MacKay and Alex Olmedo. Only the presence of Neale Fraser, winning both singles plus the doubles with Emmo, saved us.

Now I had to talk to Fraser, the successor as captain to Hopman. A good friend, but very practical. Was I up to it? And how would the other guys feel about a newcomer at this stage? They had won two series to lift the team to the semis.

Happily, I was accepted by my mates: Newcombe, Rosewall, Geoff Masters, Ross Case, Mal Anderson. They just wanted to win for Australia. If I could help, fine.

But could I? Fraser wasn't at all sure. The acid test prior to the semifinal against Czechoslovakia was the Australian Indoor Championships in Sydney. Captain Fraser made it clear that I'd have to do well to have any chance to play against the Czechs.

I worked my bum off to get fitter than I'd been in almost a year. The lineup of would-be Laver-flatteners was daunting. In the quarters, it was Raul Ramirez, the quick, sharp-volleying Mexican, and I got him, 6-3, 6-4. Next, world No. 6 Rosewall. Where did they find him? I barely escaped, 6-4, 3-6, 8-6. Finally, it was No. 2 Newcombe, in a roaring five sets, 3-6, 7-5, 6-3, 3-6, 6-4.

Captain Fraser shook my hand with, "Rocket, welcome to the team."

It couldn't have been a nicer setting after gloomy, rickety Hordern Pavilion, site of the Indoor. We were in Melbourne for the semi, plenty of November sunshine heralding the onset of summer on the famed grass courts of Kooyong. The Czechs would have preferred clay, but Jan Kodes, a future Hall of Famer, could handle the lawn. He'd won Wimbledon and was finalist to Newcombe at Forest Hills only months before.

For the last time, my parents saw me play, and fortunately I didn't let them down. Or Fraser and the country. It was extremely difficult, though. After I stopped Kodes, 6-3, 7-5, 7-5, Jiri Hrebec, wildly erratic, put it all together to stun the crowd as well as Newcombe – on grass! – 6-4, 8-10, 6-4, 7-5. Now Rosewall and I were on the same side for a change, and we needed each other in a long, demanding go-ahead doubles over Vladimir Zednik and Kodes, 6-4, 14-12, 7-9, 8-6. That left it up to me to tame Hrebec (seldom heard from again) 5-7, 6-3, 6-4, 4-6, 6-4, settling it.

We were on our way to Cleveland, a quartet called, by my co-author, "Captain Fraser's Antique Show" – Rosewall, 39; Laver, 35; Mal Anderson, 38; Newcombe, 29. Rosewall had been away from Cupping for 17 years, Anderson for 15, Laver, as I said, for 11, Newcombe for six, Fraser for 10. Never been anything like it.

We were old enough to go out alone, but nobody wanted to in the December chill of downtown Cleveland. What a place for a Cup final. Old, vast, drafty Public Hall, attracted few people to see us do our stuff: a 5-0 triumph that ended the U.S. streak of five years and a record 15 encounters. A terrible promotion. Some writers were calling us the greatest of all Davis Cup teams, yet nobody wanted to see us (maybe 7,000 for three days) or the home heroes.

It didn't matter to us. We wanted Yank heads to show that the, shall we say mature, Aussies were still breathing. And we got them on an overly drawn out Friday night and a brief Saturday afternoon. Newcombe led off with a mixture of uncharacteristic spins, soft stuff, plus his usual muscle to overcome Stan Smith in five 6-1, 3-6, 6-3, 3-6, 6-4. Then Tom Gorman and I went at it furiously, charging the net, serving-and-volleying for five more sets. A bit of revenge for Wimbledon '71 was mine, 8-10, 8-6, 6-8, 6-3, 6-1.

Fraser decided he wanted two forehands down the middle plus troublesome serving in picking me and Newc to conclude the assignment. We fast-finished the Yanks, Erik van Dillen and Smith, 6-1, 6-2, 6-4.

How pleasant to have the company of our old friend, the Cup, again, and swill victory grog from it. Long time no guzzle for all of us. My Davis Cup itch had been unexpectedly scratched.

ALMOST "HEAVYWEIGHT CHAMPION"

AFTER JIMMY CONNORS WON HIS FIRST U.S. TITLE IN 1974 AT Forest Hills, he shouted, "Get me Laver!"

Maybe. Maybe not. But that's what his shrewd manager, Bill Riordan, reported, and who wants to spoil a good story with the facts? He and Jimmy, who was No. 1, wanted a showdown with me to decide what Riordan baptized as the "Heavyweight Championship of Tennis." It caught on.

Riordan, a clever promoter of the U.S. indoor circuit that opposed Lamar Hunt's WCT, had grown up as a boxing fan. His father had managed a few fighters, and Bill was adept with the ballyhoo to sell a bout. He got CBS and Caesar's Palace in Las Vegas behind it as the site Feb. 2, 1975. The publicity was terrific.

Why not? One generation's champion clashing with another's. Of course neither Jimmy nor I qualified as heavyweights in a boxing sense (175 pounds or over), but we trained hard. I was all for it because the pay day was the best I'd seen for punching a tennis ball -- $60,000 as my end. Connors got $100,000. A lot of money then.

CBS would get into trouble later for billing the so-called prize money as "Winner take all!" But, like prizefighters, we came to terms – Riordan and my agents negotiating -- beforehand.

The title, heavyweight champion, sounded great, but had no real meaning. Jimmy and I wouldn't have traded our Wimbledon titles for it. All it meant was that a 22-year-old could beat a 36-year-old.

And he did, 6-4, 6-2, 3-6, 7-5. But it was fun to test myself against the current strongboy. I felt I played well, made him work for it. The crowd was with me, and that displeased Jimmy, who raised the well-known finger to toward one sector.

But he was in the early unpopular phase of his career that blossomed when the U.S. Open moved to Flushing Meadow in 1978. His competitive zeal made him deservedly an all-time favorite. When he, a 10-to-1 favorite, lost his Wimbledon championship to Arthur Ashe in 1975, I must admit I was pleased because Arthur was really fulfilling his promise.

Riordan kept the "Heavyweight Championship" going against John Newcombe, Ilie Nastase and Spaniard Manolo Orantes. Jimmy knocked us all out, but the concept had seen its day. Revelations that the "winner take all" pitch was phony tarnished the idea. Jimmy and Riordan parted.

Later in the year, I again dipped into the new generation in matches with the surging Swedish teenager Bjorn Borg. He was obviously going places, but I wasn't unhappy with my losses to him. It took him five long sets to beat me in the WCT semis at Dallas, and four to knock me out of the fourth round of the U.S. Open. Forest Hills had torn up the grass courts of my 1962 and 1969 titles to lay green clay, and also installed floodlights. Since 1978, Flushing Meadow has been paved with hard courts, and their color is now blue.

Wooden rackets were becoming extinct, and many manufacturers of metal clubs were popping up. One of them, short lived, was Chemold aluminum that I endorsed, and you could buy for $15. Imagine that. But I did win the Italian Open with one in 1971.

In 1990, the ATP killed the WCT circuit and playoffs, and now controls the men's tour other than the majors. It was an unkind, ungrateful act to drop Lamar Hunt from tennis, the man to whom so much was owed. Lamar, who died in 2006 and is in the International Tennis Hall of Fame, led the professionalization of the men's game.

From 1976 to 1978, I played World Team Tennis for the San Diego Friars. At age 38 in 1976, I even earned WTT "Rookie of the Year" honors. With such teammates as Cliff Drysdale, Ross Case, Terry Holladay, Kerry and Raz Reid, the team was high on camaraderie. It was most enjoyable. My last official pro match was on April 24, 1979 when I lost to countryman John Alexander 6-7, 6-3, 6-1 in the first round of the Alan King Classic at Caesar's Palace in Las Vegas.

29

THE STROKE

IT WAS AN ORDINARY DAY, I HAD NO PREMONITIONS WHAT lay ahead. Was it a day to die? No, but it would be the hardest part of my life.

The hardest part of my life, the terrible feeling of being unable to do anything, was being knocked out – almost knocked off – by a stroke.

How much do I remember about the stroke? Not much. It occurred while I was doing a TV interview at a hotel in downtown Los Angeles, July 27, 1998.

Suddenly my fingers got numb. I didn't have control. I know a lot of crazy things happened to me including explosive vomiting and collapsing. A lucky thing was that the producer had witnessed his father suffering a stroke, and knew what was happening. He phoned for help immediately, and another bit of luck was that we were two blocks from the UCLA (University of California Los Angeles) medical center. A neurosurgical stroke team was with me in about a quarter of an hour.

Dr. John Lill, a former first-class cricketer and currently president of the National Stroke Foundation of Australia, says, "Immediacy of treatment is a vital element in recovery." Apparently that quick response to the stroke was very beneficial to me.

[Anybody who watched then 66-year-old "Rocket" perform ably in an exhibition doubles with Andre Agassi, Tony Roche and John Newcombe at the International Tennis Hall of Fame, Newport, Rhode Island, in 2004 wouldn't believe the physical and mental ordeal that he overcame.]

I wasn't aware of the vomiting on camera, but I'm glad it was tape, not a live show. But later, doctors told me that it's a valuable tape to study - unique - because they'd never witnessed somebody actually having a stroke. I don't want to see it. Personally I'd rather see a tape of me hitting a backhand winner.

A month after the attack, Mary told me, "It was rough on all of us. Rod, you were in intensive care for three weeks, and at least one of us [she, their son and daughter-in-law] was in there around the clock, to let you know we were there, to calm you when you were conscious. It wasn't a great place for your 60th birthday [Aug. 9]."

There were seizures, awfully high blood pressure, a fever they had trouble controlling - 106 degrees for a few days - swelling of the brain. I had to be restrained at times, they tell me. I guess I wanted out. Sometimes I ripped out the IVs. I was rough on everybody.

I do remember being aphasic, blurring, slurring words. I looked terrible, lost 30 pounds to 130. I couldn't form words. One of the toughest was "dog." I was like a kid again, had to re-learn to tell time, and a lot of other things.

My right side was paralyzed for a while. I had no use of the right hand. Sometimes I'd be sitting on it without even noticing. But the left was OK. They had me on a bed of ice when I had the fever and pneumonia. But the bleeding in the brain had stopped on its own without requiring surgery. Lucky. One day they sent me for a CAT scan of the brain, to see how that was going. The technician who had run it said, "Your brain? There's nothing there." I thought he was trying to be funny, but he meant it was blood free. That was good news. There was a lot of therapy - physical, speech, memory. Exhausting.

Mary said, "The therapists were exhausted, too. Rod wore them out he was so determined to recover. They'd never worked with someone like him. His super determination as a player was showing itself."

A couple of years later, Bud asked me how I was feeling.

"Well, I've got a sore knee."

"Oh, too bad."

"No, very good," I told Bud, "It's the first time I've had any feeling it it since the stroke."

The muscle memory from tennis was a great help as I got my feet moving again, and my arms. I graduated from a walker and presently was able to resume tennis, golf, gardening and making public appearances.

I was nearly a scratch golfer pre-stroke. Now I'm at 10. When I was able to go onto a tennis court, hitting with Tommy Tucker, an excellent teaching pro at Mission Hills Country Club, I was able to hit for only five minutes at first. But we built up to a half-hour. Tommy was hitting balls within reach on my left side. But one day my right foot moved – a thrill – and I had more mobility. A great improvement. Mary was instrumental in getting Tommy to come every morning pick me up at our home and make sure I didn't get into bad habits with my strokes. Tommy would tell me "You're playing like Tommy Tucker, but pretty soon you'll be Rod Laver, and I'll still be Tommy Tucker."

We were living in Rancho Mirage then, on the golf course, and I got so I could play two holes, one up and one back, using a cart and carrying a cell phone in case something went wrong. Well, something did. My ball went into a sand trap, and without thinking I took my wedge and went after it. Trouble was I wasn't strong enough then to walk out, and the phone was in the cart. Nobody was around, and I had a helluva time finally crawling up and out. Sand traps took on a new, hazardous meaning to me.

Speech therapy was very hard, but my therapists and I worked at it. As I got better I might utter odd words that had no relationship to anything, and Mary would say, "Where did that come from?" and we'd laugh. If it happens now it means I'm tired, and she says, "Time for a nap."

I'm frequently asked to address stroke patients, and I'm happy to do it. I tell them, don't accept. You're a viable entity. Try. Work at your therapy. I hope it helps. Said Mary, "As always, Rod doesn't take himself or his accomplishments very seriously. He remains unassuming, the humble Queensland farm boy who fell off a few horses, started out on a home-made ant bed court and was sarcastically nicknamed 'Rocket' by his Davis Cup captain, Harry Hopman, simply because he wasn't. Hopman recalled he was anything but a rocket: 'Scrawny and slow when I first saw him. But he worked at it harder than anybody else.' "He's the redheaded guy who slammed back when the slam of his life tried to bury him."

EPILOGUE

I WONDER WHEN ANOTHER GRAND SLAMMER WILL APPEAR and join me. I look forward to it, and will welcome whoever it is just as Don Budge welcomed me in 1962. I was glad to see Steffi Graf as the latest in 1988. Roger Federer and Rafa Nadal seem to have the best chance, along with Serena Williams. I wish them success.

The days of scrounging to find eight or ten guys for a pro tournament are long gone and the game has taken off around the world involving millions of dollars and terrific players from all corners of the globe. In 1963, eight men showed up for that U.S. Pro Championship which went broke at Forest Hills (Rosewall, Laver, Gonzalez, Olmedo, Hoad, Trabert, Buchholz, Segura). That was pro tennis. We kept it alive. Barely.

Hail, farewell, good luck, and here's fuzz in your eye. The yellow fuzz of a tennis ball. Keep your eyes on it, whether you're a hacker, a champion, or a witnessing bystander, caught up in hopelessly loving this game as Bud and I have been for decades.

APPENDIX A

The Grand Slams
(World ranking of opponents, when so rated, in parentheses)

DON BUDGE of Oakland, Calif., at age 22 in 1938

AUSTRALIAN CHAMPIONSHIPS AT MEMORIAL DRIVE COURTS, ADELAIDE–
defeated:
Les Hancock, Australia, 6-2, 6-3, 6-4
Harold Whillans, Australia, 6-1, 6-0, 6-1
Len A. Schwartz, Australia, 6-4, 6-3, 10-8
Adrian Quist (6), Australia, 5-7, 6-4, 6-1, 6-2
John Bromwich (3), Australia, 6-4, 6-2, 6-1

FRENCH CHAMPIONSHIPS AT ROLAND GARROS, PARIS–
defeated:
Antoine Gentien, France, 6-1, 6-2, 6-4
Ghaus Mohammed, India, 6-1, 6-1, 5-7, 6-0
Franz Kukuljevic, Yugoslavia, 6-2, 8-6, 2-6, 1-6, 6-1
Bernard Destremeau, France, 6-4, 6-3, 6-4
Josip Pallada, Yugoslavia, 6-2, 6-3, 6-3
Roderich Menzel (7), Czechoslovakia, 6-3, 6-2, 6-4

THE CHAMPIONSHIPS AT WIMBLEDON, LONDON–
defeated:
Kenneth Gandar-Dower, England, 6-2, 6-3, 6-3
Henry Billington, England, 7-5, 6-1, 6-1
George Lyttleton-Rogers, Ireland, 6-0, 7-5, 6-1
Ronald Shayes, England, 6-3, 6-4, 6-1
Franz Cejnar, Czechoslovakia, 6-3, 6-0, 7-5
Franjo Puncec, Czechoslovakia, 6-2, 6-4, 6-0

Henry Austin (2), England, 6-1, 6-0, 6-3

U.S. CHAMPIONSHIPS AT FOREST HILLS, NEW YORK–
defeated:
Welby Van Horn, United States, 6-0, 6-0, 6-1
Bob Kamrath, United States, 6-3, 7-5, 9-7
Charles Hare, England, 6-3, 6-4, 6-0
Harry Hopman, Australia, 6-3, 6-1, 6-3
Sidney Wood (5), United States, 6-3, 6-3, 6-3
Gene Mako (9), United States, 6-3, 6-8, 6-2, 6-1

MAUREEN CONNOLLY of San Diego, at age 18 in 1953

AUSTRALIAN CHAMPIONSHIPS AT KOOYONG, MELBOURNE–
defeated:
Carmen Boreilli, Australia, 6-0, 6-1
Alison Burton Baker, Australia, 6-1, 6-0
Pam Southcombe, Australia, 6-0, 6-1
Mary Bevis Hawton, Australia, 6-2, 6-1
Julie Sampson, United States, 6-3, 6-2

FRENCH CHAMPIONSHIPS AT ROLAND GARROS, PARIS–
defeated:
Christiane Mercelis, Belgium, 6-1, 6-3
Raymonde Verber Jones, United States, 6-3, 6-1
Susan Partridge Chatrier, France, 3-6, 6-2, 6-2
Dorothy Head Knode (6), United States, 6-3, 6-3
Doris Hart (2), United States, 6-2, 6-4

THE CHAMPIONSHIPS AT WIMBLEDON, LONDON–
defeated:
Dora Killian, England, 6-0, 6-0
Jean M. Petchell, England, 6-1, 6-1
Anne Shilcock, England, 6-0, 6-1
Erika Vollmer, Germany, 6-3, 6-0

Shirley Fry (4), United States, 6-1, 6-1
Doris Hart (2), United States, 8-6, 7-5

U.S. CHAMPIONSHIPS AT FOREST HILLS, NEW YORK–
defeated:
Jean Fallot, United States, 6-1, 6-0
Pat Stewart, United States, 6-3, 6-1
Althea Gibson, United States, 6-2, 6-3
Shirley Fry (4), United States, 6-1, 6-1
Doris Hart (2), United States, 6-2, 6-4

ROD LAVER of Rockhampton, Australia, at age 24 in 1962

AUSTRALIAN CHAMPIONSHIPS AT WHITE CITY, SYDNEY–
defeated:
Fred Sherriff, Australia, 8-6, 6-4, 6-2
Geoff Pares, Australia, 10-8, 18-16, 7-9, 7-5
Owen Davidson, Australia, 6-4, 9-7, 6-4
Bob Hewitt (8), Australia, 6-1, 4-6, 6-4, 7-5
Roy Emerson (2), Australia, 8-6,0-6, 6-4,6-4

FRENCH CHAMPIONSHIPS AT ROLAND GARROS, PARIS–
defeated:
Michele Pirro, Italy, 6-4, 6-0, 6-2
Tony Pickard, England, 6-2, 9-7, 4-6, 6-1
Sergio Jacobini, Italy, 4-6, 6-3, 7-5, 6-1
Marty Mulligan (7), Australia, 6-4, 3-6, 2-6, 10-8, 6-2
Neale Fraser (4), Australia, 3-6, 6-3, 6-2, 3-6, 7-5
Roy Emerson (2), Australia, 3-6, 2-6, 6-3, 9-7, 6-2

THE CHAMPIONSHIPS AT WIMBLEDON, LONDON–
defeated:
Naresh Kumar, India, 7-5, 6-1, 6-2
Tony Pickard, England, 6-1, 6-2, 6-2
Whitney Reed, United States, 6-4, 6-1, 6-4

Pierre Darmon, France, 6-3, 6-2, 13-11
Manolo Santana (3), Spain, 14-16, 9-7, 6-2, 6-2
Neale Fraser (4), Australia, 10-8, 6-1, 7-5
Marty Mulligan (7), Australia, 6-2, 6-2, 6-1

U.S. CHAMPIONSHIPS AT FOREST HILLS, NEW YORK–
defeated:
Eleazar Davidman, Israel, 6-3, 6-2, 6-3
Eduardo Zuleta, Ecuador, 6-3, 6-3, 6-1
Bodo Nitsche, Germany, 9-7, 6-1, 6-1
Antonio Palafox, Mexico, 6-1, 6-2, 6-2
Frank Froehling, III, United States, 6-3, 13-11, 4-6, 6-3
Rafe Osuna (6), Mexico, 6-1, 6-3, 6-4
Roy Emerson (2), Australia, 6-2, 6-4, 5-7, 6-4

ROD LAVER of Rockhampton, Australia, at age 31 in 1969
AUSTRALIAN OPEN AT MILTON COURTS, BRISBANE–
defeated:
Massimo di Domenico, Italy, 6-2, 6-3, 6-3
Roy Emerson (8), Australia, 6-2,6-4, 3-6, 9-7
Fred Stolle (7), Australia, 6-4, 18-16, 6-2
Tony Roche (2), Australia, 7-5, 22-20, 9-11, 1-6, 6-3
Andres Gimeno, Spain, 6-3, 6-4, 7-5

FRENCH OPEN AT ROLAND GARROS, PARIS–
defeated:
Koji Watanabe, Japan, 6-1, 6-1, 6-1
Dick Crealy, Australia, 3-6, 7-9, 6-2, 6-2, 6-4
Pietro Marzano, Italy, 6-1, 6-0, 8-6
Stan Smith (9), United States, 6-4, 6-2, 6-4
Andres Gimeno, Spain, 3-6, 6-3, 6-4, 6-3
Tom Okker (5), Netherlands, 4-6, 6-0, 6-2, 6-4
Ken Rosewall (6), Australia, 6-4, 6-3, 6-4

THE CHAMPIONSHIPS AT WIMBLEDON, LONDON–
  defeated:
  Nicola Pietrangeli, Italy, 6-1, 6-2, 6-2
  Premjit Lall, India, 3-6, 4-6, 6-3, 6-0, 6-0
  Jan Leschly, Denmark, 6-3, 6-3, 6-3
  Stan Smith (9), United States, 6-4, 6-2, 7-9, 3-6, 6-3
  Cliff Drysdale, South Africa, 6-4, 6-2, 6-3
  Arthur Ashe (4), United States, 2-6, 6-2, 9-7, 6-0
  John Newcombe (3), Australia, 6-4, 5-7, 6-4, 6-4

U.S. OPEN AT FOREST HILLS, NEW YORK–
  defeated:
  Luis Garcia, Mexico, 6-2, 6-4, 6-2
  Jaime Pinto-Bravo, Chile, 6-4, 7-5, 6-2
  Jaime Fillol, Chile, 8-6, 6-1, 6-2
  Dennis Ralston, United States, 6-4, 4-6, 4-6, 6-2, 6-3
  Roy Emerson (8), Australia, 4-6, 8-6, 13-11, 6-4
  Arthur Ashe (4), United States, 8-6, 6-3, 14-12
  Tony Roche (2), Australia, 7-9, 6-1, 6-2, 6-2

MARGARET SMITH COURT of Albury, Australia, at age 28 in 1970
AUSTRALIAN OPEN AT WHITE CITY, SYDNEY -
  defeated:
  Caroline Langsford, Australia, 6-0, 6-0
  Kerry Wilkinson, Australia, 6-0, 6-1
  Evonne Goolagong, Australia, 6-3, 6-1
  Karen Krantzcke (8), Australia, 6-1, 6-3
  Kerry Melville (6), Australia, 6-3, 6-1

FRENCH OPEN AT ROLAND GARROS, PARIS -
  defeated:
  Marijke Schaar-Jansen, Netherlands, 6-1, 6-1
  Olga Morozova, Russia, 3-6, 8-6, 6-1
  Lesley Hunt, Australia, 6-2, 6-1

Rosemary Casals (3), United States, 7-5, 6-2
Julie Heldman (7), United States, 6-0, 6-2
Helga Niessen (5), West Germany, 6-2, 6-4

THE CHAMPIONSHIPS AT WIMBLEDON, LONDON -
defeated:
Sue Alexander, Australia, 6-0, 6-1
Maria Guzman, Ecuador, 6-0, 6-1
Vlasta Vopickova, Czechoslovakia, 6-3, 6-3
Helga Niessen (5), West Germany, 6-8, 6-0, 6-0
Rosemary Casals (3), United States, 6-4, 6-1
Billie Jean King (2), United States, 14-12, 11-9

U.S. OPEN AT FOREST HILLS, NEW YORK -
defeated:
Pam Austin, United States, 6-1, 6-0
Patti Hogan, United States, 6-1, 6-1
Pat Faulkner, Australia, 6-0, 6-2
Helen Gourlay, Australia, 6-2, 6-2
Nancy Richey (10), United States, 6-1, 6-3
Rosemary Casals (3), United States, 6-2, 2-6, 6-1

STEFFI GRAF of Bruhl, Germany, at age 19 in 1988
AUSTRALIAN OPEN AT FLINDERS PARK, MELBOURNE -
defeated:
Amy Jonsson, Norway, 6-3, 6-1
Janine Thompson, Australia, 6-0, 6-1
Cammy MacGregor, United States, 6-1, 6-2
Catarina Lindqvist (13), Sweden, 6-0, 7-5
Hana Mandlikova (5), Czechoslovakia, 6-2, 6-2
Claudia Kohde Kilsch (8), Germany, 6-2, 6-3
Chris Evert (3), United States, 6-1, 7-6 (7-3).

FRENCH OPEN, AT ROLAND GARROS, PARIS -
defeated:
Natalie Guerree, France, 6-0, 6-4
Ronni Reis, United States, 6-1, 6-0
Susan Sloane, United States, 6-0, 6-1
Nathalie Tauziat, France, 6-1, 6-3
Bettina Fulco, Argentina, 6-0, 6-1
Gabriela Sabatini (4), Argentina, 6-3, 7-6 (7-3)
Natalia Zvereva (13), USSR, 6-0, 6-0.

THE CHAMPIONSHIPS AT WIMBLEDON, LONDON
defeated:
Hu Na, United States, 6-0, 6-0
Karine Quentrec, France, 6-2, 6-0
Terry Phelps, United States, 6-3, 6-1
Mary Joe Fernandez (16), United States, 6-2, 6-2
Pascale Paradis, France, 6-3, 6-1
Pam Shriver (4), United States, 6-1, 6-2
Martina Navratilova (2), United States, 5-7, 6-2, 6-1.

U.S. OPEN AT FLUSHING MEADOW, NEW YORK –
defeated
Elizabeth Minter, Australia, 6-1, 6-1
Manon Bollegraf, Netherlands, 6-1, 6-0
Nathalie Herreman, France, 6-0, 6-1
Patty Fendick, United States, 6-4, 6-2
Katerina Maleeva (14), Bulgaria, 6-3, 6-0
Chris Evert (3), United States, default (illness)
Gabriela Sabatini (5), Argentina, 6-3, 3-6, 6-1.

APPENDIX B

The Complete Year of Laver's Grand Slam
(● = *The four major tournaments that constitute the Slam*)

JANUARY

Sydney, Australia, New South Wales Open—lost final to Tony Roche,
6-4, 4-6, 9-7, 12-10

● Brisbane, Australia, *Australian Open*—won final over Andres
Gimeno, 6-3, 6-4, 7-5

FEBRUARY

Auckland, New Zealand, New Zealand Open—lost final to Roche,
6-1, 6-4, 4-6, 6-3

Philadelphia, Pa., Philadelphia Indoor Open—won final over Roche,
7-5, 6-4, 6-4

Orlando, Fla., Orlando Pro event—won final over Ken Rosewall,
6-3, 6-2

Hollywood, Fla., Burger King Pro Cup—lost final to Roche,
6-3, 9-7, 6-4

Oakland, Calif., Oakland Pro event—lost final to Roche,
4-6, 6-4, 11-9

Portland, Ore., one-night stand—defeated Pancho Gonzalez,
7-5, 6-8, 8-6

MARCH

Seattle, Wash., one-night stand—defeated Gonzalez, 10-8, 6-3

Los Angeles, Calif., Los Angeles Pro event—won final over Marty
Riessen, 6-4, 10-8

New York, Madison Square Garden Open—lost first round to Cliff
Richey, 6-4, 3-6, 6-3

APRIL

Johannesburg, South Africa, South African Open—won final over
Tom Okker, 6-3, 10-8, 6-3

Anaheim, Calif., Anaheim Pro event—won final over Ron Holmberg,
31-16, 31-28 (VASSS scoring)

MAY

Tokyo, Japan, Japanese Pro Championships—finished third in
round-robin tournament, winning third-place match over Butch
Buchholz, 5-6, 6-2, 6-5

New York, Madison Square Garden Pro Invitation—won final over
Roy Emerson, 6-2, 4-6, 6-1

London, Wembley Pro event—won final over Ken Rosewall, 8-6, 6-0

Amsterdam, Netherlands, Dutch Pro Championships—finished
fourth in round-robin tournament, losing third-place match to
Roche, 6-3, 3-6, 6-2

JUNE

• Paris, *French Open*—won final over Rosewall, 6-4, 6-3, 6-4

Bristol, England, West of England Open—lost third round to Cliff
Drysdale, 4-6, 6-2, 7-5

London, London Open (Queens)—lost semifinal to John Newcombe,
6-4, 6-4

JULY

• London, *The Championships at Wimbledon*—won final over
Newcombe, 6-4, 5-7, 6-4, 6-4

Boston, Mass., U.S. Professional Championships—won final over
Newcombe, 7-5, 6-2, 4-6, 6-1

AUGUST

St. Louis, Mo., St. Louis Pro event—won final over Fred Stolle,
7-5, 3-6, 7-5

Binghamton, N. Y., Binghamton Pro event—won final over

Gonzalez, 6-1, 6-2

Ft. Worth, Tex., Colonial Pro Championships—won final over
Rosewall, 6-3, 6-2

Baltimore, Md., Baltimore Pro event—won final over Gonzalez,
6-3, 3-6, 7-5, 4-6, 8-6

SEPTEMBER

- New York, *U.S. Open* (Forest Hills)—won final over Roche,
7-9, 6-1, 6-1, 6-2

Los Angeles, Pacific Southwest Open—lost second round to Ray
Moore, 7-5, 3-6, 6-2 (ending 31-match win streak)

OCTOBER

Las Vegas, Nev., Howard Hughes Open—lost quarterfinal to Stan
Smith, 6-2, 6-4

Cologne, Germany, Spoga Pro Championships—lost first round to
Riessen, 6-4, 10-12, 9-7

Hamburg, Germany, one-night stand—lost to Rosewall, 2-6, 7-5, 8-6

NOVEMBER

Barcelona, Spain, Barcelona Pro event—lost final to Gimeno,
2-6, 8-6, 4-6, 6-3, 6-1

London, British Covered Courts (Indoor) Open—won final over
Roche, 6-4, 6-1, 6-3

Stockholm, Sweden, Stockholm Indoor Open—lost quarterfinal to
Stolle, 7-5, 8-10, 6-4

DECEMBER

Basel, Switzerland, one-night stand—defeated Emerson,
6-3, 6-8, 6-4, 3-6, 6-2

Madrid, Spain, Madrid Pro event—won final over Roger Taylor,
6-3, 6-2

APPENDIX C

ROD LAVER

TOURNAMENT WINS (TOTAL 196)
Amateur Period (1957-1962) - 52
Pro Period (1963-1967) - 68
Open Era (1968-1976) - 76

MAJOR SINGLES CHAMPIONSHIPS – 11
Australian Championships – 3 (1960, 1962, 1969)
French Championships – 2 (1962, 1969)
Wimbledon – 4 (1961, 1962, 1968, 1969)
U.S. Championships – 2 (1962, 1969)

TOTAL PROJECTED CAREER TOURNAMENT WIN-LOSS (1,437-358)
Amateur Period - 535-122
Pro Period - 317-82
Open Era - 585-154

TOURNAMENT WINS YEAR-BY-YEAR
1957 (2)
    Redcliffe QLD, Central Queensland (Rockhampton)
1958 (3)
    Redcliffe QLD, Nambour QLD, Southport QLD
1959 (1)
    Central Queensland (Rockhampton)
1960 (9)
    Australian Champs, Wynnum QLD, Nambour QLD, Lausanne
    SUI, Haverford PA, Southampton. N.Y., South Orange NJ,
    Newport RI, Queensland Hard Court

1961 (15)

South Australian, NZ Champs (Auckland), Kingston JAM,
Caracas VEN, Houston TX, Wimbledon, Deauville Kuntz Cup,
Deauville Centennial Cup, Bad Neuenahr FRG, Hamburg German
Champ., Sydney Metropolitan, Queensland Hard Court,
Queensland Champs, Victorian Champs, NSW Champs.

1962 (22)

Seaside Champs (Sydney), Australian Champs, Tasmanian,
Caracas VEN, Houston TX, Chingford GBR Connaught,
Bournemouth BHC, Palermo ITA, Rome Italian Champ., Lugano
SUI, French Champs, Oslo NOR, London Queen's Club,
Wimbledon, Irish Champs, Gstaad SUI, Hilversum NED, German
Champs, US Champs, Queensland Hard Court, Australian Hard
Court, Victorian.

1963 (6)

Kitzbühel AUT, Cannes FRA, Noordwijk-on-Sea NED, Rhodesian
(Salisbury), Johannesburg RSA, Western Province (Cape Town)

1964 (11)

Perth (4 man event), Monterrey CA, Boston US Pro, Biarritz FRA
(4 man), Geneva SUI, Salisbury RSA, Johannesburg RSA,
Port Elizabeth, Marseille (4 man), Cairo (4 man), Wembley
London Pro

1965 (16)

Adelaide, Perth, Melbourne, Hobart (4 man), Oklahoma City
(4 man), New York US Pro Indoor, Los Angeles Masters R.R.,
San Rafael CA, Lake Tahoe, Newport R.R., Cannes, Wembley
London Pro, Nairobi, Rhodesian (Salisbury), Durban, Cape Town,

1966 (16)

Brisbane, Melbourne, Perth, Nancy (4 man), Cannes (4 man),
Forest Hills R.R., Boston US Pro, Binghamton, Oporto POR,
Wembley London Pro, Milan (4 man), Johannesburg, Cape Town,
Durban, Abidjan (4 man), Dakar (4 man)

1967 (19)

New York US Pro Indoor, San Juan, Orlando, Miami Beach,

Boston Garden, Montreal, Marseille (4 man), Paris Indoor, San Diego, New York Madison Square Garden, Oklahoma, Boston US Pro, Newport R.R., Binghamton, Fort Worth, Wimbledon Pro, Johannesburg, Paris French Pro, Wembley London Pro.

1968 (12)

Sao Paulo, Buenos Aires, London BBC 2 (4 man), London Indoor, New York Madison Square Garden, Boston US Pro, Wimbledon, Paris French Pro, Los Angeles PSW Open, Corpus Christi, La Paz RR, São Paulo RR.

1969 (18)

Australian Open, Philadelphia US Pro Indoor, Orlando, Los Angeles, South African Open, Anaheim, New York Madison Square Garden Invitational, London BBC 2 (4 man), French Open, Wimbledon, Boston US Pro, St. Louis, Binghamton, Fort Worth, Baltimore, US Open, Wembley British Indoor, Madrid.

1970 (15)

Philadelphia US Pro Indoor, New York Champions Classic RR, Sydney, South African Open, St. Louis WCT, Queen's Club, Louisville WCT, Bretton Woods, Canadian Open, Fort Worth WCT, South Orange, Los Angeles PSW Open, Vancouver WCT, Germany (Berlin, Bonn, and Saarbrücken) Round Robin (4 man), Wembley British Indoor.

1971 (7)

New York Champions Classic RR, London Indoor, Rome Italian Open, Fort Worth WCT, Hilton Head CBS Classic (4 man), Berkeley WCT, Bologna WCT.

1972 (5)

Richmond WCT, Philadelphia US Pro Indoor, Toronto WCT, Houston WCT, Denver WCT

1973 (7)

Miami WCT, Richmond WCT, Toronto WCT, Hilton Head, Hilton Head CBS Classic (4 man), Hong Kong, Sydney Australian Indoor

1974 (6)

Philadelphia US Pro Indoor, Palm Desert WCT, Tokyo WCT, Houston WCT, Las Vegas, Bretton Woods.

1975 (5)

Puerto Rico CBS Classic, La Costa WCT, São Paulo WCT, Caracas WCT, Orlando WCT

1976 (1)

Detroit (RR 4 man)

- Compiled by Andrew Tasiopoulos

INDEX

ALSO FROM NEW CHAPTER PRESS

The Bud Collins History of Tennis–By Bud Collins

Compiled by the most famous tennis journalist and historian in the world, this book is the ultimate compilation of historical tennis information, including year-by-year recaps of every tennis season, biographical sketches of every major tennis personality, as well as stats, records, and championship rolls for all the major events. The author's personal relationships with major tennis stars offer insights into the world of professional tennis found nowhere else.

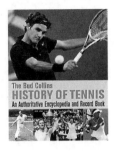

The Roger Federer Story, Quest For Perfection–By Rene Stauffer

Regarded by many as the greatest tennis player in the history of the sport, this authoritative biography is based

on many exclusive interviews with Federer and his family as well as the author's experience covering the international tennis circuit for many years. Completely comprehensive, it provides an informed account of the Swiss tennis star from his early days as a temperamental player on the junior circuit, through his early professional career, to his winning major tennis tournaments, including the U.S. Open and Wimbledon. Readers will appreciate the anecdotes about his early years, revel in the insider's view of the professional tennis circuit, and be inspired by this champion's rise to the top of his game.

On This Day In Tennis History–By Randy Walker

Fun and fact-filled, this compilation offers anniversaries, summaries, and anecdotes of events from the world of tennis for every day in the calendar year. Presented in a day-by-day format, the entries into this mini-encyclopedia include major tournament victory dates, summaries of the greatest matches ever played, trivia, and statistics as well as little-known and quirky happenings. Easy to use and packed with fascinating details, this compendium is the perfect companion for tennis and general sports fans alike.